Charles Seale-Hayne Library
University of Plymouth
(01752) 588 588
LibraryandITenquiries@plymouth.ac.uk

HUMAN ABILITIES
Their Nature and Measurement

HUMAN ABILITIES
Their Nature and Measurement

Edited by

Ian Dennis
Patrick Tapsfield
University of Plymouth

LEA LAWRENCE ERLBAUM ASSOCIATES, PUBLISHERS
1996 Mahwah, New Jersey

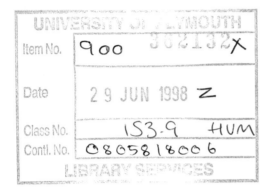
Lawrence Erlbaum Associates, Inc., Publishers
10 Industrial Avenue
Mahwah, New Jersey 07430

Cover design by Gail Silverman

Library of Congress Cataloging-in-Publication Data

Human abilities: their nature and measurement/ edited by Ian
Dennis, Patrick Tapsfield.
     p. cm.
  Papers originally presented at a symposium held at the
University of Plymouth, 1993
  Includes bibliographical references and index.
  ISBN 0-8058-1800-6 (cloth : alk. paper)
  1. Ability—Congresses. 2. Intellect—Congresses. 3.
Cognition—Congresses. 4. Factor analysis—Con-
gresses. I. Dennis, Ian, 1952- . II. Tapsfield, Patrick.
BF431.H7474 1996
153.9—dc20   96-5260
                             CIP

Books published by Lawrence Erlbaum Associates are printed
on acid-free paper, and their bindings are chosen for strength
and durability

Printed in the United States of America
10 9 8 7 6 5 4 3 2 1

Dedicated to the memory of Raymond Christal

Contents

Contributors

John W. Berry
Queen's University
Kingston, Ontario

John B. Carroll
University of North Carolina at Chapel Hill

James A. Earles
Armstrong Laboratory
Brooks Air Force Base, Texas

Susan E. Embretson
University of Kansas

Gerhard H. Fischer
University of Vienna, Austria

Michael J. A. Howe
University of Exeter, England

Patrick C. Kyllonen
Armstrong Laboratory
Brooks Air Force Base, Texas

David F. Lohman
The University of Iowa

Samuel Messick
Educational Testing Service, Princeton

Malcolm James Ree
Armstrong Laboratory
Brooks Air Force Base, Texas

Robert J. Sternberg
Yale University

Introduction: The Abilities of Man Revisited

Ian Dennis
Patrick Tapsfield
University of Plymouth

Many readers of this book will recognize an allusion in its title to that of Spearman's (1927) classic work, *The Abilities of Man: Their Nature and Measurement*. This volume arises out of a seminar held at the University of Plymouth in the summer of 1993. It is hoped that this will become the first in a regular series of symposia in the area of human abilities. The proposed series was named in honor of the founding father of the study of abilities—Charles Spearman. The inaugural seminar—and in consequence this book—was organized around the theme of revisiting issues raised in Spearman's seminal work and considering the progress that has been made on them since 1927.

Much of the early part of *The Abilities of Man* is taken up with a consideration of the nature of intelligence and the structure of human abilities. This is echoed in this volume. The two-factor theory, the articulation and advocacy of which form the core of Spearman's book, can be seen as the first product of the effort to gain a better understanding of the structure of human abilities from considering the patterns of correlations that arise amongst collections of ability tests. In Spearman's own words, two-factor theory holds that:

> Every individual measurement of ability can be divided into two parts which possess the following momentous properties. The one part has been called the "general factor" and denoted by the letter g; it is so named because, although varying freely from

individual to individual, it remains the same for any one individual in respect of all the correlated abilities. The second part has been called the "specific factor" and denoted by the letter s. It not only varies from individual to individual, but even for any one individual from each ability to another. (pp. 74–75)

Even more succinctly, "All branches of intellectual activity have in common one fundamental function (or groups of functions), whereas the remaining or specific elements seem in every case to be wholly different from that in all the others"(p. 76).

The work that led Spearman to two-factor theory provided the beginnings of the development, and application to human abilities, of factor analysis (although, as Loehlin, 1992, commented, Spearman's analysis of tetrad differences as a method of testing two-factor theory was more in the spirit of confirmatory than exploratory factor analysis).

John B. Carroll has devoted a lifetime's work to the application of exploratory factor analysis to human abilities culminating in the publication of an exhaustive review and meta-analysis of the literature on this topic (Carroll, 1993). It was fitting, therefore, that he should inaugurate the Spearman symposia with the lecture from which the first chapter of this volume derives. Carroll characterizes two-factor theory as "a glorious and honorable first approximation." His chapter explains how the three-stratum theory arising from his exhaustive survey of the factor-analytic literature refines that first approximation and contrasts three-stratum theory with the positions of other modern theorists, especially Humphreys (1985).

Mike Howe emphasizes the fact that factor analysis describes rather than explains the patterns that are found in individual variation in abilities and cautions against treating factors, such as g, as explanations rather than findings that themselves need to be explained. Howe further highlights the context dependency of the levels of ability that are revealed in mental tests. An important limitation, not only of Spearman's work but of much of the tradition to which it gave rise, lies in the restriction of its empirical base to performances on tests taken in classroom type settings in Europe and North America. Howe argues for the dependence of performance, even on g-saturated measures, on an individual's educational history and draws attention to the disparities in performance that can occur between classroom settings and those that are achieved on equivalent problems when they present as an important part of the individual's everyday life. The theme of the contextual and cultural specificity of ability is further developed by John Berry.

The need, which Howe identifies, for an explanation of g was recognized by Spearman (although Howe would probably caution against his way of expressing it): "But even the most complete demonstration ... that therefore g and s certainly exist, would not of itself afford the smallest indication as to what these two factors represent. To reveal this nature is quite a different business, and one that leaves room for widely divergent views" (p. 87).

The point is reinforced and the sense in which g can be said to exist is clarified earlier: "But notice must be taken that this general factor g, like all measurements anywhere, is primarily not any concrete thing but only a value or a magnitude.

Furthermore, that which this magnitude measures has not been defined by declaring what it is like, but only by pointing out where it can be found" (p. 75).

The accounts of why *g* is observed considered by Spearman include both the psychological and physiological, although to the modern reader the latter appear to be biologically simplistic. Although he claimed to make no attempt to decide amongst these explanations, Spearman's preferred account is based on the metaphor of mental energy, variations in *g* among individuals being attributable to variations in this quality. Spearman was handicapped in his attempts to elaborate this idea by the lack of the conceptual framework and technical vocabulary that were developed by cognitive psychologists during the 1950s and 1960s. The contribution made by these developments to the issues raised by Spearman form the second theme of this volume.

Possibly one of the most important contributions emerging from recent work in cognitive psychology was anticipated by Spearman in a remarkably prescient chapter entitled "Universal Mental Competition." In this chapter, Spearman drew attention to the limitations of what might now be called processing capacity and bemoaned what he believed to be the insufficient consideration that had been paid to these in earlier psychological theorizing. His preferred explanation of the basis of capacity limitations lies in the restrictions of "mental energy."

Thus, variation between individuals in mental energy leads to variations in their capability for concurrent processing. These impinge on their performance across a whole variety of tasks leading to the phenomenon of *g*. In his discussion in "Universal Mental Competition," Spearman considered experimental evidence related to limitations on concurrent perceptual processing but seemed more struck by the consequences of the limitations on the number of ideas that can be considered simultaneously:

> Hegel likewise speaks of the "limitless pit" for the storage of ideas. Yet of all of this potential immensity, what a beggarly pittance is available at any one moment! A man may have spent a lifetime in memorizing the whole Bible,and still remain unable to call to mind any half dozen lines quite simultaneously. As Fortlage said:
>
> > "Our soul is like a full treasury vault, in which a wretched lamp is burning, whose glimmer can only reach to illuminate a scanty number of objects at a time."
>
> So too Herbart:
>
> > "Reproduction by memory and imagination betrays indeed, that no idea once created is ever quite lost. . . But when we compare the multitude of all that the mind of an adult man has collected with that of which he is conscious in any single moment—we must be astounded at the disproportion between the former's wealth and the latter's poverty."
>
> And if the intensity of the competition is astonishing, no less so is its universality. Not reproduction alone, but perhaps in even higher degree all insightful and creative operations are also governed by it. (p. 101)

Thus, the essence of Spearman's view is that g arises from the very general impact of individual variations in what would now be referred to as working memory. This is precisely the conclusion reached in an influential paper by Kyllonen and Christal (1990) and further developed in Kyllonen's chapter in this volume. Whether Spearman's invocation of mental energy as a mediating factor in the link between working memory and g adds anything useful is open to question, although it foreshadows more modern treatments of attention and capacity limitations such as that of Kahneman (1973). Messick's chapter expands on the links between Spearman's views and more modern theories of attention and discusses the complications that individual variation in attentional mode brings for the measurement of abilities. In his chapter, Lohman further pursues the issue of the nature of g and its relationship to working memory capacity, approaching this question from the perspective of the close relationship between measures of g and some spatial tests.

Spearman's two-factor theory was important, not only because of its psychological substance, but also because in his efforts to prove it, Spearman showed how testable conclusions could be drawn from models that assume that observed performances are determined in some well-specified way by variables that cannot be directly measured (in Spearman's case g and the various s's). In this respect two-factor theory represented an early example of latent variable modeling. Latent variable modeling has advanced massively since that time. One key manifestation has been the development of item response theory. In its original form this relates the pattern of responses on a series of items to a single hidden ability. The chapters by Susan Embretson and Gerhard Fischer examine models that in different ways remove the restriction that the same single ability determines responses on all items.

The last two chapters of this volume each visit one of the applied areas discussed by Spearman. Spearman was skeptical as to whether the measurement of specific abilities could play a useful part in job selection and had the following to say of group factors and their role in occupational selection: "They are of immense importance not only theoretically but practically. By dint of nothing else can all those who claim to measure 'special abilities'—holding out magnificent promises to industry—be saved from the charge of living in the fool's paradise of faculties" (p. 222).

Malcolm Ree and James Earles argue that the "magnificent promises" remain unfulfilled and that there is little or nothing beyond the measurement of g that is useful in occupational selection.

Although the term *aptitude–treatment interaction* had not been coined in 1927, Spearman hinted at the concept when he discussed apparent disparities between educational achievement and cognitive test performance (and hence g). One possible factor in such disparities is that talents that will flourish under one educational regime may languish under another. The attention given to such interactions has been limited since a major review by Cronbach and Snow (1977) concluded that there was little evidence for interactions of practical significance. In the final chapter Bob Sternberg revisits this topic and argues that, given an appropriate theoretical foundation, the benefits of matching instructional regime to aptitudes may be greater than previously supposed.

In the final paragraphs of his main text Spearman expressed his hopes concerning the effects of his book:

> Nevertheless, science is never final. All the preceding conclusions ... will probably in the course of time suffer at least modification. The very formulation of them here, will it is hoped, serve to elicit further and still more searching inquiry.
>
> In fact our essential aim throughout has been to stimulate psychologists towards investigation of more fundamental and therefore more fruitful kind than is now customary. (p. 415)

This volume provides evidence, we hope, of the very considerable extent to which Spearman's ambitions have been fulfilled in the intervening period.

ACKNOWLEDGMENTS

We are indebted to many people who contributed to the organization of the symposium on which this volume is based, and to the production of this volume. Sidney Irvine conceived the symposium and was the driving force behind both it and the present volume. Wendy Tapsfield handled the not inconsiderable organizational burden of the symposium brilliantly. Gill Butland dealt with all the correspondence relating both to the symposium and this volume for which she also prepared the manuscript with her usual quiet efficiency. The Dean of Human Sciences at Plymouth, Geoffrey Payne, gave both his encouragement and financial support to the symposium.

To all of these individuals, and of course to our contributors, our sincere thanks are due.

REFERENCES

Carroll, J. B. (1993). *Human cognitive abilities: A survey of factor-analytic studies.* New York: Cambridge University Press.

Cronbach, L. J., & Snow, R. E. (1977). *Aptitudes and instructional methods: A handbook for research on interactions.* New York: Irvington.

Humphreys, L. G. (1985). General intelligence: An integration of factor test and simplex theory. In B. B. Wolman (Ed.), *Handbook of intelligence: Theories, measurements and applications* (pp. 119–157). New York: Wiley

Kahneman, D. (1973). *Attention and effort.* Englewood Cliffs, NJ: Prentice-Hall.

Kyllonen, P. C., & Christal, R. E. (1990). Reasoning ability is (little more than) working memory capacity?! *Intelligence, 14,* 389–433.

Loehlin, J. C. (1992). *Latent variable models: An introduction to factor, path, and structural analysis.* Hillsdale, NJ: Lawrence Erlbaum Associates.

Spearman, C. (1927). *The abilities of man: Their nature and measurement.* London: Macmillan.

CHAPTER 1

A Three-Stratum Theory of Intelligence: Spearman's Contribution

John B. Carroll
University of North Carolina at Chapel Hill

It is most gratifying to have been accorded the status of "the Spearman lecturer" in the first of a projected series of seminars concerned with intellectual abilities. I hope that the thoughts I express in this chapter are not considered in any way to devalue or detract from the enormous contribution of Charles Spearman to the study of intelligence. Spearman, after all, laid the groundwork for practically every research endeavor in this domain from his time up to the present, and his influence will certainly continue to be felt for a long time into the future. I find myself in agreement with much of Spearman's thinking, as expressed in his various works such as *The Nature of Intelligence and the Principles of Cognition* (1923) and *The Abilities of Man: Their Nature and Measurement* (1927). Where I (or anyone) could justifiably differ with him consists chiefly in matters that have become clearer through the research of the past seven decades, that has been accomplished with more precise and comprehensive methods than were available to him. Even so, it is remarkable how much our present-day theories and methods rely on principles and procedures that he established during his lifetime. Although some discussions might suggest that his ideas were challenged in fundamental ways by subsequent investigators such as L. L. Thurstone, P. E. Vernon, R. B. Cattell, and J. P. Guilford, it now appears that these later investigators merely refined and elaborated Spearman's views, in some ways for the better, and in some ways, I think, for the worse.

A THREE-STRATUM THEORY OF COGNITIVE ABILITIES

These, at any rate, are the thoughts that I have come to hold as a result of a thorough review of factor-analytic studies of cognitive abilities that I have made in the past few years, summarized in a book, *Human Cognitive Abilities* (Carroll, 1993). What I developed in that survey was what I call a *three-stratum theory* that depicts the total domain of intellectual abilities in terms of three levels or *strata* (see Fig. 1.1).

At the top stands a single factor at Stratum III, identified as 3G, General Intelligence, conceptually equivalent to Spearman's g. Obviously, Spearman's g is his major contribution to a theory of cognitive abilities.

Following, there appear eight broad factors at Stratum II, including 2F (or Gf), Fluid Intelligence, 2C (or Gc), Crystallized Intelligence, and several other broad factors of ability. Lines connect the Stratum III General Intelligence factor with Stratum II abilities to suggest that the g factor dominates the Stratum II abilities to varying extents. That is, phenotypic measurements of the second-stratum abilities are likely to be correlated with phenotypic measurements of g to greater or lesser extents. The relative sizes of these correlations are suggested by the relative nearness of a Stratum II factor to the Stratum III general factor. For example, Factor 2F, Fluid Intelligence, appears to be more highly related to g than Factor 2T, Processing Speed, if the latter relation is in fact other than zero. Later I discuss the question of whether Fluid Intelligence is to be taken to be identical to g, as postulated by some writers.

Finally, it appears that each of the Stratum II factors dominates a series of "narrow" factors assigned to Stratum I. In Fig. 1.1, I have listed a number of such factors under each of the Stratum II factors. Ordinarily such factors appear at the first order of analysis; some of them, for example, are Thurstone's "primary" factors.

It is pertinent at this point to mention that all factors can appear in either of two forms, depending on the nature of the matrices that contain loadings of variables on factors or loadings of factors on higher order factors. What may be called *phenotypic* factors are generally oblique to each other, in the sense that they are correlated with each other. Loadings on such factors are shown in either reference vector or pattern matrices, and the correlations among such factors are shown in higher order correlation matrices. In contrast, what may be called *genotypic* factors are orthogonal to each other because their covariance with factors at other orders has in effect been partialed out. It follows that the correlations among such factors are zero. Loadings on such factors are shown in hierarchical factor matrices produced by the

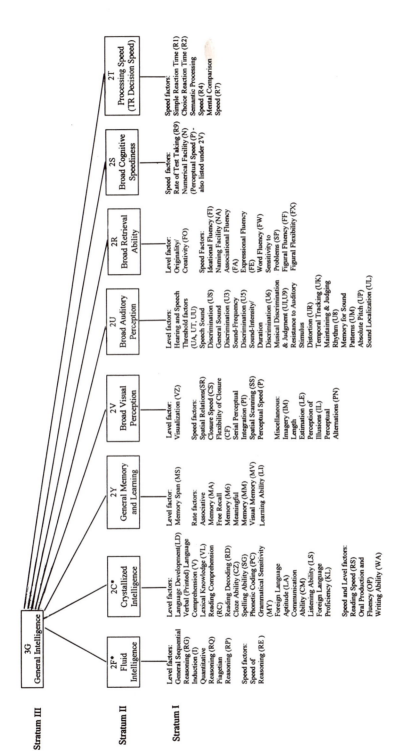

Stratum III

3G
General Intelligence

Stratum II

2F*
Fluid Intelligence

2C*
Crystallized Intelligence

2Y
General Memory and Learning

2V
Broad Visual Perception

2U
Broad Auditory Perception

2R
Broad Retrieval Ability

2S
Broad Cognitive Speediness

2T
Processing Speed (TR Decision Speed)

Stratum I

Level factors:
General Sequential Reasoning (RG)
Induction (I)
Quantitative Reasoning (RQ)
Piagetian Reasoning (RP)

Speed of Reasoning (RE)

Level factors:
Language Development(LD)
Verbal (Printed) Language Comprehension (V)
Lexical Knowledge (VL)
Reading Comprehension (RC)
Reading Decoding (RD)
Cloze Ability (CZ)
Spelling Ability (SG)
Phonetic Coding (PC)
Grammatical Sensitivity (MY)
Foreign Language Aptitude (LA)
Communication Ability (CM)
Listening Ability (LS)
Foreign Language Proficiency (KL)

Speed and Level factors:
Reading Speed (RS)
Oral Production and Fluency (OP)
Writing Ability (WA)

Level factor:
Memory Span (MS)

Rate factors:
Associative Memory (MA)
Free Recall Memory (M6)
Meaningful Memory (MM)
Visual Memory (MV)
Learning Ability (L1)

Level factor:
Visualization (VZ)

Speed factors:
Spatial Relations(SR)
Closure Speed (CS)
Flexibility of Closure (CF)
Serial Perceptual Integration (PI)
Spatial Scanning (SS)
Perceptual Speed (P)

Miscellaneous:
Imagery (IM)
Length Estimation (LE)
Perception of Illusions (IL)
Perceptual Alternations (PN)

Level factors:
Hearing and Speech Threshold factors (UA, UT, UU)
Speech Sound Discrimination (US)
General Sound Discrimination (U3)
Sound-Frequency Discrimination (U5)
Sound-Intensity/ Duration Discrimination (U6)
Musical Discrimination & Judgment (U1,U9)
Resistance to Auditory Stimulus Distortion (UR)
Temporal Tracking (UK)
Maintaining & Judging Rhythm (U8)
Memory for Sound Patterns (UM)
Absolute Pitch (UP)
Sound Localization (UL)

Level factor:
Originality/ Creativity (FO)

Speed Factors:
Ideational Fluency (FI)
Naming Facility (NA)
Associational Fluency (FA)
Expressional Fluency (FE)
Word Fluency (FW)
Sensitivity to Problems (SP)
Figural Fluency (FF)
Figural Flexibility (FX)

Speed factors:
Rate of Test Taking (R9)
Numerical Facility (N)
(Perceptual Speed (P) - also listed under 2V)

Speed factors:
Simple Reaction Time (R1)
Choice Reaction Time (R2)
Semantic Processing Speed (R4)
Mental Comparison Speed (R7)

* In many analyses, factors 2F and 2C cannot be distinguished: they are represented, however, by a factor designated 2H, a combination of 2F and 2C.

FIG. 1.1. The structure of cognitive abilities (from Carroll, 1993. Reprinted with the permission of Cambridge University Press).

3

Schmid–Leiman orthogonalization procedure (Schmid & Leiman, 1957). I am not sure that genotypic is the best word for characterizing such factors; I use it mainly because it contrasts to phenotypic, which seems to characterize a factor that would be manifested in scores directly derived from test scores by any of several procedures discussed in treatises on factor analysis, and would thus contain variance from factors at different orders. For example, a score on a phenotypic factor could contain variance from a general factor, a second-stratum factor, and a first-stratum factor. A score on a genotypic factor, on the other hand, would constitute an estimate of a person's score on that factor, with variance from other strata partialed out. I find it useful to note loadings of variables on orthogonal genotypic factors, which show the extent to which they contain variances independent from genotypic factors at different strata. To my mind, genotypic factors represent latent causal elements in test scores. For example, in interpreting data in a hierarchical factor matrix, a variable with a loading of .6 on a general factor, .5 on a fluid intelligence factor at Stratum II, a loading of .4 on a Stratum I verbal factor and a loading of .3 on a Stratum I induction factor, could be assumed to be independently influenced by each of those factors, to the extent indicated by the loadings.

Considering that Fig. 1.1 represents a structure of correlated factors, it represents phenotypic factors. Underlying it, at another level of presentation, so to speak, one can assume a structure of orthogonal genotypic factors that differ principally in their generality over the domain of cognitive abilities. The g factor is most general, second-stratum factors are less general, and first-stratum factors are least general. Actually one can envisage a structure in which all factors are orthogonal, differing *only* in their degree of generality. This type of structure is in fact represented in the "nested" designs postulated by Gustafsson and Undheim (1992) and specified in orthogonal factor matrices input to confirmatory analyses. My use of stratum arises from my methodological preference for exploratory factor analysis as an initial heuristic procedure.

For this and other reasons, the structure presented in Fig. 1.1, therefore, should not be taken too literally or precisely. It is only a conceptually ideal structure suggested by the total array of data that I have analyzed—more than 460 datasets found in the factorial litera-ture. My approach is analogous to what has been called "meta-analysis" in other fields of psychological and educational research, in the sense that it attempts to establish or estimate the "true" structure of intellectual abilities that would be revealed if one were able to use an infinite set of ideal measures in factor analysis. In practice, the third-stratum g factor does not always show up in the analysis of a particular dataset, and often, second-stratum factors either do not appear or cannot be distinguished from one another. Furthermore, the Stratum I factors appearing for a particular dataset are not always related to Stratum II factors in the manner suggested by Fig. 1.1. Either they are related to different Stratum II factors from those indicated in Fig. 1.1, or they may be related to two or more such factors. These complications are undoubtedly the result of the design of particular datasets—that is, the variables that were chosen to be included in the dataset, not all the variables being adequately "pure" in a factorial sense, and the variables not being chosen to cover all the possible domains of cognitive ability. It is for this reason that I would urge that factor-analytic research needs to be greatly expanded and refined in order to approximate more closely the true structure of cognitive abilities, to the extent that factor analysis could make such an approximation possible. Expansion would come from the inclusion of a greater variety of variables over the postulated domains of ability, and refinement would come from more focused work on the manner in which ability constructs are measured—possibly through the greater use of item response theory and applications of basic measurement theory.

From this perspective, Spearman's work can be viewed as contributing a glorious and honorable first approximation to the true structure of cognitive abilities—an approximation that in many ways has stood the test of time, but that contrarily, has over the years since then been shown to be grossly inadequate. Spearman cannot be faulted for being unable to go much beyond his first approximation. Going beyond what he established has required decades of further research, and even now we have only perhaps a second or third approximation.

GROUP AND SPECIFIC FACTORS

It is pertinent to inquire just how far Spearman's glorious approximation went in achieving the kind of structure suggested in Fig. 1.1. In *The Abilities of Man*, we find considerable discussion of what Spearman called "group factors," attributed by him to "overlap between specific factors" (pp. 79–82). A series of chapters in Part II was devoted to various possible special abilities and group factors of this sort. But Spearman was at all times skeptical about them. "They make their appearance here, there, everywhere; the very Puck of psychology," he wrote. "On all sides contentiously advocated, hardly one of them has received so much as a description, far less any serious investigation" (p. 222). Almost grudgingly, Spearman acknowledges the existence of "a very large additional factor common to the tests of Reasoning and of Generalization" (pp. 225–226). "Here then," he wrote, "we appear to have discovered a 'special ability' or group factor, broad enough to include a sphere of mental operations that is very valuable for many purposes in ordinary life. Quite possibly, indeed, this special logical ability may not be innate, but acquired by training or habit. Even so, its importance would not lose in degree, but would only shift from the region of aptitude to that of education." Would this "group factor" be what R. B. Cattell later recognized as Gf, fluid intelligence? Or would the "spatial cognition" factor that Spearman recognized (p. 229) in the work of McFarlane (1925) be the Space factor identified later by Thurstone (1938)? Similarly, could we not cross-identify a group factor of arithmetical abilities that Spearman (p. 230) recognized in the work of Collar (1920) with the N (Numerical Facility) factor of Thurstone and many other investigators? It is unfortunate, in a way, that Spearman could not properly appraise various results that he discussed in this chapter on special abilities. He was limited to use of his tetrad equation in evaluating these findings. His final comment in the chapter was as follows:

> The main upshot of this chapter is negative. Cases of specific correlations have been astonishingly rare. Over and over again, they have proved to be absent even in circumstances when they would most confidently have been anticipated by the nowadays prevalent *a priori* "job analysis."
>
> Among the exceptional cases where, on the contrary, specific correlations and group factors do become of appreciable magnitude, the four most important have been in respect of what may be called the logical, the mechanical, the psychological, and the arithmetical abilities. In each of these a group factor has been discovered of sufficient breadth and degree to possess serious practical consequences, educational, industrial, and vocational.
>
> The same may be said of yet another important special ability which was reluctantly omitted from our preceding account for want of space; this is the ability to appreciate music. (pp. 241–242)

I will not take time to refer to further instances of Spearman's recognition, in *The Abilities of Man*, of possibly important group factors beyond g, including, for example, a group factor of "retentivity" that is possibly similar to Memory factors identified by Thurstone and others. Instead, I turn to the volume by Spearman and Wynn Jones (1950), for more evidence of the extent to which Spearman admitted the existence of group factors. From the preface to this volume, one learns that it was in the main jointly written by Spearman and Wynn

Jones beginning in 1942 and ending in 1945, when Spearman died. Thus it may be taken as Spearman's final statement on the structure of cognitive abilities. Nevertheless, it is evident that probably due to delayed circulation of scientific writings in the war years, the volume was very limited in its reference to studies published in the United States after about 1940.

In Chapter II of this book we find the following statement: "As regards the statistical results of this method (of factorizing), these have only been outlined. They have consisted of (1) a general factor; (2) an unlimited number of narrow specific factors; and (3) very few broad group factors" (p. 15).

The casual reader might interpret this passage as almost an exact description of a three-stratum theory of cognitive abilities. Such an interpretation, however, would not be quite correct. To be sure, the general factor forms the third stratum of the theory, and the "broad group factors" form the second stratum. But in speaking of "an unlimited number of narrow specific factors" Spearman seemed to have in mind not necessarily the narrow first-stratum factors of the theory, but rather, the specifics that can be associated with particular variables. Spearman and Wynn Jones recognized that the term *specific factor* has had "at least three different versions," namely:

(a) As used originally by the senior writer: that is to say, the whole content of any ability other than its general part.
(b) The non-recurrent part; that is to say, the part of any ability which does not recur in any other of any given set of abilities.
(c) Any ability content which cannot recur in any other ability whatever. (p. 77)

On the whole, it is exceedingly difficult to interpret Spearman and Wynn Jones' discourse about specific factors without translating it into a discourse using s in the sense defined by later writers, including Thurstone, as an ability that is independent of any error, but also independent of any common factor identified in a particular set of ability measurements. Such a definition recognizes, as did Spearman, that what may be a specific factor in a particular battery may become a common factor in a second battery if such a specific factor is measured by more than one variable in the second battery.

Subsequent chapters of this book discuss various "broad factors" that Spearman and Wynn Jones recognized, though with much caution. They were aware of Thurstone's study of primary abilities as published in 1938, and of Holzinger's studies (e.g., Holzinger & Swineford, 1939) conducted in the "Unitary Trait" program of researches. Among the broad factors treated were a Verbal factor (Chapter XI), a Mechanical factor (Chapter XII), and Arithmetical, Fluency, Psychological, and Retentivity factors (Chapters XIII, XV, XVII). From a present-day perspective, one might say that Spearman and Wynn Jones were limited both by inadequate methodology and by an inadequate amount of experimental evidence that they were able to consider. But if they had not been limited in these respects, I would not think that they would be opposed to a three-stratum theory. A three-stratum theory, at least, tends to fit the evidence they had at hand.

Nowadays the conventional wisdom is that the general factor is by far more important than lower-stratum factors. Possibly Spearman's emphasis on the importance of the general factor has been responsible for this "conventional wisdom," but it has also resulted from the frequent finding that lower-stratum factors seldom add much predictive validity to what can be obtained from measures of the general factor. I believe that the conventional wisdom is to some extent incorrect, however, because there are many types of learning or performance that can be shown to depend not only on the general factor but also on lower-stratum factors. Examples that come to mind are foreign language learning ability and musical performance. I would point out that although Spearman attached great importance to the general factor, he regarded some lower-stratum factors as being of educational or occupational significance.

INTERPRETATION OF THE GENERAL FACTOR

Spearman established a tradition of trying to interpret factors in terms of what biological, psychological, or educational constructs underlie them. In Chapter VII of *The Abilities of Man*, titled "Proposed Explanations of G," Spearman devoted much attention to the interpretation of the general factor. His preferred explanation seems to have been derived from what he called "the adventurous step of deserting all actually observable phenomena of the mind, and proceeding instead to invent an underlying something which—by analogy with physics—has been called mental energy." Later, in Chapter IX, "The Hypothesis of Mental Energy," he expanded this hypothesis by assigning mental energy to the interpretation of the g factor, while regarding the specific factors as "engines" promoting the application of mental energy to specific domains of mental activity. These ideas were further summarized: "We found that the whole of psychology would be illuminated if they could be taken, g as the amount of a general mental energy, and the s's as the efficiency of specific mental engines'' (p. 137).

These rather vague and fanciful ideas were to my knowledge never elaborated on or subjected to experimental proof by Spearman and his immediate followers. Indeed, in the volume by Spearman and Wynn Jones, it is argued that the concept of mental energy has the same hypothetical status as fundamental concepts of physics such as force, gravity, temperature, and so on. And that volume says nothing about specific factors as "engines." The authors label specific factors with such terms as "verbal," "mechanical," and "retentivity" with little attention to spelling out their meanings.

Nevertheless, it is becoming obvious, as shown by Matarazzo (1992), that various kinds of biological indicants are proving to have significant and interesting relationships with intelligence, or more specifically with the g factor. Many such indicants could be regarded as measures of some sort of mental energy, in that they reflect properties of such responses as average evoked potentials, reaction times, inspection times, and rates of glucose metabolism in the brain. Perhaps, then, Spearman's concept of mental energy as explaining the g factor is finally coming into its own. I would point out, however, that in my model of cognitive ability structure, the second-stratum factors Gs (broad cognitive speediness) and Gt (processing speed) have only modest correlations with the general factor. This must mean that, contrary to Spearman's opinion, speed is not a central characteristic of the general factor, or that numerous extraneous variables not related to intelligence affect the biological indicants examined in recent research studies.

Let me now turn to a broader discussion of contemporary views of the factorial analysis of intelligence.

The first part of Wolman's *Handbook of Intelligence* (1985) deals with theories and conceptual issues related to intelligence. Many of the authors of chapters in this part seem to accept the previously described conventional wisdom about intelligence. For example, Vandenberg and Vogler (1985), writing on genetic determinants of intelligence, stated that "there is much to recommend the conception of intelligence as one general entity" (p. 5), but they also discussed possible genetic determinants of special abilities. Similarly, Hynd and Willis (1985) viewed intelligence as "a general class of behavior" with g as a "unifying element" (p. 135).

Authors who have been closely associated with the factor-analytic approach to intelligence, however, differ not only in their emphases but also, to a considerable extent, in their theoretical positions. J. P. Guilford (1985) appealed strongly to his structure of intellect (SOI) model to suggest that intelligence should be defined as "a systematic collection of abilities or functions for processing information of different kinds in various forms" (p. 238). In his chapter, he introduced a hierarchical model that he had recently developed for SOI abilities, using techniques quite different from the Schmid–Leiman orthogonalization. Nevertheless, one gathers that he would reject any notion of g or general intelligence because, he says, "there is no good evidence for anything more general than the third-order factors" (p. 238). He would expect to find 16 such third-order factors, each associated with one of the SOI categories (five operations, five contents, and six products).

Horn (1985) regarded intelligence as "a mixture of quite different things" (p. 268), and apparently rejected the notion that anything like g exists. In fact, he claimed that "studies that have been adequately designed to test Spearman's theory have demonstrated time and time again that the theory does not describe human intellectual capacities" (p. 271). Instead, he tentatively supported the idea that at least four or five broad factors are needed to account for the diversity of results in the factorial analysis of intelligence—certainly fluid intelligence (Gf) and crystallized intelligence (Gc), but also visual intelligence (Gv), auditory intelligence (Ga), and general speediness (Gs). He also recognized the need for narrow, first-stratum factors.

In contrast, Humphreys (1985) strongly supported the finding of a general factor of intelligence, as evidenced, for him, by the uniformly positive correlations between intellectual tests, even tests that are far from the central region of Guttman's (1954a) radex representation, and far apart from each other in such a representation.

In some ways, Humphreys' views on the structure of cognitive abilities are similar to mine. We agree, for example, on a hierarchical view, and on the importance of a general factor. There are, however, many differences, and I think it valuable to discuss them because they stem from basic differences in our assumptions about the meaning of factorial results. Let me consider, therefore, not only Humphreys' chapter in the Wolman *Encyclopaedia* but also a series of Humphreys' writings over the years, starting from a paper published in the *American Psychologist* (Humphreys, 1962).

In the 1962 paper, Humphreys noted that he was disturbed by the proliferation of factors claimed by various investigators. He also noted his discomfort with the tendency of many investigators to regard first-order factors as primary and of great importance, and the frequent failure of these investigators to pursue factor analysis into higher orders. As a consequence, few investigators (at least, authors using Thurstonian techniques) recognized anything like a general factor. In this matter Humphreys was undoubtedly correct. Possibly as a result of

Humphreys' writings, some investigators became more ready to adopt a hierarchical view of intelligence, and began using the Schmid and Leiman (1957) orthogonalization procedure. Humphreys (1982) pointed out that "in the hierarchical model all factors are defined by the original variables" (p. 229). However, as early as 1962, Humphreys concluded that a facet approach, similar to Guttman's (1954b), might be more useful in the interpretation of factors than the conventional approach whereby factors are interpreted in terms of overall characteristics of test tasks. He noted that if one assumes a small number of facets—say eight, each with a small number of levels—it would be possible to generate 8,640 different factors by using the Cartesian product of these facets. For Humphreys, the implication was that many lower-order factors were merely adventitious combinations of facets. Note that Guilford (1985) explicitly defined factors in terms of combinations of facets (five operations, five contents, and six products) and therefore claimed the possibility of defining 150 factors. Humphreys, however, assumed many more facets than Guilford did. "The ultimate factor in the Guilford sense," Humphreys (1981, p. 89) wrote, "is defined by two or more parallel forms of the same test." Apparently from such considerations, Humphreys (1985, p. 207) proposed that "tests are invented; therefore factors are invented." Further, "Nice, clear first and second order factors reflect mainly our habits of test construction and our selection of the tests to factor" (Humphreys, 1981, p. 90). In the 1962 paper, Humphreys had illustrated the construction of a four-order hierarchy for different tests of mechanical information.

All this is related to Humphreys' concept of intelligence, which in one place (1971, p. 31) he defined as "the entire repertoire of acquired skills, knowledge, learning sets and generalization tendencies considered [by experts] as intellectual in nature that are available at any one period of time." Later (1982, p. 236) he defined intelligence as "the resultant of the processes of acquiring, storing in memory, retrieving, combining, comparing and using in new contexts information and conceptual skills; it is an abstraction." He stated that intelligence so defined is not an entity like Spearman's mental energy. Instead, he believed that his definition assumed something like Thomson's (1916, 1919) multiple bonds approach. Humphreys thus seemed to view intelligence as a large collection of acquired knowledges and skills, more or less undifferentiated except to the extent that the particular skills exhibited by an individual depend on the particular experiences that the individual has had and the knowledge and skills that the individual has acquired through these experiences. Actually, Humphreys said little about explaining the appearance of lower-order factors such as the verbal factor, the spatial factor, and other factors recognized by Thurstone and others, but I assume that he might have explained them by associating them with particular classes of experiences that different individuals are likely to have had, and the fact that items in certain classes of knowledge and skill tend to be learned together. His support of the notion of a general factor arises mainly from his observation of positive correlations of intellectual measurement, even though they may be widely different with respect to the facets that they may involve. At no point, unless I have missed something, did he attempt to describe or explain the general factor in more specific terms, or to differentiate the general factor from lower-order factors except in a mathematical sense.

Humphreys is especially insistent that intelligence is not a capacity. If intelligence measures appear to predict future learning, this is only because for him intelligence is a phenotypic trait that is relatively stable over time. Humphreys drew support for this view from the work of Anderson (1940) and Roff (1941), who found that gains in mental age appeared to be uncorrelated with initial status at a given chronological age. Nevertheless, Humphreys was willing to admit that intelligence has biological and psychosocial substrates; the biological substrate can include a genetic component, and the psychosocial substrate has mainly environmental components (Humphreys, 1971). These, then, are Humphreys' views on the nature and structure of intelligence. I now spell out my disagreements with certain aspects of Humphreys' views.

As I have already mentioned, we agree that intellectual abilities are structured hierarchically, or perhaps more precisely, that some abilities are more general than others. Spearman's g is the most general because it covers a greater range and diversity of intellectual tasks. Both Humphreys and I use hierarchical analysis because it offers a convenient heuristic device for establishing factors at different orders or strata, or at different levels of generality. Generally, I find that no more than three orders are necessary to account for the structure of typical datasets, and consequently I postulate that factors can be assigned to no more than three strata. Humphreys (1962) concocted an example that would require four strata, but the variables of this example were measures of different types of mechanical information, some highly specific, others more general. I regard this example as not typical of data likely to be employed in studying intelligence. Instead, I regard the three strata that I have postulated as reflecting the true structure of intellectual abilities as measured by typical tests. For me, the evidence for a general factor comes not from the positive correlations among rather dissimilar tasks, but rather, from the three-stratum model that, for a well-designed dataset, yields factors at different strata, including a general factor.

Admittedly, it might be possible to find or construct examples of empirical data that would demand more than three strata—a stratum of highly specialized abilities below Stratum I. The fact is, however, that such specialized abilities only very rarely appear, if at all, in typical datasets. I can cite many instances in which variables measuring a Stratum I ability appear to differ in one or more facets, but there is rarely any evidence that separate factors of any interest or significance can be established for such facets. For example, memory span tests (measuring the first-stratum factor MS) may differ in a number of ways—for example, in whether the stimuli are visual or auditory, or letters or digits—but I do not find a corresponding visual–auditory subfactor, or a letter–digit subfactor. Therefore, I do not share Humphreys' pessimism about lower-order factors, or agree with his claim that factors can be almost indefinitely divided according to a facet analysis.

Another reason for doubting Humphreys' disdain for lower-order factors is that generally I find, in the common factor variance of variables, considerable amounts of variance from lower-order factors. For example, in the variables used in Thurstone's (1938) primary mental abilities study, on average about half the common factor variance comes from lower-order factors found in a hierarchical analysis. Although it has been widely claimed that predictive validities of mental tests are chiefly due to a general factor, I have encountered many instances in which lower-order factors add significantly to predictive validity. In my view, lower-order factors (both at Stratum I and II) are worthy of scientific study, not only for themselves, but also for their possible social and practical importance.

Almost parenthetically, I want to express disagreement with Humphreys' (1985) notion that "tests are invented; therefore factors are invented" (p. 207). For one thing, the conclusion does not follow. One could invent a series of tests, but whether one or more factors are found in such tests depends on characteristics of the population studied, not on whether the tests are invented. In fact, it could be argued that all tests—or for that matter, all measurements—are in some sense invented, but this by no means disqualifies their results, as analyzed by factor analysis or other means, as chimerical.

Now consider Humphreys' concept of intelligence, whether it be general intelligence or the entire range of intellectual abilities. On a superficial level, one can agree that intelligence is a large collection of acquired skills and knowledge. Or one can agree that intelligence reflects a repertoire of intellectual response tendencies. But what seems to me of more importance, from a scientific point of view, is to identify parameters in the individual that account for the acquisition of skills and knowledge of different kinds. A first step in the identification of such parameters, in my opinion, is to postulate models for abilities. Considering the entire history of psychological testing, it should be apparent to anybody that psychological testing has always tacitly assumed a model for an ability. That is, an ability is assumed to refer to variations in individuals' capacities to respond successfully to a class of tasks that differ in difficulty, and in the likelihoods that individuals can perform these tasks, as a function of their difficulties. Binet's mental age scale exemplifies one such model of ability; tasks are assigned to different mental ages on the basis of the likelihood that a child of a given chronological age could exhibit successful performance of the tasks. Only in more recent years has *item response theory* formulated a more precise mathematical model of an ability, for example the three-parameter model proposed by Birnbaum (1968).

Of most importance here is that ability models of this kind serve to organize the collection of intellectual skills that can be observed. Not only do they emphasize that skills differ widely in their difficulties or their prevalences in the population, but they provide a model for the likelihood that an individual with a given ability parameter (the *b* parameter in the typical equation for response probability) can pass an item.

In my view, factors isolated by factor analysis reflect abilities that can be described by an appropriate ability model. That is true for an ability at any level of the postulated three-stratum model. In principle, the general factor can be described in terms of where on a general ability continuum a given task falls, with consequent predictions of individuals' likelihoods of performing the task successfully. Similar remarks can be made for lower-order factors, except that it is necessary to correct the predictions for the influence of one or more higher-order factors. At several points, Humphreys (1985) urged that test theory must be modified to take care of factorial results. But my claim is that test theory needs to be modified not so much to provide good general factor measurements from heterogeneous items (which is what concerned Humphreys), but to accommodate the fact that test scores frequently have multifactorial determinants (as shown, e.g., by significant loadings of tests on first-, second-, and third-stratum factors in a hierarchical orthogonalized factor matrix).

My view of intelligence thus contrasts with Humphreys' in that it prescribes an organization of intellectual tasks in terms of abilities that conform to a precise model with respect to how particular tasks play a role.

I also differ from Humphreys in that I allow for the possibility that many abilities may be viewed as capacities. For one thing, I believe that Humphreys was in error in accepting Anderson and Roff's views on the stochastic nature of gains in abilities. Cronbach and Snow (1977) showed that Anderson and Roff ignored the role of measurement errors in finding that gains in mental age were uncorrelated with initial states at a given chronological age. More than this, however, it is possible to cite many instances where validities of psychological tests can be interpreted as indicative that capacities are involved. Indeed, the very definition of an ability (e.g., in the three-parameter model of item response theory) implies the operation of a capacity, at least at a given point of time.

I hope you agree with me that my conception of intelligence is more congruent with Spearman's than with Humphreys'. I do not claim that mental energy underlies the general factor, as Spearman speculated, but I do claim that underlying each factor of the three-stratum theory there is a specific state or substrate that exists in the individual and that accounts for his or her ability or inability to perform tasks in which that ability is called for. Incidentally, I believe that a resolution of the famous controversy between Spearman and Thomson on the nature of a factor might come from an analysis of the implications of item response theory. It is difficult for me to imagine how test intercorrelations could be explained by Thomson's theory when test scores are constrained by parameters of item response theory. The resolution of that controversy, however, must await another day.

FUTURE RESEARCH

I end with one or two thoughts about future research, which I envisage as necessarily being very extensive in order to settle all the questions that can be raised even now about the structure of human abilities. One important question has to do with the status of g, Gf, and Gc. Gustafsson (1984, 1988), using confirmatory techniques, raised the possibility that g, at the third stratum, is identical to Gf at the second stratum. He may very well be correct, but I would urge that it may require more focused experimental work to establish the identity of g and Gf. In my view it is possible that measures of Gf feature attributes that require specific skills in inductive and deductive reasoning that are not necessarily present in other measures of g.

On the status of Gc, crystallized intelligence, I suggest that effort should be devoted to show that measures of environmental opportunity are specifically related to Gc in such a way as to account for changes in factor loadings on Gc as a function of environmental opportunity.

Recently, for example, I have been impressed with several studies (McBride-Chang, Manis, Seidenberg, Custodio, & Doi, 1993; Stanovich & Cunningham, 1993) that suggest that performance on reading tests depends on the amount of "print exposure" the individual has had, when the effects of general intelligence are partialed out. It might be possible to show that variables have loadings on Gc when they can be affected by environmental exposure, but on Gf otherwise, particularly for individuals with minimal environmental exposure. If so, Cattell's (1971) interpretation of Gc as reflecting the "investment" of Gf ability in learning would be better confirmed. No doubt all this leaves you with many unanswered questions.

REFERENCES

Anderson, J. E. (1940). The prediction of terminal intelligence from infant and preschool tests. In G. M. Whipple (Ed.), *Intelligence: Its nature and nurture* (pp. 385–403). Bloomington, IL: National Society for the Study of Education.

Birnbaum, A. (1968). Some trait models and their use in inferring an examinee's ability. In F. M. Lord & M. R. Novick, *Statistical theories of mental test scores* (pp. 395–479). Reading, MA: Addison-Wesley.

Carroll, J. B. (1993). *Human cognitive abilities: A survey of factor-analytic studies.* New York: Cambridge University Press.

Cattell, R. B. (1971). *Abilities: Their structure, growth and action.* Boston: Houghton Mifflin.

Collar, D. J. (1920). A statistical survey of arithmetical ability. *British Journal of Psychology, 11,* 135–138.

Cronbach, L. J., & Snow, R. E. (1977). *Aptitudes and instructional methods: A handbook for research on interactions.* New York: Irvington.

Guilford, J. P. (1985). The structure-of-intellect model. In B. B. Wolman (Ed.), *Handbook of intelligence: Theories, measurements and applications* (pp. 225–266). New York: Wiley.

Gustafsson, J. E. (1984). A unifying model for the structure of intellectual abilities. *Intelligence, 8,* 179–203.

Gustafsson, J. E. (1988). Hierarchical models of individual differences in cognitive abilities. In R. J. Sternberg (Ed.), *Advances in the psychology of human intelligence* (Vol. 4, pp. 35–71). Hillsdale, NJ: Lawrence Erlbaum Associates.

Gustafsson, J. E., & Undheim, J. O. (1992). Stability and change in broad and narrow factors of intelligence from ages 12 to 15. *Journal of Educational Psychology, 84,* 141–149.

Guttman, L. (1954a). A new approach for factor analysis: The radex. In P. F. Lazarsfeld (Ed.), *Mathematical thinking in the social sciences* (pp. 258–348, 430–433). Glencoe, IL: The Free Press.

Guttman, L. (1954b). *An outline of some new methodology for social research.* Paper presented at World Association for Public Opinion Research and American Association for Public Opinion Research, Asbury Park, NJ.

Holzinger, K. J., & Swineford, F. (1939). *A study in factor analysis: The stability of a bi-factor solution.* Supplementary Education Monographs No. 48. Chicago: University of Chicago, Department of Education.

Horn, J. L. (1985). Remodeling old models of intelligence. In B. B. Wolman (Ed.), *Handbook of intelligence: Theories, measurements and applications* (pp. 267–300). New York: Wiley.

Humphreys, L. G. (1962). The organization of human abilities. *American Psychologist, 17*, 475–483.

Humphreys, L. G. (1971). Theory of intelligence. In F. Cancro (Ed.), *Intelligence: Genetic and environmental influences* (pp. 31–42). New York: Grune & Stratton.

Humphreys, L. G. (1981). The primary mental ability. In M. P. Friedman, J. P. Das, & N. O'Connor (Eds.), *Intelligence and learning* (pp. 87–102). New York: Plenum.

Humphreys, L. G. (1982). The hierarchial factor model and general intelligence. In N. Hirschberg & L. G. Humphreys (Eds.), *Multivariate applications in the social sciences* (pp. 223–239). Hillsdale, NJ: Lawrence Erlbaum Associates.

Humphreys, L. G. (1985). General intelligence: An integration of factor, test and simplex theory. In B. B. Wolman (Ed.), *Handbook of intelligence: Theories, measurements and applications* (pp. 201–224). New York: Wiley.

Hynd, G. W., & Willis, W. G. (1985). Neurological foundations of intelligence. In B.B. Wolman (Ed.), *Handbook of intelligence: Theories, measurements and applications* (pp. 119–157). New York: Wiley.

Matarazzo, J. D. (1992). Psychological testing and assessment in the 21st century. *American Psychologist, 47*, 1007–1018.

McBride-Chang, C., Manis, F. R., Seidenberg, M. S., Custodio, R. G., & Doi, L. M. (1993). Print exposure as a predictor of word reading and reading comprehension in disabled and nondisabled readers. *Journal of Educational Psychology, 85*, 230–238.

McFarlane, M. M. (1925). A study of practical ability. *British Journal of Psychology, Monograph Supplement 8.*

Roff, M. (1941). A statistical study of the development of intelligence test performance. *Journal of Psychology, 11*, 371–386.

Schmid, J., & Leiman, J. M. (1957). The development of hierarchical factor solutions. *Psychometrika, 22*, 53–61.

Spearman, C. (1923). *The nature of intelligence and the principles of cognition.* London: Macmillan.

Spearman, C. (1927). *The abilities of man: Their nature and measurement.* New York: Macmillan.

Spearman, C., & Wynn Jones, L. (1950). *Human ability: A continuation of "The abilities of man."* London: Macmillan.

Stanovich, K. E., & Cunningham, A. E. (1993). Where does knowledge come from? Specific associations between print exposure and information acquisition. *Journal of Educational Psychology, 85*, 211–229.

Thomson, G. H. (1916). A hierarchy without a general factor. *British Journal of Psychology, 8*, 271–281.

Thomson, G. H. (1919). On the cause of hierarchical order among correlation coefficients. *Proceedings of the Royal Society, A, 95*, 400–408.

Thurstone, L. L. (1938). Primary mental abilities. *Psychometric Monographs*, No. 1.

Vandenberg, S. G., & Vogler, G. P. (1985). Genetic determinants of intelligence. In B. B. Wolman (Ed.), *Handbook of intelligence: Theories, measurements and applications* (pp. 3–57). New York: Wiley.

Wolman, B. B. (Ed.). (1985). *Handbook of intelligence: Theories, measurements and applications.* New York: Wiley.

CHAPTER 2

A Cultural Ecology of Cognition

John W. Berry
Queen's University, Kingston, Ontario

In this chapter, the position is taken that human cognitive abilities develop in contexts that are both ecological and cultural. It is thus necessary to understand variations in these contexts if we are to arrive at a valid understanding of variations in cognitive development. This position has been referred to as the Law of Cultural Differentiation (Irvine & Berry, 1988), and is rooted in the early assertion by Ferguson (1956) that "cultural factors prescribe what shall be learned and at what age; consequently different cultural environments lead to the development of different patterns of ability" (p. 121).

Although this position emphasizes variations in cultural experience, and resultant differential learning, the position nevertheless allows for both cultural and biological adaptations in human populations to ecological press, and the transmission of characteristics between generations by both cultural and biological mechanisms (i.e., enculturation and genetic). The approach thus differs little, except for a change in terminology and the implied social engineering, from the way it was phrased by Spearman (1927):

> The question appears to be cardinal for all human improvement. This is at present everywhere blocked by the rivalry between two plans of procedure. Any serious enterprise to better man by means of more effective breeding always breaks against the opposition of those who seek, instead, for betterment by means of more effective training. Conversely, all great efforts to improve human beings by way of training are thwarted through the apathy of those who hold the sole feasible road to be that of stricter breeding. (p. 376)

CROSS-CULTURAL PSYCHOLOGY

The approach taken in this chapter is that of cross-cultural psychology, which has attempted to describe and explain human psychological diversity as a function of cultural diversity. The notion of *culture* has usually been taken to include concepts that are both broader than culture, such as ecology, and notions that are less broad, such as ethnicity. That is, there is considered to be a range and network of contexts for human development and behavior that need to be understood if human psychological functioning is to be properly interpreted. This complex includes whole ecosystems (physical environments in which human and other animals engage in an endless process of cultural and biological adaptation), nation states and societies (with comprehensive economic and political institutions), ethnocultural groups (with cultural traditions transmitted over generations), and evolving relationships among these contexts. An attempt has been made to capture the essence of this diverse enterprise in the following definition of the field: "Cross-cultural psychology is the study of similarities and differences in individual psychological functioning in various cultural and ethnic groups; of the relationships between psychological variables and socio-cultural, ecological and biological variables; and of ongoing changes in these variables" (Berry, Poortinga, Segall, & Dasen, 1992, p. 2).

Many cross-cultural psychologists adopt the theoretical position of *universalism*. From this perspective, it is assumed that psychological *processes* are shared, specieswide characteristics of human populations everywhere. Variations in the development and display of human behavior are considered to be largely the result of cultural factors that vary from one group to another. The main task of cross-cultural psychology is to understand how culture affects human development and performance, while acknowledging fundamental underlying similarities. To accomplish this task, it is necessary to elaborate a framework that permits an examination of behavior in cultural context.

An Ecological Framework

An ecological framework for cross-cultural psychology is presented in Fig. 2.1. This framework is a conceptual scheme, rather than a theoretical model from which specific testable hypotheses can be derived. It is a general guide to classes of variables, and their relevance for the explanation of similarities and differences in human behavior and experience to be found across cultures.

This framework derives from earlier models proposed by Berry

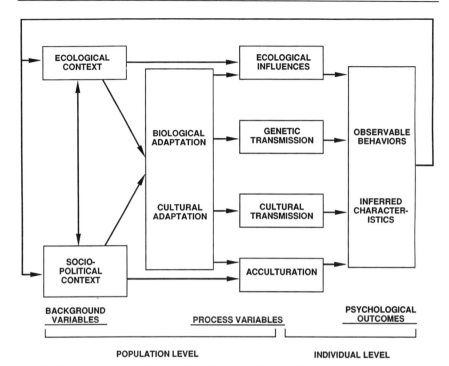

FIG. 2.1.   An ecological and cultural framework for understanding psychological development (from Berry, Poortinga, Segall, & Dasen, 1992).

(1966, 1975, 1976, 1986) where it was called an "ecocultural model." However, the roots of this model go back to the point of view of Whiting (1974) who was working in the field of culture and personality (Berry, 1995).

The framework distinguishes between the *population* level and the *individual* level of analysis with the former on the left of the framework, and the latter on the right. The *flow* is from left to right, with population-level variables (left part) conceived of as influencing the individual outcomes (right part). This general flow is intended to correspond to the interests of cross-cultural psychology; we wish to account for individual and group differences in psychological characteristics as a function of population-level factors. However, it is obvious that a full model (i.e., one that attempts to specify completely relationships in the real world) would have many more components and numerous feedback arrows, representing influences among components, and by individuals on the other variables in the framework.

The notion of feedback is necessary in order to recognize the individual as an actor, and to avoid viewing the developing and behaving individual as a mere *pawn* in such a framework. However, for ease of presenting the framework, only two feedback relationships are illustrated in Fig. 2.1 (individuals influencing their ecological and sociopolitical contexts), and this should be taken to signal the presence of feedback in the framework more generally, even though not all relationships are indicated in Fig. 2.1.

At the extreme left are two major classes of influence (background variables of ecological context and sociopolitical context), and at the extreme right are the psychological characteristics that are usually the focus of psychological research (including both observable behaviors and inferred characteristics, such as motives, abilities, traits, and attitudes). The two middle sets of variables (process variables) represent the various forms of transmission or influence from population variables to individuals. For completeness, both biological and cultural factors are included; however, the usual emphasis in cross-cultural psychology is on cultural influences.

In more detail, the ecological context is the setting in which human organisms and the physical environment interact; it is best understood as a set of *relationships* that provide a range of life possibilities for a population. Such an interactive point of view is the essence of an ecological approach, and allows us to avoid the pitfalls of earlier approaches, such as that of environmental determinism (Berry, 1976; Feldman, 1975). Because the organism interacts with its habitat primarily to exploit resources to sustain individual and collective life, the basic feature of this ecological context is *economic activity*. This variable involves nonindustrial cultural groups being rated with respect to their degree of reliance on five kinds of economic activity: hunting, gathering, fishing, pastoralism, and agriculture. Urban-industrial societies have a way of life in which other dimensions of economic activity have emerged and which are rated on other dimensions (the most common being socioeconomic status). However, each form of economic activity implies a different kind of relationship between the local human population and the resources of their habitat. These relationships in turn imply varying cultural, biological, and psychological outcomes.

With respect to adaptation at the population level, we take the position that individual behavior can be understood across cultures only when both cultural and biological features of our species are taken into account. This joint interest in cultural and biological influences on behavior appears to be not only balanced but indeed the only possible point of view to adopt; the exclusion of either culture or biology as factors in the explanation of human psychological variation makes little sense (Boyd & Richerson, 1985). These two major sources of influence are together adaptive to the contexts in which individuals live. Culture is transmitted by the central processes of *enculturation* and *socialization*.

However, not all outcomes can be seen as being the result of ecological relationships. Also depicted in Fig. 2.1 is the view that culture and individual behavior are affected by influences stemming from culture contact in the sociopolitical context of one's group. These come about with *acculturation*, due to such historical and contemporary experiences as colonial expansion, international trade, invasion, and migration.

It is important to note that not all relationships between the two major background variables and psychological outcomes are mediated by cultural or biological adaptation. Some influences are direct and rather immediate, such as environmental learning in a particular ecology (leading to a new performance), nutritional deficiency during a famine (leading to reduced performance), or a new experience with another culture (leading to new attitudes or values). These direct influences are indicated by the upper and lower arrows that bypass the two forms of population adaptation. Many of these direct influences have been the focus of the work of Barker (1968) and Brunswik (1957) in the field of ecological psychology. Because individuals can recognize, screen, appraise, and alter all of these influences, whether direct or mediated, there are likely to be wide individual differences in the psychological outcomes.

To summarize, it is proposed that the distribution of psychological characteristics within and across groups can best be understood with the help of a framework such as this one. When ecological, biological, cultural, and acculturational factors are identified and taken into consideration, it should be possible to account for how and why people differ from one another and also why they are the same.

Indigenous Cognition

Most studies of cognition have adopted concepts (e.g., "intelligence") and measures (e.g., "IQ tests") that are rooted in one culture (e.g., Western Euroamerican) and then employed in other cultures (e.g., African or Indigenous American). It should be evident that these studies are very much at odds with the ecological approach that was just outlined. An important alternative to this outsider's approach is to take an insider's view by situating observations within an *indigenous psychology* (Kim & Berry, 1993) or by taking an *emic* rather than an *etic* approach (Berry, 1989). When it is done with respect to cognition specifically, then the field of *indigenous cognition* is created (see Berry, Irvine, & Hunt, 1988).

Although not yet precisely defined, indigenous cognition is what people do cognitively in their daily lives, whether in our own or some other culture, and which has usually escaped the attention of psychologists who work in formal settings with standard cognitive assessment procedures. In addition to emphasizing the mundane aspects of cognitive life, indigenous cognition involves the cognitive study of cognitive life, in the sense that it not only takes into account cognitive performances by individuals but is also concerned with how people understand what they are doing and how they interpret it. Implicit also is the view that these subjective interpretations require investigation guided by the emic tradition of research in cross-cultural psychology and cognitive anthropology (Headland, Pike, & Harris, 1990; Schliemann, Carraher, & Ceci, in press).

Put in these terms, the study of indigenous cognition is first clearly part of a current trend in cognitive psychology that can be identified by the notions of "everyday cognition" (Goodnow, 1980; Rogoff & Lave, 1984; Wassmann & Dasen, 1993) and "practical intelligence" (Sternberg & Wagner, 1986). In these theoretical and empirical statements, there is a focal concern for how individuals develop and display their cognitive activity in mundane (nonformal, nonacademic) situations, such as working on the job, doing the shopping, playing games, or waiting on tables. In such situations, there is the opportunity to observe cognitive activity in natural settings, and in a wider variety of contexts than psychologists have traditionally employed in their research. Two of the obvious consequences of this approach are that although such studies are likely to be more generalizable to others within a culture, they may also be less comparable across cultures and encounter more difficulties in making inferences from the data obtained; this is the classical trade-off known well to field workers in many disciplines.

To avoid idiosyncrasies based on a single informant, the study of indigenous cognition must also attend to local cultural (collective, as distinct from individual) interpretations. Cognitive life is not merely an individual phenomenon but is influenced by the cultural norms and practices with which one grows up (Rogoff, 1991). Hence, collective views need to be studied and drawn into the interpretation of the data obtained. Cultural values and goals for cognitive development in the community need to be understood so that development toward these goals and eventual competence can be assessed. This is where the crux of the issue lies. Such an approach, of course, is an emic one, in which indigenous views are extremely useful in the interpretation of any body of psychological data. In a field such as cognition, however, the Western notion of general intelligence so dominates the research and practice of cognitive assessment that we need to be reminded constantly of the problem.

Bricoleurs and Bricolage

To capture some of these ideas, in our paper "Bricolage: Savages Do It Daily," we concluded that "bricolage is basic, and savages are everywhere" (Berry & Irvine, 1986, p. 298). To understand this cryptic conclusion, we need to develop some shared notions about the term *bricolage*. The term bricolage was used by Lévi-Strauss (1962) to refer to work of an odd-job sort. The worker (bricoleur) is "someone who works with his hands and uses devious means compared to those of the craftsman" (Lévi-Strauss, 1962, pp. 16–17). The translator adds that the term bricoleur has no precise equivalent in English. He is a man who undertakes odd jobs and is a Jack-of-all-trades, or a kind of professional do-it-yourself man, but he is of a different standing from, for instance, the English odd job man or handyman (in Lévi-Strauss, 1962, p. 17). The term was introduced as an analogy to highlight a contrast between "the savage mind" and contemporary scientific thinking; for example, "cash-crop agriculture is hardly to be confused with the science of the botanist" (Lévi-Strauss, 1962, p. 3). Although promoting this contrast in cognitive life, Lévi-Strauss nevertheless affirmed the psychic unity of cognitive activity: Magic and science are "the same sort of mental operations and they differ not so much in kind as in the different types of phenomena to which they are applied" (Lévi-Strauss, 1962, p. 13).

The approach taken in this chapter is that cognitive processes are very likely to be universal (a view now widely espoused in crosscultural psychology, and one based on a considerable amount of research; see Berry, Poortinga, Segall, & Dasen, 1992), but that these day-to-day survival skills are not to be so lightly dismissed; rather, they are the very stuff on which we may be able to build a more culturally relevant, more comprehensive, and less ethnocentric conception of human cognitive functioning.

Cognitive Values

Cognitive values comprises the set of cognitive goals that are collectively shared and toward which children are socialized in a particular society. It is essential to understand these goals, because we cannot assess how far a person has gone unless we understand where he or she is going. Studies of the meaning of intelligence in differing cultures (see Berry, 1984, for a review), and of socialization more generally (e.g., Rhys-Williams, 1983), constitute an important set of data in our attempt to understand the kinds of cognitive competence children are directed toward. These studies exhibit a wide and diverse set of cognitive goals, often diverging sharply from the Western "quick, analytic, abstract" cluster so much inculcated by our school system and so thoroughly incorporated in our assessment devices.

Another approach to understanding these values or goals is to engage in an ecological analysis (Berry, 1980) in which one attempts to find out what has to be accomplished, not only cognitively, but also socially and emotionally, in order to live in a particular cultural context. This kind of "job analysis" for the task of life has proven to be extraordinarily fruitful for the fields of ethology, population biology, and ecological anthropology. Within these traditions the question is asked: "What sorts of knowledge and abilities are needed in order to carry on life in this part of the world?" In anthropology, the ecological approach has grown in recent years, so that it is now common to find explanations of cultural phenomena in terms of their interrelationships with natural phenomena in a particular ecosystem.

In psychology, ecological analysis was stimulated by the observations of Ferguson (1956), quoted at the beginning of this chapter. Expanding this notion of cultural prescription of cognitive development, one can seek and discover (in the terms used by Berry, 1966), the *ecological demands* made on people living in a particular ecosystem, and the *cultural aids* available that permit the cultural transmission and individual learning of particular abilities. This approach is also implicit in Bruner's (1966) notion of cultural amplifiers, and the subsequent work of Berland (1982, 1983) with them: "Every ecocultural system has a curriculum of basic experiences and attendant skills provided through a variety of lifelong socialization strategies" (Berland, 1982, p. 50).

A model proposing four levels of ecological analyses has been developed by Berry (1980, and revised in Berry et al., 1992). Fig. 2.2 illustrates four environmental (ecological and cultural) contexts and four human effects related through a human organism. The structure of the diagram places the various contexts at the left and the various effects at the right. Toward the top are natural and holistic contexts and effects, and at the bottom are more controlled and reductionistic contexts and effects. It is a hierarchical model, in the sense that lower levels are nested in the levels above them.

Looking in more detail at the environmental contexts, the *ecological context* is the "natural-cultural habitat" of Brunswik (1957). It consists of all the relatively permanent characteristics of a cultural system that provide the context for human action (e.g., climate, topography, resources). Nested in this ecological context are two levels of the "life

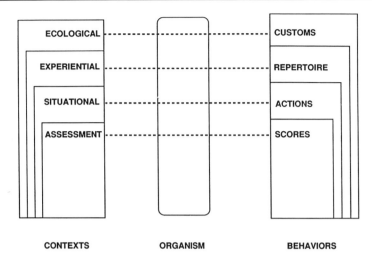

FIG. 2.2. A framework for ecological analyses (from Berry, 1980).

space" or "psychological world" of Lewin (1936). The first, the *experiential context*, is that pattern of recurrent experiences and deliberate training (enculturation and socialization) that provides a basis for learning; it is essentially the set of independent variables that cross-cultural psychology tries to spot as being operative in a particular habitat in the development of behavioral characteristics. The other, the *situational context*, is the limited set of environmental circumstances that may be observed to account for particular behaviors (e.g., recreational and other daily activities); these are immediate in space and time, and "set the stage" for a particular performance. The fourth context, the *assessment context*, represents those environmental characteristics that are designed by the researcher (e.g., cognitive tasks or questions) to elicit a particular response or test score. The assessment context may or may not be nested in the first three contexts; the degree to which it is nested represents the ecological validity of the experimental task or test item.

Paralleling these four contexts are four psychological outcomes or effects. The first, *customs*, refers to the complex, long-standing, and shared behavior patterns that are developed and in place in a population as an adaptive response to the ecological context. It includes all the established and shared patterns of behavior that are distributed in a cultural group and constitute the culture of the group. The second, *repertoire*, is the set of behaviors that has been learned over time in the recurrent experiential context. Included here are the abilities, traits, and attitudes that have been nurtured in particular roles, or acquired by specific training or education, whether formal or informal. A third effect, *actions*, are those performances that appear in response to immediate stimulation or experience. In contrast to one's repertoire, they are not a function of role experience or long-term training, but appear in fleeting reply to immediate experiences. The fourth effect, *scores*, is comprised of those behaviors that are observed, measured, and recorded during psychological experiments or testing. If the assessment context is nested in the other contexts, then the scores may be representative of the behaviors, repertoire, and customs of the individual and the culture. If the assessment instrument has ecological validity, then the scores will have behavioral validity.

Relationships can be traced between the elements across the model. The *ecological arc* operates across the top of the model. It is concerned with the life situation (in physical environmental and cultural terms) of human beings and their accomplishments. At the second level, the *experiential arc* is concerned with tying together recurrent independent variables in the experience of individuals with their characteristic behaviors. The third level, that of the *situational arc*, involves understanding more specific acts as a function of immediate and current experience. And at the fourth level, the *assessment arc* relates to the laboratory or other systematic study of relationships between controlled stimulation (experimental problems or test items) and test scores. These latter relationships are known to be variable, depending on the other contexts in the model (e.g., Irvine, 1983).

Whether from anthropological or psychological sources, the essence of this ecological approach in cross-cultural psychology (Berry, 1975) is one that views cognitive (and other psychological) functioning as situated in an ecological and cultural context; the task is to specify the general life requirements for the group as a whole, and then to identify how these are communicated to the developing individual prior to assessment. It is basically making sure that we know the cognitive values or goals being pursued by a particular cultural group, which are being transmitted to developing members of the group, before assessment is begun.

Cognitive Development

Once the goals have been identified, it should be possible to attempt to discover how far individuals have traveled toward them. Because, in the perspective of indigenous cognition, groups may have radically different goals, these can be diagrammed as being radically different.

Figure 2.3 is an attempt to capture this variation by drawing paths from a common underlying (universal) cognitive process toward varying goals along a number of radii. Although no diagram can

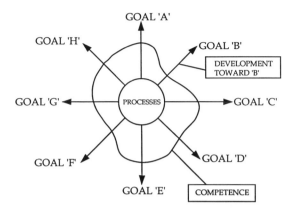

FIG. 2.3.   Variations in cognitive development in relation to differing cognitive goals.

capture the complexity of natural phenomena, Fig. 2.3 does manage to show in graphical form the goals of development and the extent of development toward them that may be reached. The essential point is that if assessment of "progress" toward one goal is attempted, when ecological or cultural evidence informs us that the individual is headed for another goal, then serious underestimation of cognitive development will occur.

To make this view more concrete, evidence from reviews of cultural definitions of intelligence (Berry, 1984) shows clearly that in some groups holistic rather than analytic problem solving is culturally valued, and that deliberation rather than haste is the proper course of action; moreover, collective discussion, rather than individual reflection may be the preferred mode. In a society with this cluster of cognitive values, an individual confronted with a standardized Western psychological test may exhibit "minimal development" toward the analytic-fast-individualistic criterion, but be maximally developed toward the holistic-reflective-collectivistic criterion. The tragedy, of course, is that most psychologists would not discover this, given their nonrecognition of alternative cognitive goals.

An Empirical Example

Our recent work among the Cree of Northern Ontario (Berry & Bennett, 1989, 1991) has focused on the distribution and use of literacy in the syllabic script as a function of historical and cultural factors, and on its relationship to cognitive test performance. One result of this project has been the realization that there is a need for a more fine-grained and locally based understanding of how the Cree themselves conceive of cognitive competence, how they identify it and transmit it to their children, and how they know when it has been successfully inculcated in the matured individual (cf. Dasen, 1984).

To accomplish this task we (Berry & Bennett, 1992) used both ethnographic and psychometric procedures to uncover what the Cree understand by notions such as "intelligent," "smart," "clever," "able," and "competent." The first stage was to work with a small set of key informants to elicit Cree concepts for these and similar terms, and to seek both linguistic and contextual elaborations of them. We collected a list of 20 words dealing with cognitive competence through a series of very loosely structured interviews conducted with Cree speakers in Big Trout Lake (Northern Ontario).

The sample consisted of 32 males and 28 females (mean age = 41.3) with varying levels of formal schooling: 23.3% had virtually no schooling (2 years or less), 28.4% had completed primary school; and 48.3% had some high school or more (mean of 6.97 years, standard deviation of 3.55).

Card Sorting

The 20 words were written out in the Cree syllabic script on cards. The cards were given to participants, all of whom were able to read syllabics. We asked them to put the cards into piles on the basis of similarity of meaning. Multidimensional scaling revealed two dimensions (see Fig. 2.4). Reading from left to right (on the horizontal axis) there is a movement from negative to positive evaluation, with the

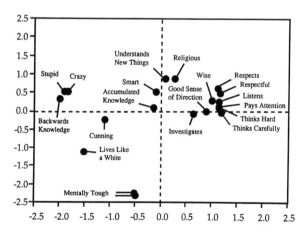

FIG. 2.4.   Two dimensions of meanings of cognitive competence among the Cree (from Berry & Bennett, 1992).

possible inclusion of a moral aspect as well. That is to say, words on the left side of the diagram are not only disliked (stupidity and craziness are not positively valued) but they are probably considered to be morally reprehensible as well (viz. "cunning" and "backwards knowledge").

The vertical dimension is more difficult to label. At one extreme we have two words for "mentally tough" in the sense of brave, of having courage or fortitude. At the other extreme are "religious" and "understands new things." This dimension may have something to do with openness or sensitivity. The paucity of words in the lower half of the diagram makes it difficult to be more specific.

Looking further at Fig. 2.4, there is a cluster of words on the right side and slightly above center (i.e., both sensitive and morally good) containing the words we have rendered in English as wise, respects, respectful, listens, pays attention, thinks hard, and thinks carefully. This cluster, we suggest, constitutes the core meaning of what we will refer to as "thinking well in Big Trout Lake." All of the words in this cluster need some elaboration as most have a distinctly Cree flavor and do not translate easily into English.

It is interesting to note that the word most directly opposite the core cluster, the word that is therefore most distant from it on both dimensions (i.e., insensitive and morally bad) is we-mi-ti-ko-shi-wa-ti-se. This has been rendered as "lives like a White," in the sense of behaving, thinking, and comporting oneself like a White person. It would be tempting to regard this as something like the Cree version of being a "klutz" (particularly because clumsy boorishness features in so many stories of White men in the bush), and has some quite derogatory overtones. Its very position on the diagram should alert us to look for meanings of negative moral content and insensitivity. Its closeness to words like cunning, stupid, crazy, and backwards knowledge (wisdom turned to the service of disruption and disharmony) underlines this view.

We now look more closely at the meaning of terms in this core cluster:

Wise, Thinks Hard, Thinks Carefully.   Two items were invariably among the first that were given to us for smart or intelligent. The first was *ka-gi-ta-wen-tam* (he is smart, he is wise). The second were words deriving from *ma-mi-ta-nej-i-gan* (mind).

We have rendered *ka-gi-ta-wen-tam* as wise in order not to confuse it with another word, *ki-ken-da-so* (smart in Fig. 2.4), which also means smart, but without some of the loftier connotations of good thinking that attach to *ka-gi-ta-wen-tam*. *Ki-ken-da-so* was the word most usually given to describe smartness displayed at school. The closeness of *ki-ken-da-so* to understands new things and accumulated knowledge, both of which describe mental abilities that Euro-Canadians feel are crucial in classroom education, lends support to this more school-like interpretation. All three words are at some distance from the core cluster of good thinking.

Respects, Respectful. The idea of respect centers around knowledge of and personal engagement with people, animals, objects (both manmade and natural), the Creator, the land, and so on. European notions of submission and exaggerated deference, both of which derive from attaching importance to unequal status, do not appear to be involved. Discussions of respect, and disrespect, in Big Trout Lake invariably shade off into areas English designates with words or phrases such as understanding, deep knowledge, enjoyment, enthusiasm, self-control, and following advice.

Paying Attention. The word we have rendered "pays attention," *ka-ya-kwom-si-kan-tak* was just as often translated as "discipline" or "self-control." Its closeness to the two words for respect, discussed earlier, is shown by the fact that when we asked for a word meaning the opposite of "paying attention" or "discipline" we were usually given *ma-nen-chi-ge*, "disrespect."

Again, as with the words we translated as "respect" this notion of discipline lacks the European nuances of coercion, force, obligation, or social duty, all of which reflect the idea of power exercised between persons of unequal status. The people of Big Trout Lake are not saying that individuals have a moral duty to listen to others and carry out what they say. They are telling us that listening to others is smart.

In discussions of the words in the core cluster three very strong emphases developed: taking time, being self-sufficient, and allowing abilities to develop.

Taking Time. There is an emphasis in all "good thinking" on going slowly and thoroughly, on eschewing rapid action and decision. This is close to what we would call, in English, deliberation. Patience is also frequently mentioned as an attribute of good thinking but it is patience with a heavy admixture of perseverance. The patient person is one who sticks with a task, who does not give up when he starts feeling lazy, who is hard working but not in a hurry. The patient person is the tortoise and not the hare.

Independence, Self-Sufficiency. The goal of traditional socialization was to make a person self-sufficient, to develop a person who would be able to look after oneself, someone who could survive without being a drain on others. The theme of survival is a constant one in any discussions of Cree traditional ways of life, not without good reason. Unnecessary dependence on others was seen as irresponsible and immature behavior.

Development. The commodity or transactional model of knowledge (the idea that knowledge is some kind of substance that can be acquired, collected, exchanged, and stored, that it is something you can get more of from a teacher or a library, and that the more of it you have the better you are and the better off you are) is a model that is foreign to the traditions of Big Trout Lake. Certainly, Cree people expect that guidance and advice will go from old to young; certainly they expect some sharing of experience. But essentially "good thinking" is seen as something that develops within each individual. A person can hinder, or even misdirect, this development (using knowledge for evil or disruptive purposes, for instance) but in the proper circumstances, for ordinary people, knowledge will grow in its own good time. There is a sense here of allowing experience to work on you, of not closing yourself off from your own wisdom. There is also a sense of trust in the process that reinforces a social predilection for letting people go about things in their own way and not constantly trying to supervise, direct, and interfere.

Cognitive Competence

To continue the argument, the cognitive competence of an individual in a particular culture may be conceived of as actual progress toward a number of culturally valued cognitive goals. In terms of Fig. 2.3, distance out from the center along a culturally valued radius is the measure of development and thus implies competence of a particular sort. Of course, competencies are usually multiple, and so the full picture of an individual's competence would be represented by a space enclosed by a line joining the various points of development on each radius (indicated by the globular form in Fig. 2.3). In this example, developed competence in Ability C is substantially greater than in Ability B.

Indigenous and Universal Cognition

Any science seeks generalizations, and cognitive science is no exception. In terms of the present discussion, we wish not only to uncover indigenous cognition, but also to discover what might be common or universal about cognitive functioning among all human groups. This tension, between the local and the universal, is the core problem in cross-cultural psychology, and is clearly present in studies of cognition. Without denying this conflictual quality, it is also possible to view the difference as two complementary functions. Such a view has been proposed by Berry (1984), and is illustrated in Fig. 2.5.

Down the left is a set of cognitive domains or topics that can be identified in various cultures. These can be discovered by ecological analysis or by the study of cognitive values in various societies. Across the top is a broad range of cultures selected to represent variation in human societies, in which one might carry out cognitive research. Integrating information down a column (across topics within a society), we develop a local indigenous psychology of cognition. Integrating information across a row (over societies within a topic), we develop a psychological universal for that topic. Integrating both across and down will eventually yield a universal cognitive psychology.

At the present time we have perhaps achieved an indigenous psychology in a few (mainly Western) cultures, and we may have achieved some degree of comprehensive knowledge about a few areas of cognitive functioning across a range of cultures (a universal for the particular cognitive function), but we have clearly not achieved a fully universal cognitive psychology. This will continue to be true well into the future if we persist in ignoring both the bricolage and the indigenous conceptions of other cultures, remaining fixated on conceptions based on our bricolage to carry out research on their cognitive functioning.

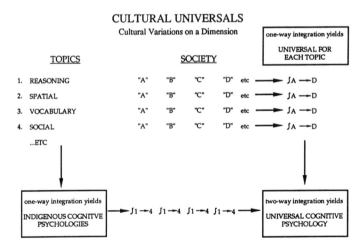

FIG. 2.5.   Toward a universal cognitive psychology (from Berry, 1984).

CONCLUSION

Adopting the position of cultural ecology permits psychologists to describe and understand cross-cultural variations in cognitive development and performance, at the same time asserting the presence of common, species-wide cognitive processes. This universalist orientation, in turn, permits psychologists to interpret cognitive performance differences across cultures in their own terms, and as being adapted to the ecological and cultural context in which the cultural group carries out its life. The indigenous approach permits psychologists to understand these local contexts and meanings, and to avoid the use of *imposed etic* terms such as "general intelligence," and the associated ethnocentrism, bias, and harm that can be inflicted on differing cultural groups.

The empirical example presented in this chapter is only one of many explorations of indigenous conceptions of cognitive competence now being carried out within the conceptual framework of cross-cultural psychology. It has taken this field a long time to begin to move from a singular notion of general intelligence, and of its assessment by standard IQ tests. Patterns of cognitive abilities are now being studied both in context and with culturally informed psychometric procedures. The task of incorporating these more culturally sensitive ideas and findings has really only just begun, and so we remain a long way from attaining the panhuman understanding of cognitive functioning that most of us believe is possible.

REFERENCES

Barker, R. (1968). *Ecological psychology*. Stanford, CA: Stanford University Press.

Berland, J. (1982). *No five fingers are alike: Cognitive amplifiers in social context*. Cambridge, MA: Harvard University Press.

Berland, J. (1983). Dress rehearsals for psychological performance. In S. H. Irvine & J. W. Berry (Eds.), *Human assessment and cultural factors* (pp. 139–154). New York: Plenum.

Berry, J. W. (1966). Temne and Eskimo perceptual skills. *International Journal of Psychology, 1*, 207–229.

Berry, J. W. (1975). An ecological approach to cross-cultural psychology. *Nederlands Tijdschrift voor de Psychologie, 30*, 51–84.

Berry, J. W. (1976). *Human ecology and cognitive style: Comparative studies in cultural and psychological adaptation*. London: Sage.

Berry J. W. (1980). Ecological analyses for cross-cultural psychology. In N. Warren (Ed.), *Studies in cross-cultural psychology* (Vol. 2, pp. 157–189). London: Academic Press.

Berry, J. W. (1984). Towards a universal psychology of cognitive competence. *International Journal of Psychology, 19*, 335–361.

Berry, J. W. (1986). The comparative study of cognitive abilities: A summary. In S. E. Newstead, S. H. Irvine, & P. L. Dann (Eds.), *Human assessment: Cognition and motivation* (pp. 57–74). Dordrecht, Netherlands: Martinus Nijhoff.

Berry, J. W. (1989). Imposed etics, emics, derived etics. *International Journal of Psychology, 24,* 721–735.

Berry, J. W. (1995). The descendants of a model. *Culture and Psychology, 1,* 373–380.

Berry, J. W., & Bennett, J. A. (1989). Syllabic literacy and cognitive performance among the Cree. *International Journal of Psychology, 24,* 429–450.

Berry, J. W., & Bennett, J. A. (1991). *Cree syllabic literacy: Cultural context and psychological consequences.* Tilburg, Netherlands: Tilburg University Press Monographs in Cross-Cultural Psychology.

Berry, J. W., & Bennett, J. A. (1992). Cree conceptions of cognitive competence. *International Journal of Psychology, 27,* 73–88.

Berry, J. W., & Irvine, S. H. (1986). Bricolage: Savages do it daily. In R. Sternberg & R. Wagner (Eds.), *Practical intelligence: Nature and origins of competence in the everyday world* (pp. 271–306). New York: Cambridge University Press.

Berry, J. W., Irvine, S. H., & Hunt, E. B. (Eds.). (1988). *Indigenous cognition: Functioning in cultural context.* Dordrecht, Netherlands: Martinus Nijhoff.

Berry, J. W., Poortinga, Y., Segall, M., & Dasen, P. (1992). *Cross-cultural psychology: Research and applications.* New York: Cambridge University Press.

Boyd, R., & Richerson, P. J. (1985). *Culture and the evolutionary process.* Chicago: University of Chicago Press.

Bruner, J. S. (1966). On cognitive growth. In J. S. Bruner, R. Oliver, & P. M. Greenfield (Eds.), *Studies in cognitive growth* (pp. 1–67). New York: Wiley.

Brunswik, E. (1957). Scope and aspects of the cognition problem. In A. Gruber (Ed.), *Cognition: The Colorado Symposium.* Cambridge, MA: Harvard University Press.

Dasen, P. R. (1984). The cross cultural study of intelligence: Piaget and the Baoulé. *International Journal of Psychology, 19,* 407–434.

Feldman, D. (1975). The history of the relationship between environment and culture in ethnological thought: An overview. *Journal of the History of the Behavioural Sciences, 110,* 67–81.

Ferguson, G. A. (1956). On transfer and the abilities of man. *Canadian Journal of Psychology, 10,* 121–131.

Goodnow, J. (1980). Everyday concepts of intelligence and its development. In N. Warren (Ed.), *Studies in cross-cultural psychology* (Vol. 2, pp. 191–219). London: Academic Press.

Headland, T., Pike, K. L., & Harris, M. (Eds.). (1990). *Emics and etics: The insider/outsider debate.* Newbury Park, CA: Sage.

Irvine, S. H. (1983). Testing in Africa and America: The search for routes. In S. H. Irvine & J. W. Berry (Eds.), *Human assessment and cultural factors* (pp. 45–58). New York: Plenum.

Irvine, S. H., & Berry, J. W. (Eds.). (1988). *Human abilities in cultural context.* New York: Cambridge University Press.

Kim, U., & Berry, J. W. (Eds.). (1993). *Indigenous psychologies.* Newbury Park, CA: Sage.

Lévi-Strauss, C. (1962). *La pensée sauvage* [The savage mind]. Paris: Plon.

Lewin, K. (1936). *Principles of topological psychology.* London: Methuen.

Rhys-Williams, R. (1983). *Socialization.* Englewood Cliffs, NJ: Prentice-Hall.

Rogoff, B., & Lave, J. (Eds.). (1984). *Everyday cognition: Its development in social context.* Cambridge, MA: Harvard University Press.

Rogoff, B. (1991). *Apprenticeship in thinking: Cognitive development in social context.* London: Oxford University Press.

Schliemann, A., Carraher, D., & Ceci, S. (in press). Everyday cognition. In J. W. Berry, P. R. Dasen, & T. S. Saraswathi (Eds.), *Handbook of Cross-Cultural Psychology: Vol. 2. Basic Processes and Human Development*. Boston: Allyn & Bacon.

Spearman, C. (1927). *The abilities of man: Their nature and measurement*. London: Macmillan.

Sternberg, R., & Wagner, R. (Eds.). (1986). *Practical intelligence: Origins of competence in the everyday world*. New York: Cambridge University Press.

Wassmann, J., & Dasen, P. (Eds.). (1993). *Alltagswissen/Les savoirs quotidiens/Everyday cognition*. Freiburg, Switzerland: Universitatsverlag Freiburg.

Whiting, J. W. (1974). *A model for psychocultural research* (annual report, 1–14). Washington, DC: American Anthropological Association.

CHAPTER 3

Concepts of Ability

Michael J. A. Howe
University of Exeter

Acquiring a human ability is a time-consuming and sometimes arduous activity. In some research being undertaken by John Sloboda, Jane Davidson, and myself, looking at the early progress of young musicians, we have found that 16-year-olds who are seriously committed to music practice for 4 hours per day, on average. By the time they are 18, those youngsters who have made sufficient progress to have a good chance of being able to enjoy careers as professional musicians will already have spent up to 9,000 hours practicing—a very substantial amount of time.

I sometimes find myself wishing that I could painlessly "read in" to my brain a new skill or a new body of knowledge, much as I can install a new item of software into my computer. Many people harbor the illusion that this is actually possible, as is demonstrated by the healthy sales of so-called "subliminal tapes" in Britain and the United States. The idea is that you play these recorded auditory tapes, and messages that you are not aware of hearing find their way into your brain, making you healthier, slimmer, more attractive to the opposite sex, better at remembering, more self-confident, or whatever, depending on the particular contents of the subliminal messages. The only problem with all this is that it does not work. Neither do other ways of trying to read knowledge or skills into the brain, such as so-called "learning in one's sleep." Unlike computers, human brains have developed in ways that do not make this possible, in part, perhaps, because they have evolved from earlier brains in which the capacity to acquire and use new information and skills did not have quite the priority that it has for us today.

I want to raise some conceptual issues that arise when we think about human abilities. Thinking about such matters can be useful because it can help prevent us going off in an unpromising direction, or proceeding in a way that depends on assumptions that are incorrect. Dennett (1993) noted that one of the most difficult things to do when trying to understand human consciousness is to discover what are the right questions to ask about it, and he suggested that we have not yet managed to do that. We are no longer at quite that stage where human abilities are concerned, but it is worth pondering whether the questions that come to mind, when we are thinking about people's abilities, are always the ones that offer the best ways of extending our understanding.

Efforts to understand human abilities are plagued by conceptual problems. One difficulty stems from the fact that there is more than one way in which we can use the word *ability*. Two ways we can use the word are these. First we can use it in order to make statements about what a person can do. For example, we can say that a person who plays the piano has musical ability, or possibly piano-playing ability. In this context the word ability is being used in a purely descriptive way. By saying a person has musical ability, we may be simply saying that the person is someone who can do musical things.

Second, and alternatively, we can use the word ability when we make statements that purport to explain why someone can do something that person demonstrates he or she can do, in other words to say what the person has that makes it possible for him or her to do something. So we can say that someone plays the piano because he or she has musical ability, or alternatively, piano-playing ability. Here we are using the concept of ability to explain something. Explanatory uses of concepts are often more problematic than purely descriptive ones, and there are occasions where we might want to argue that a concept, which is in reality only a descriptive one, is being inappropriately used as though it were a descriptive one. It would be possible to debate at length about whether or not one can have a concept of ability that is genuinely explanatory, and I myself have argued, that in the case of the related concept of intelligence, that is not really possible (Howe, 1988, 1989b, 1990). Although Spearman would have regarded abilities, and general intelligence especially, as being causal qualities, some people nowadays would be unconvinced about this.

In the ways in which the word ability is used in everyday life, the distinction between descriptive and explanatory uses of the term is not always clear. If someone says that a person succeeds in math because they have mathematical ability, we should not rush to assume that they necessarily think they have discovered the underlying reason for the person's success. All that may actually be intended is a vague statement that the person has what it takes to succeed in math. In real life, descriptive and explanatory uses of terms sometimes overlap.

But it is important to realize that, even if we can choose between alternative conceptions of ability, a construct such as ability cannot function as both a descriptive and an explanatory one at the same time. We ought not to fall into the trap of thinking that when we say someone has musical ability we are simultaneously implying that the piano playing demonstrates the existence of musical ability and that the presence of the ability provides the reason why the person is able to play the piano. If we do that, we get into all kinds of trouble, and we all too easily start going around in circles. For better or worse, however, in the folk psychology of common sense and everyday life, people do this all the time. On several occasions individuals have insisted to me that such or such a person has a real gift for music, and when I have asked them how they know, my informant has told me that the fact that person plays so well provides firm evidence that the gift exists. The same individual has gone on to insist that the reason the person plays music so well is that he or she has a gift for it. When I have suggested that although they think they are explaining something they are actually doing nothing of the kind, they are most offended.

We do need to try to keep a clear head and avoid getting into muddles like this. Although we do not always succeed, it is worth making the effort. When we introduce particular words and concepts, it is important to make it clear how we are using them. We cannot keep switching around.

What actually is an ability? That is partly an unanswerable question, or if there is an answer it has to be something unhelpful like, "It depends on the kind of ability concept that we happen to be using." One point that almost everyone agrees with is that an ability is not a thing, although people have a tendency to talk about abilities as though they were things despite the fact that they know that they are really not. That seems to be one example of the way in which a nonscientific folk psychology persists in permeating our thoughts about psychological issues even when we are aware that we ought to be more rigorous. Certainly, you cannot touch an ability or describe its physical nature. Attempts to go beyond saying what the ability achieves on behalf of its user and describing how what is achieved actually gets done quickly become stuck.

On the other hand, unless we believe in some kind of dualism we have to accept that there is some kind of physical embodiment corresponding with any psychological capacity, so even if an ability is not a thing it is not true to say that there is not any material event or mechanism that corresponds with the notion of an ability (in the explanatory usage of the concept): it is just that we almost certainly will not have identified it. To confuse matters a little more we are sometimes presented with clear evidence of the material aspects of an ability, for instance when, perhaps as a consequence of brain damage, certain capabilities disappear. Corresponding with—and to some extent supporting—the claim that some of the processing systems that contribute to the brain's learned activities are at least partly modular, and operate with a degree of independence and autonomy, is the fact that the computational mechanisms necessary for various mental capacities are physically located in particular brain areas. Distinct parts of the brain seem to house the processes that correspond with distinct capacities. Whereas abilities are not things, in the sense that we can point to them, the psychological processes that correspond to them do nonetheless have physical embodiments, just as the word processing capacities that are being used on my computer as I struggle to compose these words have physical embodiments in the physical events that are made to happen by the word processing software that has been installed into the computer.

Thinking about computers and software in connection with human abilities brings to mind two further issues that it is useful to be aware of when we are trying to increase our understanding of abilities. One is that it is difficult to decide how and where to place the boundaries between different abilities. That is true in a way even in a computer. If a computer has a word processing package installed, would we say that the computer has word processing ability, or would we say that the word ability is better suited for smaller groupings of the much more specific operations that combine to make word processing possible. And if we choose the latter, how specific do we want to be? Where do we draw the line between one ability and another? There is no obvious answer to that question: To some extent it is a matter of taste how small or large a segment of processing capacities we decide to designate as being an ability. There is a large element of arbitrariness here. If we are using the concept of ability in a purely descriptive way, based on measures of performance, we can look for patterns of performances that go together, possibly through the use of factor analysis. But when we do this we must remember that we are starting and ending with information that refers to patterns of performance. It is important not to assume that the factors that emerge will necessarily tell us much about processes that underlie, or cause, or give rise to those patterns of performance.

The other issue that comes to mind, when we introduce computer analogies in our efforts to understand human abilities, concerns the relationships between psychological capacities and the corresponding physical events in the brain. Computers and brains operate at more than one level. Two of those levels are the level of performance (the kinds of phenomena that psychologists examine and measure) and the physical level, broadly corresponding to the hardware of the computer and the anatomy and physiology of the brain. But the fact that both these levels demonstrably do exist does not necessarily mean that there are direct links between them, or correspondingly, that knowledge and understanding at one level will greatly contribute to our knowledge and understanding at another level.

In a computer it is quickly apparent that there is no direct mapping between these two levels. We can find plenty of physical characteristics to assess, ranging from crude indications of the computer's size or weight to much more refined indications of various aspects of its electronic functioning, but none of these measures will be much help for predicting whether the performance of one computer is better than another at, say word processing or doing mathematical calculations or statistics or whatever. It is even more unlikely that the physical measures will do much to help explain the difference in the computers' performance. Whereas that is most clearly the case when the two computers are similar in their physical hardware, even when they are not, it is still largely true to say that differences in measures of physical functioning may provide only the crudest indication about how different computers will actually perform at the kinds of tasks we set them.

There are real grounds for questioning the assumption, which is implicit in a fairly large body of psychological research, that looking for correlations between human performance and observations that are intended to provide direct measures or indirect indications of the human brain's physical functioning will prove to be as fruitful a scientific activity as some researchers believe it to be. The reason for my doubts stems from the observation by scientists such as Marr and Pylyshyn that, in human brains as well as in computers, there is no direct mapping between the psychological and the physical levels. Scientific progress demands that we depend on at least a third level of analysis, which may be called the computational level and which broadly corresponds to the program level (or, more accurately, levels) in computers and artificial intelligence systems. In other words, psychological and physiological levels of knowledge do not link together in the direct manner that they would need to in order for physiological knowledge to translate into psychological insights or vice versa.

Traditional approaches to abilities are concerned with questions about why and how people differ in what they achieve, and computer-based approaches that have links with work on artificial intelligence, also attempt to answer questions about why and how certain achievements become possible. But the latter approaches tend to be highly pragmatic, relatively unconcerned with theory, and tend to give little emphasis to concepts of ability as distinct from what is actually achieved. The idea of some kind of more or less general ability that underlies more specific capacity is not at all prominent in research and developments within the newer computational tradition.

A similar pragmatism, and a similar lack of emphasis on abilities (general or specific) as such, is seen in a largish and growing recent body of work on what its practitioners call *expertise*, or the *expert systems* approach. Here the aim is to describe the structure of expert performance in specific domains, and understand the mechanisms mediating the superior performance in various areas of competence, including chess, music, sports, dance, mathematics, and medicine. One assumption is that when we can describe precisely what it is that an expert is actually doing, we will be in a good position to help other people to do it. Some, but not all, researchers who utilize this approach regard expert performance as essentially a reflection of acquired skill that is gained over years of training and practice and involves the acquisition of specific knowledge and mental methods. It would not be entirely wrong to say that with this approach the notion of ability is to some extent bypassed, and that although practitioners are interested in some of the same questions that are raised when writers discuss abilities, the trend is to confine discussion to descriptions of the performances achieved, and the kinds of acquired knowledge and specific skills that give rise to those performances or achievements.

Even when we restrict ourselves to using the concept of ability as a purely descriptive one, and keep away from all the problems that emerge when we think of an ability as an explanatory construct, we do not entirely avoid conceptual problems. One source of difficulty that makes abilities hard to define and elusive to our efforts to get a conceptual grip on them, is that they seem to be in some respects less fixed or firm than we would like them to be. There is a growing body of evidence that what people are capable of doing may depend to a very considerable extent on the particular context in which they were asked to do it. This fact first impressed itself on my mind when I was looking at special skills in mentally retarded individuals. For example, one young man was no good at all at doing subtraction tasks if we asked them in the form "What is 14 minus 5" or "What is 12 minus 3" and hardly any better if we made the problems more concrete by saying something like "If I had 14 apples, and someone took 5 away, how many would that leave?" But if we gave him subtraction tasks that involved calendar dates he would do much better, even when the problems were much more complex, such as "If a man was born in 1879 how old would he have been in 1926?" (Howe, 1989a; Howe & Smith, 1988). So if I was asked to describe that individual's ability to subtract, I would find it extremely difficult. It just would not be possible to give a clear indication of the person's subtracting ability as such; one would have to point out that it depends on the context in which the subtracting is being undertaken.

Of course, mentally retarded individuals are untypical of people in general, and it is generally true that their capacity to solve problems is more dependent than that of other people on the contexts in which the task is set. All the same, there are many instances of context-dependent capacities in ordinary people. For instance, in a study of Liberian tailors who attempted arithmetic problems, Lave (1977) obtained measures of both the numbers of years of schooling each tailor had received and also the number of years tailoring experience. She gave them pairs of problems in arithmetic that were formally the same, but expressed either in a school context or in a tailoring context. Lave found that when a problem was communicated in a school task context the best predictor of how well a tailor would do was the number of years of schooling received. But when the identical arithmetic problem was expressed in tailoring context the best predictor of performance was the number of years of experience in tailoring. Again, if one wanted to make a statement about one of these individual's arithmetic ability, one would have to say that it depended on the context in which the arithmetic tasks were presented. Similar findings have emerged in research by Schliemann (1988) and others who have observed Brazilian "street children" who make a living selling lottery tickets. To buy and sell lottery tickets, these children have developed a sophisticated understanding of probabilities. But if you give them school-type problems, aimed at testing the same probability skills, they cannot do them at all. Conversely, students who have had lessons at school in which they learned about probability, permutations, and combinations, are not successful at all, and worse than street children involved in buying and selling the gambling tickets, when given tasks in which they have to apply the rules they have learned at school in out-of-school contexts.

Even when the tasks are absolutely identical, the physical and psychological contexts in which they have to be done may have a big effect on performance. Ceci and Bronfenbrenner (1985) gave children identical monitoring tasks which they performed either in their own homes or in a university laboratory. It was found that the children performed better, and used more effective strategies when they did the tasks at home than when in the other context. So again, even the apparently reasonable idea that an ability is fixed and plainly measurable seems to be something we cannot count on. If we cannot, that makes things rather difficult if we want concepts of ability to play a part in some kind of quantitative or broadly scientific enterprise. Abilities really do raise tricky conceptual problems. It is bad enough that they are hard to define and that it is so difficult to make nonarbitrary decisions about where to draw the boundaries between different abilities. When we add to that the problem that abilities—or, at least, people's capacities to do various tasks—often seem to have the "now it's here, now it's not here" quality that emerges in the experiments examining contextual effects, the difficulties multiply.

It would be easier to make firm statements about certain abilities if we could identify ones that are especially stable, or basic, or fundamental. Obviously, to some extent some abilities are more basic than others. For instance, if we do not possess the ability to identify numbers, various arithmetic skills will be impossible. Can we identify certain abilities that are particularly stable and resistant to change?

Even that turns out to be more difficult than we might expect. Take measured intelligence, for example, which for various reasons should be at least as stable and fixed as any more specific abilities. General intelligence, surely, ought to be hard to change. But even that may not be altogether the case. For instance, a number of studies investigating the influence of the summer vacation on IQ have shown a small but reliable decrement during the summer vacation months, especially among low-income youngsters whose summer activities are least likely to be similar to those in school. Similar results have emerged from studies of the effects of dropping out of school. When comparisons were made between boys who were equated in IQ, socioeconomic status and school grades at age 13, those who dropped out had a loss of 1.8 IQ points on average for each year of high school (in Sweden) not completed.

It is also possible to conduct investigations relating IQ scores to the age of starting school. One investigation capitalized on the fact that children in the German school system were required to be 6 years of age by April 1st on the year of entering school. So some children of very similar age (if their birthdays were around this date) could have up to a year difference in schooling. It was found that highly schooled 8-year-olds were closer in mental abilities to the least schooled 10-year-olds than they were to the least schooled 8-year-olds (Baltes & Reinert, 1969).

A number of studies have demonstrated that missing school is associated with low IQ; the more school missed the bigger being the drop. Interpreting that finding raises problems, of course, but some of them are avoided in studies that were in remote U.S. "hollows" in the Blue Ridge Mountains. Some communities are very cut off from the rest of the world, with school only infrequently being open. One school was only open for 16 months between 1918 and 1930. It was found that children who had the most schooling had IQ advantages of 10 to 30 points compared with children who had the least. Also, it was found that children born in one community in 1940, and who had relatively good schooling, had IQs on average 11 points higher than children born in the same community in 1930, and who did not have as much schooling. Again, studies conducted in South Africa, where schooling was cut short or delayed for reasons outside the family's control, had similar results—the earlier the schooling, and the more the schooling, the higher the IQ. Some of these findings suggest that IQ may be influenced by schooling just as much as other achievement measures—and this tends to contradict the assumption that IQ is necessarily more basic or more fundamental than other measures of achievement (Ceci, 1990). The idea that general intellectual ability underlies or constrains more specific abilities is at least open to question.

If we were asked how human abilities are organized, many people would share the view that there are numerous relatively specific abilities, and also a smaller number of broader and more general ones, that to some extent underlie the more specific, narrower, and broader abilities by some quality of general ability or intelligence. As a statement about the concept of ability that restricts itself to statements about our performance, or what we can do, that is fine, and there is no reason for taking exception to it. But we all too easily make the assumption that it is a statement that must refer to whatever makes that performance possible, that is to say, the reasons why we are able to do things. In other words, this widely shared mental model of human abilities refers not just to what we can do, but to whatever we have that enables us to do what we do. I think that the arguments in the preceding pages demonstrate that however attractive and commonsensical that way of thinking about human abilities is, and however widely that view is shared, it needs to be seriously questioned. If it is found wanting, where do we look for alternatives? I am not at all sure, but we might do worse than examining some of the systems that have been invented by scientists who have been working on computer-based artificial intelligence.

REFERENCES

Baltes, P., & Reinert, G. (1969). Cohort effects in cognitive development in children as revealed by cross-sectional sequences. *Developmental Psychology, 1,* 169–177.

Ceci, S. J. (1990). *On Intelligence . . . more or Less: a bio-ecological theory of intellectual development.* Englewood Cliffs, NJ: Prentice-Hall.

Ceci, S. J., & Bronfenbrenner, U. (1985). Don't forget to take the cupcakes out of the oven: Strategic time-monitoring, prospective memory, and context. *Child Development, 56,* 175–190.

Dennett, D. C. (1993). *Consciousness explained.* London: Penguin.

Howe, M. J. A. (1988). Intelligence as an explanation. *British Journal of Psychology, 79,* 349–360.

Howe, M. J. A. (1989a). *Fragments of genius: The strange feats of idiots savants.* London: Routledge & Kegan Paul.

Howe, M. J. A. (1989b). Separate skills or general intelligence: The autonomy of human abilities. *British Journal of Educational Psychology, 59,* 351–360.

Howe, M. J. A. (1990). Does intelligence exist? *The Psychologist, 3,* 490–493.

Howe, M. J. A., & Smith, J. (1988). Calendar calculating in "idiotic savants": How do they do it? *British Journal of Psychology, 79,* 371–386.

Lave, J. (1977). Tailor-made experiments and evaluating the intellectual consequences of apprenticeship training. *The Quarterly Newsletter of the Institute for Comparative Human Development, 1,* 1–3.

Schliemann, A. (1988). Understanding the combinatorial system: Development, school learning, and everyday experience. *Quarterly Newsletter of the Laboratory for Comparative Human Cognition, 10,* 3–7.

CHAPTER 4

Is Working Memory Capacity Spearman's g?

Patrick C. Kyllonen
Armstrong Laboratory

> does there exist any factor of *retentivity* pure and simple . . . a unitary function broad enough to cover its entire domain? . . . to some extent *retentivity* enters into cognitive operations of all kinds . . . it must be a second universal factor alongside of g . . .
>
> —Spearman (1927, p. 286)

Charles Spearman's remarkable contributions to psychology centered around his identifying the general factor in human cognition. He developed numerous methods—still in use today—for analyzing ability test scores, including reliability and factor analysis. These methods, particularly factor analysis, enabled Spearman to establish the necessity of a general factor of cognition, that is, a factor that influences virtually every cognitive performance.

But as Jensen (1994) pointed out, Spearman clearly understood "the important distinction between objectively identifying g, which he had accomplished, and explaining the nature, or cause of g, which he had not accomplished" (p. 1013). This is not to say that Spearman failed to speculate on the nature of g. He did, in the form of his "noegenetic laws," which define the processes of cognition. For example, in 1923 Spearman suggested that intelligence involves the construction of new concepts through the "eduction of relations" and the "eduction of correlates," and that tests would be good measures of g to the degree that performance on them required those processes. Further, Spearman

49

speculated that that which underlies individual differences in g is a kind of "mental energy" that varies in level from person to person. He also speculated on other potential factors that influenced cognition, such as retentivity, fatigue, and conative control.

Still, Spearman's speculations on the nature of g have not had a serious impact on present-day speculations, and indeed, the nature of the general factor ought to be considered a theme "identified from issues raised but not resolved in [his] book, *The Abilities of Man*" (as quoted from the Spearman Seminar invitation letter, October 1992, S. Irvine). We may be in a better position today to speak about the nature of g. Information-processing approaches to the study of intelligence offer promise for shedding light on the cognitive psychological nature of the general factor.

WORKING MEMORY AND OTHER INFORMATION-PROCESSING ABILITIES

Background

Information-processing approaches to the study of human intelligence have been in vogue for the past 20 years (for a review, see Kyllonen, 1994). Initially, there was considerable speculation that the information-processing approach would lead to an overhaul in our conception of human intelligence. There was talk that processing parameters such as encoding and comparison, and strategic variables, such as serial versus exhaustive memory search would someday replace traditional psychometric factors such as verbal, spatial, numerical, and reasoning ability. More recently, as theoreticians have evaluated the practical utility of testing systems based on information-processing notions, and as data inspired by such notions have come in, there has been a growing realization that new ability frameworks will probably not turn out to be radical departures from existing, conventional ones. It now appears that a synthesis of empirical findings emerging from a century of psychometrics' research combined with newer conceptions based on an information-processing framework holds out the greatest promise for an improved model of human intelligence.

Findings From Traditional Psychometrics

The conventional human abilities model, also sometimes referred to as the factor model, is based on a methodology of exploratory structural analyses performed on the matrix of intercorrelations among scores computed from various abilities tests. Structural analysis methods, such as factor analysis, cluster analysis, or multidimensional scaling, are designed to reveal regularities in the correlational data. This exploratory methodology, primarily the factor analysis variant, has revealed a fairly robust picture of the organization of human abilities (Carroll, 1993; and chapter 1, this volume). Two features of this robust picture stand out. One is that abilities are organized hierarchically. This means that a performance score on any given test can be understood as being determined jointly by a general factor and by a more specific factor (e.g., a verbal factor), and perhaps additionally by a still more specific factor (e.g., a verbal fluency factor). There is controversy about how many strata or layers there are in this hierarchy (Carroll suggests three, others suggest more), but the key point is that there is evidence for the simultaneous influence of both a general factor and more specific ones.

A second feature of the conventional abilities model concerns the identity of these more specific factors. The human abilities literature is replete with proposals for different factors, but perhaps three of the most robust factors, factors that appear in study after study, are verbal, spatial, and quantitative ability. This feature of the conventional abilities model is probably not as universally acknowledged as the hierarchical feature, but I believe that that is due to shortcomings in the method of exploratory factor analysis.

A tenet of information-processing approaches is the content–process distinction, and thus one might expect this distinction to be reflected somehow in the psychometric literature. It is not. That, I believe, is because exploratory factor analysis is susceptible to identifying factors that confound process and content, such as reasoning and quantitative ability factors. With the use of methods that are less susceptible to this kind of problem, such as multidimensional scaling (MDS), a content (e.g., verbal, spatial, quantitative) distinction emerges clearly.

To illustrate this point, consider a multidimensional scaling reanalysis of Thurstone's (1938) primary mental abilities data (Snow, Kyllonen, & Marshalek, 1984). Recall that Thurstone identified seven factors: verbal, word fluency, number facility, spatial visualization, reasoning, memory, and perceptual speed. Figure 4.1 shows the two-dimensional scaling solution. MDS attempts to represent variables in a similarity matrix as points in space, where the interpoint distances are proportional to the similarity coefficients. In this case the similarity matrix is a correlation matrix, and the similarity coefficients are correlation coefficients. Highly correlated tests thus appear close to one another in the configuration; modestly correlated tests appear

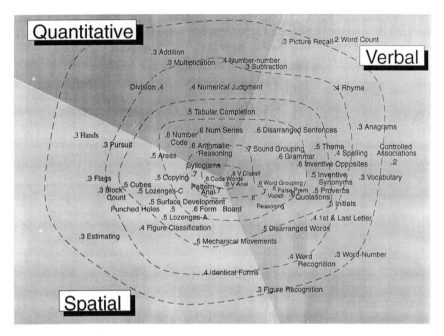

FIG. 4.1. Multidimensional scaling analysis of Thurstone's (1938) primary mental abilities data. Solution shows clear separation into content wedges, which motivates the domains dimension of the Cognitive Abilities Measurement (CAM) model.

further apart. Two interesting structural properties are clearly revealed by the analysis, as shown in Fig. 4.1. First, tests with high loadings on the general factor appear toward the center of the configuration, and loadings decrease systematically as one moves out toward the periphery. That is, MDS captures the general factor, a point originally noted by Marshalek, Lohman, and Snow (1977). Second, and more pertinent, tests are arrayed by content wedges with verbal content tests clustering together into one wedge in the configuration, spatial content tests into a second wedge, and quantitative content tests into a third wedge.

Ties to Cognitive Psychology

These two conclusions drawn from traditional psychometrics, the hierarchical organization of abilities, and the existence of something like verbal, quantitative, and spatial factors, are legitimate findings that must be accommodated by any comprehensive theory of abilities. Nevertheless, cognitive psychological, or information-processing approaches have grabbed the attention of many researchers because of perceived weaknesses in the psychometric approach. One is that the approach, although accurate in identifying robust performance dimensions, is silent on the question of the meaning of those dimensions. We know there is a general factor, for example; and we even have learned how to measure it fairly efficiently. We simply do not know what it is in any psychological sense. A related criticism is that the psychometric approach is not integrated with cognitive psychology. This is odd because both fields investigate essentially the same phenomena. One can find books in the cognitive literature dedicated to an investigation of reasoning ability, for example, that have no references to the factor-analytic literature on reasoning ability (e.g., Evans, 1982). Still another criticism is that the psychometric approach reveals the organization of the tests that are analyzed, but that is not necessarily the same as the organization of human abilities. There might be tests that could have been analyzed, but were never constructed. Psychometrics cannot discover factors underlying performance on tests that have been left out of a study.

The use of a cognitive, information-processing model can help avoid some of these problems with the traditional psychometric approach. In particular, a cognitive model can suggest factors that have been identified outside the context of psychometrics, and one can still then apply the psychometric methods to evaluate the veracity of those new factors. An additional benefit is that because cognitive psychology is concerned with the information-processing mechanisms underlying thought, there should be a better understanding of those factors discovered.

Applying such an approach depends on having a cognitive information-processing model to begin with. There is considerable debate in cognitive psychology over the details of the human information-processing system, but there is some agreement over at least the broad outlines of the system. Figure 4.2 displays what might be referred to as the "consensus information-processing model." The system consists of a short-term working memory, and two long-term memories, one containing declarative knowledge, the other procedural knowledge. In Fig. 4.2, declarative knowledge is represented by three file cabinets (one verbal, one quantitative, and one spatial) containing file folders; and procedural knowledge is represented by floppy disks (also segregated by content). Working memory, being the locus of immediate thought, contains a couple of folders and a floppy disk. This is to indicate the limited capacity of the working memory system, along with the idea that those limits pertain to the amount of material

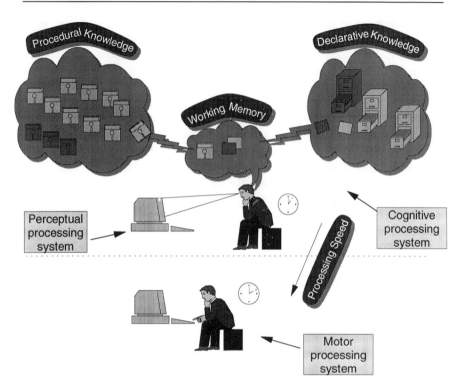

FIG. 4.2.   Consensus information-processing model, highlighting key sources of individual differences. These sources motivate the processing distinctions in the Cognitive Abilities Measurement (CAM) model.

(folders) that can be processed (floppy disk) at any one time. Another feature of Fig. 4.2 is that processing activity takes place in real time (represented by the clock in the background) and that various processing systems work together to transform incoming percepts into some kind of motoric response.

An obvious proposal is that the major components of the consensus information-processing system might serve as sources of individual differences. For example, individuals might vary in the capacity of their working memory system, in the breadth of long-term declarative or procedural knowledge they have available, or in the speed by which they are able to process information. This idea, elsewhere referred to as the four-sources model (Kyllonen & Christal, 1989), combined with the idea that the process aspects of abilities' tests can be decoupled from the content or domain aspect, together can serve as an outline for a new kind of information-processing test battery.

An Evaluation of the CAM Framework

We have referred to this proposal as the Cognitive Abilities Measurement (CAM) framework. To evaluate the viability of the CAM framework we must ask whether the descriptions of the four-source factors (working memory, processing speed, declarative, and procedural knowledge) can be specified in sufficient detail to allow for the generation of a battery of tests, and second, whether tests constructed in accordance with the description behave in a way consistent with models inspired by the framework.

We constructed a test battery by selecting tests from the literature, and supplementing those with tests developed by our in-house staff (Kyllonen, 1993). Tests were selected according to whether we considered them to be good measures of the four sources, balanced into the three domain areas (verbal, quantitative, and spatial). Figure 4.3 shows tests organized into the CAM taxonomy (version 1), a name we have applied to this work.

Under the heading "Source" are listed the four sources, Processing Speed (PS), Working Memory (WM), and so on. Under the heading "Domain" are listed the three content domains. Within each taxonomy cell are listed several tests that we used to measure the particular source. For example, in the Processing Speed row, Verbal column, there are three test names, Sentence Verification, Meaning Identity, and Category Identity. In total there are 25 tests. Each test took subjects about 15 minutes to complete, and thus the entire battery took about 6 hours.

We administered the 25-test battery to a group of 350 volunteers,

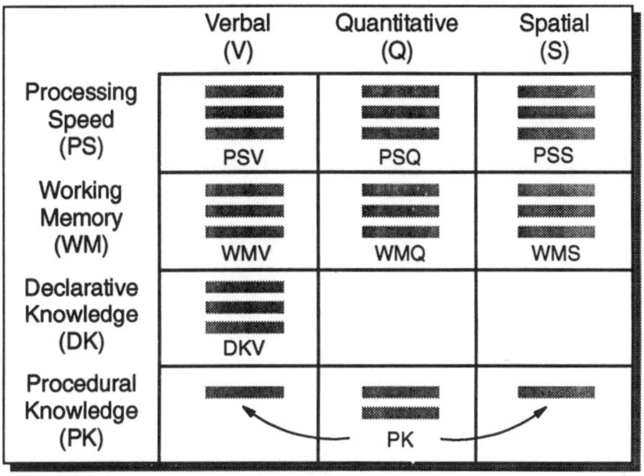

FIG. 4.3.   Cognitive Abilities Measurement (CAM) taxonomy (version 1).

whom we recruited through advertisements in local newspapers and other sources as part of a larger study on the relationship between aptitude variables and learning computer programming (more on the larger study later). For each test we computed either an accuracy score (percentage correct) or, in the case of the more highly speeded tests, an accuracy-per-unit-time score (percentage correct divided by average amount of time spent per item). From these scores we computed a 25 × 25 variance–covariance matrix, which we then analyzed using confirmatory factor analysis methods. (Interested readers may find descriptions of the tests and scoring procedures elsewhere in Kyllonen, 1994.)

There are numerous models suggested by the CAM taxonomy that can be tested against the CAM battery data. Some of these are shown in Fig. 4.4.

Figure 4.4a shows what might be referred to as a one-factor model, where each of the 25 tests is presumed to have a loading on a single general factor. (Spearman referred to this, of course, as the two-factor model, where the second factor was one specific to the particular test. Strictly, Spearman probably should have called it the one-plus-n-factor model, since the n specific factors are separate from each other.) Figure 4.4b shows what can be labeled a three content-factor model, in which the correlations among tests are presumed to be due to shared content, combined with the idea that the content factors are intercorrelated. Figure 4.4c shows the four-source model, which presumes that the correlations among tests are due to the source factors only (processing speed, working memory, etc.), which themselves are correlated.

In addition to these "pure" models, there are combination models. One is shown in Fig. 4.4d. This is a combination of the content factor model and the four-sources model. In this model, the three content factors are correlated with each other, and the four-source factors are correlated with each other, but content and source factors are orthogonal. This is done to identify the factors similar to the way in which it is done with multitrait–multimethod models, with which this model can be seen as sharing a formal structure. A second combination model, shown in Fig. 4.4e, can be called a cell factor model, because for every CAM taxonomy cell there is a factor, such as Processing Speed–Verbal (PSV), Working Memory-Spatial (WMS), and so on. Note that there is only one declarative knowledge cell (we had not constructed quantitative and spatial declarative knowledge tests for this study), and that the three domains are combined in the Procedural Knowledge factor.

Finally, most of these models can be constructed in two ways, hierarchical and flat. The models discussed to this point, shown in Fig. 4.4a to 4.4e are all flat models. A hierarchical model is different in that

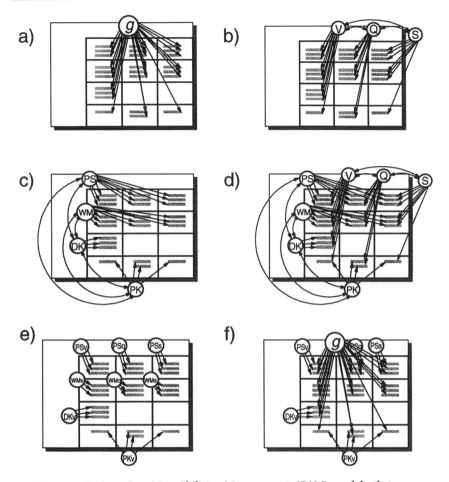

FIG. 4.4. Various Cognitive Abilities Measurement (CAM) models that were compared with one another in the Kyllonen (1993) study: (a) one-factor model; (b) three-content-factor model; (c) four-source model; (d) 4 sources + 3 domain model; (e) cell-factor model; (f) hierarchical cell-factor model.

it consists of a general factor along with the other, primary factors; the general factor is uncorrelated with the primaries. To identify the factors in a hierarchical model it is generally necessary to identify or designate one of the primary factors as the general factor (Gustafsson, 1989). Figure 4.4f shows a hierarchical version of the cell factor model (compare with Fig. 4.4e, which is the flat model version). In the hierarchical version, the three working memory cell factors (WMV, WMQ, and WMS) are identified as the general factor. This is done for two reasons. First, in earlier research, we (Kyllonen & Christal, 1990) found high correlations between working memory capacity and a general factor. Also, identifying working memory as the general factor fit the data better than did identifying any other factors as the general factor.

We tested these and other models against the test correlation matrix using confirmatory factor analysis procedures. Figure 4.5 presents the results.

The column labeled Model is self-explanatory. Degrees of freedom (*df*) are computed as the difference between the number of data points in the variance–covariance matrix (with 25 tests, that is, 25 * 26 / 2 = 325) minus the number of free parameters in the model. In these models, each variable's factor loading(s) and error (or uniqueness) variance is a free parameter (factor variances are fixed at one). Thus, for the one-factor model there are two free parameters per test for a total of 50 free parameters. For the other models, there are also free parameters for each factor intercorrelation, so, for the cell factor model, which has eight cell factors, there are 8 * 7 / 2 = 28 additional free parameters.

The last two columns are goodness of fit indexes. The non-normed fit index (NNFI) is an index based on the goodness of fit of the target model as compared with a "null model" (one that assumes that all the variables are simply uncorrelated). This index is also adjusted for degrees of freedom in the model, and takes sample size into account (chi-squared indexes are sensitive to sample size). The values for this index generally run between 0 and 1 with higher values indicating better fit. The last column is the mean residual correlation, that is, the average difference between correlation coefficients from the input and the model recovered matrices. Here, lower values indicate a better fit of the model.

There are several conclusions to be drawn from the data presented in Fig. 4.5. First, the poorest fitting models were those that included either content or source factors but not both. This means that both kinds of factors are necessary, an observation consistent both with the content–process distinction suggested by the information-processing approach, and with the Snow–Kyllonen–Marshalek MDS scaling results. Second, the best fitting models, the cell factor and the source-plus-content (or 4 + 3) factor models fit the data about equally as well. Finally, the hierarchical models fit the data slightly better than did their nonhierarchical counterparts, but the difference was not that great.

All these findings are consistent with and therefore lend support to the CAM framework. There are several almost equivalent models, in terms of goodness of fit, but rather than viewing this as an unsatisfactory outcome, this can be seen as a benefit in that these models can be useful for addressing different kinds of questions. For example, the

Model	df	nnfi	m residual
4 source	318	.857	.0458
1 factor	275	.780	.0520
3 content	272	.823	.0531
1 + 3 content	247	.931	.0364
4 + 3 factor	241	.947	.0346
cell (8) factor	247	.930	.0375
hierarchical 4 source	256	.877	.0414
hierarchical 4 + 3	228	.949	.0318
hierarchical cell factor	232	.935	.0320

pretty good fits

FIG. 4.5. Goodness of fit for various CAM models.

hierarchical models, which by definition included a general factor, fit the data slightly better than did the flat models, which did not include a general factor. This suggests that one can argue for the existence of a general factor. On the other hand, because the improvement in fit was very small, one can consider the flat models as virtually equivalent, and for some purposes, such as exploring the nature of the factors, it may be useful to consider flat models.

One might ask, for example, about the intercorrelations of the cell factors. In particular, there is controversy over whether there is a single working memory system or multiple, independent working memory systems. An idea sometimes expressed in the cognitive literature on working memory is that there are separate working memory systems for various content areas. There is no reason why one would expect these separate systems to be all that highly correlated. Yet, from the MDS results (see Fig. 4.1), one might expect the opposite. Working memory cell factors would be presumed to lie close to the center of the scaling configuration, because of their close connection to g (recall from Fig. 4.1 that highly g-saturated tests appeared closer to the center of the configuration). Objects close to the center of the configuration are therefore close to one another; and thus working memory cell factors, lying close to the center of the configuration, would be close to one another and therefore highly correlated with one another. The empirical results show exactly that. The correlations among the three working memory cell factors (WMV, WMS, and WMQ) are .96, .90, and .97.

Another question that can be usefully addressed with the cell factor model results is the issue of the relationship between CAM's cell factors and factors from the conventional abilities model. The participants in this study were also administered the Armed Services Vocational Aptitude Battery (ASVAB), which consists of 10 subtests measuring Word Knowledge, Arithmetic Reasoning, Coding Speed, and the like. Exploratory factor analyses of scores from this battery typically yield four factors, which may be labeled General Reasoning, Verbal, Perceptual Speed, and Technical Knowledge.

We computed the correlations between these four factors and the CAM cell factors, as estimated in a separate confirmatory factor analysis of the data. The correlations were generally fairly high (ranging from .31 [Declarative Knowledge, Perceptual Speed] to 1.00 [Declarative Knowledge, Verbal]). This is because the sample is a fairly heterogeneous one (many studies in the literature report on range-restricted samples), and the correlations are between factors rather than between variables. The pattern of correlations is sensible, with the lowest for example, being between Declarative Knowledge and Perceptual Speed, and the highest being between Declarative Knowledge and Verbal, which are really identical constructs from different test batteries. But clearly the most striking result from these data was that the three working memory factors correlated extremely highly with the General (Reasoning) Factor (r = .94, .96, .95). The magnitude of these correlations suggests that individual differences in working memory capacity may be what are responsible for individual differences in general ability. This is a provocative conclusion, and we now explore it in more depth.

WORKING MEMORY AND REASONING ABILITY

The individual-differences approach is potentially a powerful means for drawing conclusions about the nature of cognitive factors, such as reasoning ability, as has been suggested by psychologists from Spearman to Underwood (1975). But the use of the individual-differences approach is plagued with treacheries. One is that the conclusions drawn are often unreliable. Researchers often underestimate the number of subjects needed in individual-differences investigations, and the literature is replete with studies of hopelessly inadequate statistical power. Large samples of test subjects are required for individual-differences research. This is because the interesting conclusions often are not tests of the hypothesis that a population correlation is different from zero, but that several correlations are different from each other in a particular way. Hypotheses cast in this form require greater numbers of subjects to be tested for a given level of statistical power.

A second and very common problem plaguing individual-differences research is that researchers often mistake a variable for a construct. In the behavioral sciences, it is almost always the case that the interesting question has to do with the relationship between two constructs, not two variables. Variables are imperfect measures of constructs, which was certainly a central notion in Spearman's thinking from the concept of reliability to the concept of the general factor.

Both these potential problems were addressed in a study Christal and I conducted (Kyllonen & Christal, 1990) to investigate the relationship between working memory capacity and general reasoning ability. We thought that there might be a relationship. Reasoning ability is the central factor in psychometric theories of ability. Working memory capacity plays a central role in cognitive theories, serving as the bottleneck in learning and information processing. Variability in the capacity of working memory ought to have a broad impact on all varieties of cognitive acts.

We began by examining the factor-analytic literature on reasoning ability and found that there was evidence for the existence of several reasoning factors. For example, in Educational Testing Service's (ETS) kit of cognitive reference tests (Ekstrom, French, Harman, & Dermen, 1976), there are four reasoning factors. Reasoning, General (RG) is defined as the ability to select and organize relevant information for the solution of a problem. Reasoning, Logical (RL) is defined as the ability to reason from premise to conclusion and to evaluate the correctness of a conclusion. Induction (I) is defined as the ability to form and try out hypotheses that will fit a set of data. Integrative Processes (IP) is defined as the ability to keep in mind simultaneously or to combine several conditions or rules to produce a correct response. The ETS kit provides several tests of each of these factors, several of which we adapted for administration on the computer. (On our research project we administer almost all our tests and tasks on the computer because of the ease with which that allows us to process and score all the data we collect.) In addition to these tests, we created a number of other tests that have appeared in the literature over the years under the heading of "reasoning tests." Assembling this diverse group of reasoning tests allowed us to avoid the problem of mistaking the test for a factor.

We similarly developed a set of tests for measuring working memory capacity. To do this, we did not have the benefit of something like ETS' kit of cognitive reference tests to help us. Instead we had a definition, provided by Baddeley (1986), that working memory was measured by tasks that required the simultaneous processing and storage of information. There also have been a number of studies of the working memory construct over the last several years from which a variety of tasks could be extracted (e.g., Baddeley & Hitch, 1974; Daneman & Carpenter, 1980; Hitch, 1978; Hockey, Maclean, & Hamilton, 1981). We constructed for computer administration a variety of measures of working memory capacity based on these sources.

To avoid the problem of unreliability due to inadequate sample sizes, we administered the working memory tests and the reasoning tests to a large group of Air Force Basic trainees. Because of limitations in how long we had available to test the trainees (we could test for 3.5 hours, one time only), we divided the tests into several sets, and administered several "batteries" to successive groups of examinees. In all, we administered various reasoning tests and working memory tests to over 2,000 trainees. The results were fairly consistent. Using a confirmatory factor-analytic approach, we estimated the correlation between a reasoning ability factor and a working memory capacity factor to be

.82, .88, .80, and .82 in four independent studies, using different measures of reasoning ability, different measures of working memory capacity, and different trainees to estimate each coefficient.

These results are striking in both their consistency and in the sheer magnitude of the relationship between the two factors. However, the magnitude of the correlation between the working memory capacity factor and the general reasoning factor is lower than estimated in the Kyllonen (1994) study. I suspect that the reason is in the difference between the two kinds of samples. The Kyllonen (1994) study used an unselected sample of civilians from the San Antonio community, whereas the Kyllonen and Christal (1990) study used a sample of selected trainees screened by the Air Force. No range restriction adjustments went into the Kyllonen and Christal estimate of the correlation between reasoning ability and working memory capacity, and so those estimates are probably underestimates.

WORKING MEMORY AND CONGITIVE SKILL ACQUISITION

If working memory capacity is such an important factor in governing performance on all varieties of abilities tests, an obvious next question is what role does it play in learning? In the cognitive literature, working memory plays an important role in learning. Basically, we learn by associating previously unassociated elements in working memory, and by strengthening the connection between those elements in working memory. Thus it seems sensible that individuals with greater working memory capacity will be able to hold more to-be-associated elements in working memory and thereby increase the likelihood and the rate of learning.

Logic Gates Study

In the first study where we investigated this relationship, we (Kyllonen & Stephens, 1990) looked at the acquisition of logic gate skill. Why logic gates? Gitomer (1988) had earlier investigated a wide variety of cognitive tasks as possible predictors of proficiency in electronics troubleshooting as measured by supervisor ratings and a job sample test. Gitomer investigated many different hypotheses such as differences in component recognition times, differences in understanding of how the systems being troubleshooted fit together, and so on. But the only task that clearly separated expert from not-so-expert troubleshooters was a logic gates task he had developed. We took this as a sign that knowledge of logic gates was an important determinant of troubleshooting ability, and we therefore set off to discover what it was that led individuals to acquire skill in understanding logic gates.

We were constrained to a 3-hour examination session, and so we constructed a fairly simple logic gate learning task. It began with a "declarative" (associative) phase where students (120 Air Force enlistees) were trained to associate the logic gate symbols with the names of the logic gates (AND, OR, XOR, INVERT), the symbols with the definitions, and the names with the definitions. This was done in a study–test manner, analogous to a computerized flash card method, where students would study a set of pairs for 4 seconds, and then would get tested on each of the pairs, then study the pairs again, and they would continue doing that until they had learned them to a criterion of three successive correct responses. Following these associative trials, students were put through a "procedural" learning phase, where they were required to actually solve logic gate problems. Thus, if shown an AND gate with a "High" and a "Low" input, students would be required to press the button indicating a "Low" output. Or, if shown an OR gate with a "High" and a "Low" input, they would be required to press the button indicating a "High" output. Following these single gate problems, students were shown linked sets of gates, which were the actual types of problems that were best discriminating of good and poor troubleshooters in the Gitomer study. Figure 4.6 depicts this sequence of events.

In addition to the logic gates task, which took about an hour to complete, students were also administered a portion of the CAM battery. Because of time limits, however, we were only able to administer a couple of tests for each of the four-source factors. Results from the study are presented in Figure 4.7.

First, note that the working memory (WM) factor is defined as the general factor, in the sense that all the predictor tests were allowed to load on it. By the same token, the declarative learning (DL) factor is a general criterion outcome factor in the sense that all the criterion tests were allowed to load on it. Thus, the other predictor factors, procedural knowledge (PK) and declarative knowledge (DK) may be interpreted as pure factors, with the influence of working memory statistically removed or partialed out. Similarly, procedural learning (PL) can be properly interpreted as that part of learning specific to learning procedures (i.e., solving logic gates problems), with the general declarative or associative learning component partialed out. This technique, originally suggested by Gustafsson (1989), and sometimes referred to as the embedded factors method (Gustafsson, 1989) enables clearer factor interpretations than would be the case if the various predictor and criterion factors were simply left free to covary.

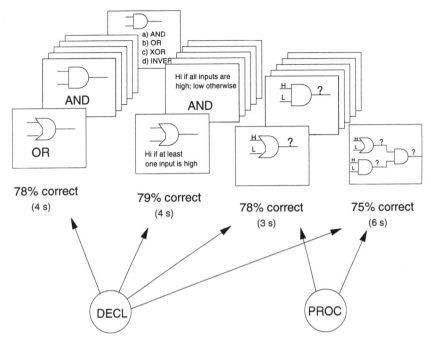

FIG. 4.6. Sequence of events in logic gates study.

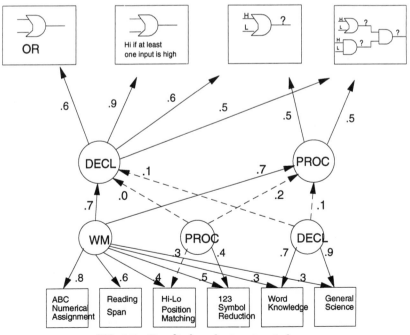

FIG. 4.7. Results from logic gates study.

The key finding in this analysis was that the working memory factor was a strong predictor of both the general declarative learning component ($r = .74$) and the more specific procedural learning component ($r = .73$). Further, the working memory factor was the only significant predictor of the two learning components. In a related study (Experiment 2, results not pictured), where, instead of logic gates, we taught people novel logical constructions (called color equations), we reached an identical conclusion.

Computer Programming Study

Results from the logic gates study were intriguing, but a pesky issue in this kind of research concerns ecological validity. That is, we showed that learning on a short-term laboratory learning task is well predicted from a working memory capacity factor, but is the task we examined realistic? Would the results we obtained have generalized to a longer-term learning task, a task that seemed less like a psychology experiment and more like a realistic classroom learning experience?

To examine this issue, we acquired a computerized tutoring system that taught the computer language Pascal to beginning programmers. The system, called BRIDGE, was developed by Bonar, Cunningham, Beatty, and Weil (1988) at the University of Pittsburgh's Learning Research and Development Center, and it taught the equivalent of about a half a semester of programming. The tutoring system was based on the idea of "computer programming as problem-solving." It required students to specify problem solutions, first, using natural language, then, after teaching about Pascal formalisms (functions, procedures, syntax, etc.), by having students write actual computer programs. The name BRIDGE refers to the learning process as a bridge between everyday, natural language reasoning, and formal programming code specification.

During initial pilot data collection with the tutor, we discovered that students did not already know many of the concepts the tutor assumed, such as the difference between a real number and an integer, a product and a sum, and so on. Consequently, Shute created a pretutor designed to instruct students on the background knowledge required to benefit from the tutor. Shute also created a posttutor set of outcome tests, designed to measure how much students learned from the BRIDGE tutor. The outcome tests required students to solve problems similar to the ones they were instructed on in the tutor, and the tests varied in how much problem-solving support they were given. A recognition test required students simply to recognize whether a program segment was correct or not; a Menu-Select test required students to solve problems by selecting Pascal statements from a menu, and a No Menus test required students to simply type in programming code to solve problems.

Students were solicited to participate in the study by advertisements we placed in local newspapers and by word of mouth. We recruited about 350 students in this manner, and we paid them the prevailing rate to participate. We tried to have the sample match the demographics of the U.S. Air Force applicant population (e.g., between the ages of 18 and 26 years; mostly male), and we disqualified anyone who already could program in the Pascal language (there were a few volunteers who could program in other languages, however; they were allowed to participate). We kept the students for almost a full week. During that time they went through the tutor and all associated tests, which took up to about 20 hours, and they also took the CAM, version 1 battery, which is described in an earlier section of this chapter.

From their performance on the tutor, the pretutor, and the posttutor outcome tests, we computed a number of scores. From the pretutor, for example, we computed the number of trials it took for a student to learn the concepts (e.g., "real number," "string," "product"). Some students were able to acquire the concepts fairly quickly, others took a fair number of trials to get through. We also computed the percentage correct on those trials, and we computed the percentage correct on an independent test of the concepts studied. From the tutor itself, which consisted of 25 problems, administered over several days, we computed the number of errors students made, and we computed the amount of time students took to get through the tutor. These two scores tended to be highly (negatively) correlated, as students making lots of errors tended to take a long time getting through the tutor. Finally, from each of the three outcome tests (Recognition, Menu-Select, and No-Menus), we computed a percentage correct score.

From these sets of scores, we estimated three factors, using confirmatory factor analysis methods. The approach taken was similar to that taken in the Kyllonen and Stephens (1990) study. That is, we first defined a general associative, or declarative learning factor. It was assumed to influence performance on all eight measures, as can be seen in Fig. 4.8. Next, we defined a procedural learning factor, orthogonal to the general declarative learning factor. It was assumed to influence performance on all measures that could be influenced by the tutor per se, that is, the scores from the tutor, and the scores from the outcome test. Because this factor was defined to be orthogonal to the declarative learning factor, this factor represents the portion of the learning that was specifically influenced by the tutor, but at the same time was not due to general (associative) learning. Finally, we defined a third factor,

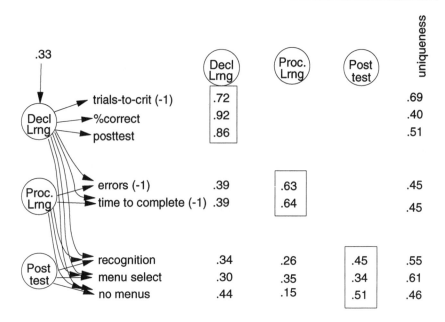

FIG. 4.8.   Results from programming study: Factor analysis of Learning factors.

which we presumed to influence performance on the outcome tests only. This factor was defined to be orthogonal to the declarative and procedural learning factors.

As Fig. 4.8 shows, all eight measures had either moderate or high loadings on the declarative learning factor, as we would expect, with the declarative learning measures having the highest loadings on that factor. The two tutoring measures, errors committed on the tutor, and time to complete the tutor, in addition to having moderate loadings on the declarative learning factor, had high loadings on the procedural learning factor. The fact that these measures had loadings on both the declarative and the procedural factors suggests that both kinds of learning processes were implicated in students' performance on the tutor. The three posttest measures, Recognition, Menu-Select, and No-Menus, had moderate loadings on all three factors, indicating that both declarative and procedural learning processes were involved in performance on these tests, in addition to processes associated specifically with performance on the posttests.

To assess the relationship between the CAM battery factors and the three learning factors, we regressed the three learning factors on the CAM factors, again, using confirmatory factor analysis methods. In the interest of saving space, I have not presented the goodness of fit results, but it is sufficient to say that the models fit the data reasonably well. In this analysis, we used the CAM factors as identified in the "Hierarchical 4 + 3" factor model (see Fig. 4.4). Hierarchical or embedded models have an advantage over flat models when analyzing the relationship between aptitude and learning-outcome variables because of the way in which variance is decomposed. In general, regression weights for orthogonal variables are easier to comprehend than are regression weights for correlated variables.

Figure 4.9 shows the results from the analysis, for the first learning factor, declarative learning, only. (In fact, the analysis was performed simultaneously with all three learning factors; using confirmatory path analysis. I am presenting results here for one variable at a time for ease of exposition.) Standardized coefficients are displayed. Again, in the interests of saving space, I do not discuss the so-called measurement portion of the model (i.e., the parameter estimates associated with the linkages between the measures and the latent factors, such as WM and DL). Instead, attention here is focused on the structural relations between the various latent aptitude and learning factors. Approximately 89% of the variance in the latent DL factor was accounted for by aptitude factors. Note, in particular, that the prediction was dominated by the WM factor, which by itself accounted for 81% of the variance in the general, declarative learning factor. Note also that no other factor contributed significantly to the prediction of general learning.

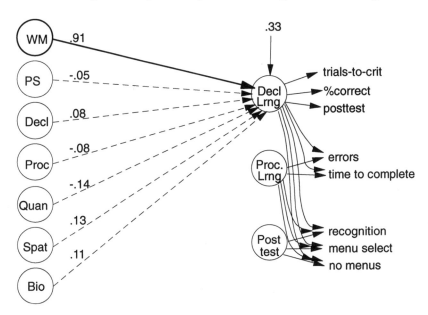

FIG. 4.9.   Results from programming study: Declarative Learning factor.

Figure 4.10 shows the results from the analysis for the second learning factor (PL). This factor was not as well predicted as was the first factor, but the prediction was still fairly strong, with the aptitude variables accounting for 63% of the variance in the PL factor. Recall that this factor is orthogonal to the first, general declarative learning factor. This factor represents that portion of learning unique to the tutor itself, that cannot be predicted on the basis of an individual's general learning ability. Still, as can be seen in Fig. 4.10, the working memory capacity factor was the most important determinant of procedural learning, accounting for 26% of the variance in the factor. One other factor, domain knowledge, also contributed significantly (18% of the variance) to the prediction of procedural learning. Results for the third factor are not displayed, but were similar to those for the procedural learning factor. Working memory and domain knowledge made significant contributions to the prediction of success.

Considered together, these results suggest that first, it is useful to break down the skill acquisition process into three stages: a declarative learning stage, a procedural learning stage, and a transfer stage. It is not necessary to assume that the kind of learning that occurs in each of these stages is different. In fact, we found it useful to assume that declarative learning, or what might also be called general associative learning, occurs during all stages. The key finding from both the logic gates and the computer programming studies is that almost all of the

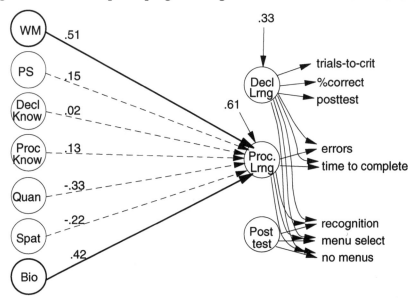

FIG. 4.10.   Results from programming study: Procedural Learning factor.

individual-differences variability in this general associative learning is related to individual differences in working memory capacity. No other cognitive factor that we measured had any impact on the success of the associative learning process.

Not all learning that occurs on tasks such as logic gates and computer programming is associative learning. For both tasks we defined procedural learning as going beyond merely associating concepts with definitions, to applying new concepts and rules to the task of solving problems in the domain. Certainly, problem-solving tasks have an associative learning component to them. But in addition, they require something else, something unique, which can be called procedural learning. Interestingly, in the computer programming study at least, we found that domain knowledge was an important determinant of success for this particular type of learning. But again, in both studies, the most important determinant of success for this type of learning was working memory capacity.

COMPONENTS OF WORKING MEMORY

Given the apparent importance of the working memory capacity factor, it seems critical to explore the question of what working memory capacity is, and how it can best be measured. One advantage the construct of working memory capacity has over a more conventional psychometric construct such as reasoning ability or g is that it is amenable to experimental research (Baddeley, 1986), and in fact, the construct has been much more thoroughly researched from an experimental rather than from an individual-differences perspective. On the other hand, there may be individual differences that shed light on the nature of working memory capacity.

For example, we can inspect the tests of working memory capacity that appear in the CAM battery, and compare them for their loadings on (i.e., correlations with) the working memory factor. The principle is that tests with higher correlations with the working memory factor are better measures of working memory. Higher correlations with the working memory factor reflect higher average correlations with other tests of working memory, which indicates higher "centrality" or "prototypicality" with respect to the working memory construct.

In the CAM battery there were nine tests of working memory: three verbal tests, three spatial tests, and three quantitative tests. The verbal test with the highest loading was a word span test where subjects were cued with the synonym of the word in the list presented immediately prior to the test probe. For example, the computer might present the words "damp," "noisy," "quick," "cold," "large," "good," "smooth," "high," "loud," in succession, then ask the subject which word followed the synonym of "fast" on the list (correct answer: "cold"). In this test, all the words used were extremely simple (solved correctly by 95% of the examinees on a pilot test). The verbal test with the lowest loading in our study was a reading span test, similar to that used by Daneman and Carpenter (1980). One of the problems with this test, as pointed out by Baddeley (1986) is that it fails to disentangle clearly the influences of prior knowledge from the effects of differences in working memory capacity per se. It is interesting that Baddeley's informal observations about the test were supported with the factor-loading data.

Of the quantitative tests, the one with the highest loading was an "Assignment" test developed by Dr. Raymond Christal, from our research group, in which examinees were given a series of assignments of either digits or equations to letters, and then were asked to solve the equations to determine the values associated with the letters. For example, an examinee might be told that $a = b/2$, $b = c + 1$, and $c = 5$ (in succession). Then the examinee would be asked $a = ?$, $b = ?$, $c = ?$. For all questions, the numbers used were small, and the equations were simple. The quantitative test with the lowest loading was a mental math test involving multiple column addition or subtraction (e.g., $142 - 79$) where examinees were not permitted to take notes or use scratch paper. This kind of test certainly measures working memory capacity; a problem with it might simply be that it is also susceptible to the use of mnemonic "tricks" for keeping track of the results of intermediate calculations. It could also reflect whether a person has memorized solutions to multiple-column addition and subtraction problems.

In both cases, the verbal and the quantitative tests, the test with the higher loading appears to have been the one that required less domain knowledge. It may be that a principle is that a test is a good measure of working memory capacity to the degree to which the role of prior knowledge in affecting performance on the test is minimized.

SUMMARY

We started this series of investigations with no preconceived notions of the role of working memory or any of the other factors in governing performance and learning. The remarkable finding is the consistency with which the working memory capacity factor has proven to be the central factor in cognitive activities. We have observed in study after study, under a variety of operationalizations, using a diverse set of criteria, that working memory capacity is more highly related to performance on other cognitive tests, and is more highly related to learning, both short-term and long-term, than is any other cognitive factor.

This finding of the centrality of the working memory capacity factor leads to the conclusion that working memory capacity may indeed be essentially Spearman's g. What is particularly exciting about this conclusion, if it turns out to be correct, is that working memory capacity is not susceptible to the criticism of being a statistical artifact in the manner that g is. The working memory capacity construct does not depend on factor analysis for its identification. The working memory system was developed theoretically not as a label for an individual-differences factor, but rather as a construct to explain experimental results in the memory literature. We know how to characterize working memory limitations independently of individual-differences results. We know how to manipulate the working memory requirements of a task without even computing correlations. Unlike the case with other conventional psychometric factors, such as reasoning ability and g, it is possible, in principle, to measure working memory capacity on an absolute rather than relative scale. This property carries with it tremendous potential for, among other things, bridging the individual differences and the cognitive engineering literatures.

An additional benefit of defining a psychometric factor in terms of a construct that does not depend on psychometrics, a construct that is amenable to independent inquiry methods, is the potential for creating synergy between the two fields of inquiry. What we know and learn about the construct from experimental investigations can inform individual-differences investigations; those can in turn inform further experimental investigations.

As a concrete example, consider the distinction between what might be called effective and true working memory capacity. We know, from the expertise literature, that individuals can increase their effective working memory capacity in a particular domain by increasing their knowledge in that domain. Consider, for example, the chess expert's superb working memory for standard board configurations. We also know, from the expertise literature, that such increases in effective working memory capacity are not accompanied by concomitant in-creases in true working memory capacity. Consider, for example, the chess expert's mediocre memory for nonstandard (random) board configurations. Are there analogies here that we can draw to help us think about the training of intelligence and the possibilities and the limitations of such endeavors?

It is clear that the empirical findings reviewed in this chapter on the relationship between working memory capacity and general intellectual ability, promising though they may be, are simply first steps. Much more needs to be done. There can be further informal work on the characteristics of good measures of working memory capacity. This can be followed up by more formal experimental tests of those characteristics. For example, we can experimentally manipulate prior knowledge requirements and observe the effects on working memory capacity factor loading. An especially fertile, and almost completely untapped line of investigations concerns the use of individual-differences methods to examine the structure of the working memory system as laid out by experimentalists such as Baddeley (1986). Investigations such as these will dissolve the boundaries between correlational and experimental literatures and lead to our capability for understanding and explaining the nature, or cause of psychometric constructs, such as g.

REFERENCES

Baddeley, A. D. (1986). *Working memory*. Oxford, England: Clarendon.

Baddeley, A. D., & Hitch, G. (1974). Working memory. In G. Bower (Ed.), *Advances in learning and motivation* (Vol. 8, pp. 47–90). New York: Academic Press.

Bonar, J., Cunningham, R., Beatty, P., & Weil, W. (1988). *Bridge: Intelligent tutoring system with intermediate representations* (Tech. Rep.). Pittsburgh, PA: University of Pittsburgh, Learning Research & Development Center.

Carroll, J. B. (1993). *Human cognitive abilities*. New York: Cambridge University Press.

Daneman, M., & Carpenter, P. A. (1980). Individual differences in working memory and reading. *Journal of Verbal Learning and Verbal Behavior, 19*, 450–466.

Ekstrom, R. B., French, J. W., & Harman, H. H., with Dermen, D. (1976). *Manual for kit of factor-referenced cognitive tests*. Princeton, NJ: Educational Testing Service.

Evans, J. St. B. (1982). *The psychology of deductive reasoning*. London: Routledge & Kegal Paul.

Gitomer, D. H. (1988). Individual differences in technical troubleshooting. *Human Performance, 1*(2), 111–131.

Gustafsson, J. E. (1989). Hierarchical models of abilities. In R. Kanfer, P. Ackerman, & R. Cudeck (Eds.), *Learning and individual differences: Abilities, motivation, and methodology* (pp. 203–237). Hillsdale, NJ: Lawrence Erlbaum Associates.

Hitch, G. J. (1978). The role of short-term working memory in mental arithmetic. *Cognitive Psychology, 10*, 302–323.

Hockey, G. R. J., Maclean, A., & Hamilton, P. (1981). State changes and the temporal patterning of component resources. In J. Long & A. D. Baddeley (Eds.), *Attention and Performance, 9*. Hillsdale, NJ: Lawrence Erlbaum Associates.

Jensen, A. R. (1994). Spearman, Charles Edward. In R. J. Sternberg (Ed.), *Encyclopedia of human intelligence* (pp. 894–907). New York: Macmillan.

Kyllonen, P. C. (1993). Aptitude testing based on information processing: A test of the four-sources model. *Journal of General Psychology, 120*, 375–405.

Kyllonen, P. C. (1994). Information processing. In R. J. Sternberg (Ed.), *Encyclopedia of human intelligence* (pp. 581–588). New York: Macmillan.

Kyllonen, P. C., & Christal, R. E. (1989). Cognitive modeling of learning abilities: A status report of LAMP. In R. Dillon & J. W. Pellegrino (Eds.), *Testing: Theoretical and applied issues* (pp. 146–173). San Francisco: Freeman.

Kyllonen, P. C., & Christal, R. E. (1990). Reasoning ability is (little more than) working memory capacity?! *Intelligence, 14*, 389–433.

Kyllonen, P. C., & Stephens, D. L. (1990). Cognitive abilities as determinants of success in acquiring logic skill. *Learning and Individual Differences, 2*, 129–160.

Marshalek, B., Lohman, D. F., & Snow, R. E. (1977). *The complexity continuum in the radex and hierarchical models of ability organization.* Unpublished manuscript, Stanford University, Stanford, CA.

Snow, R. E., Kyllonen, P. C., & Marshalek, B. (1984). The topography of ability and learning correlations. In R. J. Sternberg (Ed.), *Advances in the psychology of human intelligence* (Vol. 2, pp. 47–103). Hillsdale, NJ: Lawrence Erlbaum Associates.

Spearman, C. (1927). *The abilities of man: Their nature and measurement.* New York: Macmillan.

Thurstone, L. L. (1938). Primary Mental Abilities. *Psychometric Monograph, No. 1.* Chicago: University of Chicago Press.

Underwood, B. J. (1975). Individual differences as a crucible in theory construction. *American Psychologist, 30*, 128–134.

CHAPTER 5

Human Abilities and Modes of Attention: The Issue of Stylistic Consistencies in Cognition

Samuel Messick
Educational Testing Service

> Another important problem still unsettled is as to whether the conative influence [of attention] is always primarily enhansive, or can also be (directly) inhibitive.
>
> —Spearman (1923, p.136)

Intelligence and attention have been closely related concepts at least since the turn of the century. Indeed, "the pervasiveness of attention in cognition was accepted from the earliest days of psychology, and the term was used almost synonymously with cognition and consciousness" (Shiffrin, 1988, p.739). Specifically, "attention has been used to refer to all those aspects of human cognition that the subject can control . . . , and to all aspects of cognition having to do with limited resources or capacity, and methods of dealing with such constraints" (p.739). Early theorists of intelligence such as Spearman spoke of the sources and limits of attention in terms of mental energy and mental span, whereas modern cognitive theorists speak of mental effort and working-memory capacity. These continuities point to some enduring principles of cognition but are also open to some perennial problems posed by the occurrence of multiple and alternative modes of attention, such as broad versus narrow focusing and extensive versus concentrated scanning. That is, if intelligence and attention are intertwined and there are multiple modes or styles of attention, what are the implications for the conceptualization and measurement of intelligence?

Such stylistic modes of attention have long been discussed under the rubric of cognitive styles, or characteristic intraindividual patterns of abilities or cognitive controls (Broverman, 1960a, 1960b; Klein, 1958). Cognitive control is a term used in psychoanalytic ego psychology to refer to adaptive regulatory mechanisms for coping with environmental demands, in contradistinction to defense mechanisms for coping with anxiety and conflict. Cognitive styles are more general and comprise organizing as well as controlling functions (Messick, 1984). Furthermore, attentional behavior provides fertile ground for identifying such stylistic consistencies. According to George Klein, Riley Gardner, and their colleagues:

> When we view the workings of controls from the standpoint of the availability, mobilization, and deployment of attention, . . . the influence of cognitive controls is very much a matter of highlighting certain environmental features and reducing the effectiveness of others, [that is,] it is precisely in the regulation of attention that the influence of cognitive controls may be most apparent. (Gardner, Holzman, Klein, Linton, & Spence, 1959, p.13)

Moreover, "studies of cognitive controls have suggested . . . that several relatively independent control principles determine different aspects of attention, and that no one control is dominant in all situations" (Gardner, Jackson, & Messick, 1960, p. 28).

Individual consistencies in attentional processes in perception and memory underlie dimensions of cognitive control at the first-order factor level; modal patterns of these control dimensions constitute higher-order factors of cognitive style (Messick, 1989). In particular, in addition to the cognitive styles of field independence versus field dependence and reflection versus impulsivity, which involve consistencies in attention deployment in field articulation and restructuring as well as in analytic versus holistic processing (Globerson & Zelniker, 1989; Witkin & Goodenough, 1981), two second-order bipolar factors have been identified that contrast sharp-focus versus broad-focus scanning and signal versus information scanning (Messick, 1989). These stylistic factors, that are operative in memory as well as perception and are differentially related to personality, are discussed in more detail later.

As background for this discussion, we first briefly examine some early views of mental energy and capacity in the interplay of attention and intelligence, especially the views of Spearman and Burt. These notions serve as counterpoint to more modern treatments in terms of the allocation of attentional resources and the limits of working memory. Next, current conceptions of selective attention are summarized to illustrate the variety of processes of perceptual enhancement, filtering, and response inhibition that might exhibit consistent individual differences underlying, in various combinations, the observed dimensions of cognitive style. Special emphasis is placed on the neo-Piagetian theory of constructive operators proposed by Pascual-Leone (1969, 1989), which attempts to disentangle components of ability and capacity from the sources of style. In this context, the two styles of sharp-focus versus broad-focus scanning and signal versus information scanning are examined as performance variables as opposed to competence variables. It is noted, however, that such cognitive styles are not purely performance variables because they have implications not only for the expression of competence but also for its development. That is, styles influence the development of abilities and ability structures and hence bear on the conceptualization and measurement of intelligence.

A more straightforward way to motivate the ensuing discussion is as follows: Of the two bipolar second-order factors of scanning style recently identified, one of them—namely, broad-focus versus sharp-focus scanning—relates to attentional modes discussed by Spearman for deploying the mental energy underlying g. Hence, as background for interpreting this scanning style, we review Spearman's treatment of mental energy and mental span as determinants of both intelligence and attention, in relation to more current concepts of mental effort and working memory capacity. The other bipolar scanning factor—namely, signal versus information scanning—relates to serial selective attention as opposed to simultaneous parallel processing. Hence, as background for interpreting this second scanning style, we review theories of selective attention (which also bear on broad-focus versus sharp-focus scanning), along with work on automatic versus controlled cognitive processing. Finally, because attentional styles and intellective abilities are each inferred from consistencies in task behavior, the distinction between performance and competence is examined. This provides a basis for characterizing styles both as performance variables contaminating the assessment of abilities and as competence variables influencing the nature of ability development.

ENERGY AND CAPACITY AS ENDURING CONCEPTS OF INTELLIGENCE AND ATTENTION

In interpreting his general factor of intelligence, or g, Spearman (1923, 1927) distinguished between quantitative and qualitative aspects. On the quantitative side, g represents the amount of mental energy that an individual has available, the mobilization of which is closely linked to attention. For example, Spearman (1923, p. 162) discussed attention in terms of the conative directing of mental energy. When waxing metaphorical, he referred to the "focus" and the "fringe" of mental energy (Spearman, 1927, p. 344). He endorsed Burt's (1940, p. 217) qualification that intelligence is not merely an effect of attention but rather that attention is an effect or symptom of intelligence (Spearman & Wynn Jones, 1950). Finally, Spearman defined attention as "the application of intellectual energy" (Spearman & Wynn Jones, 1950, p. 172).

One key aspect of mental energy is its transferability, that is, "it is some force capable of being transferred from one mental operation to another" (Spearman, 1927, p. 414). This concept of transferability remains an important feature of most, if not all, modern theories of human abilities as enabling variables (Messick, 1992). Furthermore, this mental energy is constrained for Spearman by a quantitative law of mental span that is a strong version of capacity limits, namely, "every mind tends to keep its total simultaneous output constant in quantity, however varying in quality" (p. 259). This law is explicitly discussed in terms of trade-offs in the distribution of attention as well as of competition among simultaneous cognitive activities for available attentional energy. Spearman even referred to "universal mental competition" in which simultaneous affective states compete with each other and with cognitive states for attentional energy; that is, affect can interfere with cognition and vice versa (Messick, 1987). Conation is also viewed as competitive with cognition and affect, but he is less clear as to whether one conation interferes with another.

Still on the quantitative side, Spearman (1927) identified two other general factors of perseveration and oscillation. The former is related to disposition rigidity and the marshalling of the will to overcome it (Cattell, 1946a, 1946b), and the latter is negatively related to "steadiness of character" (Spearman & Wynn Jones, 1950). Spearman (1927) held that the obverse of perseveration was cleverness or originality, but not simply ideational fluency (Spearman & Wynn Jones, 1950). Guilford later showed that perseveration was opposed by measures of spontaneous flexibility or the divergent production of classes (Frick, Guilford, Christensen, & Merrifield, 1959). In terms of Spearman's quantitative formulation of intelligence, g represents the amount of mental energy, perseveration represents its inertia in shifting from one operation to another, and oscillation its facility of recuperation after mental effort.

Spearman (1927) also posited reciprocal attentional modes and considered the possibility of individual differences in each. He pointed out that mental energy, like physical energy, "has two dimensions, intensive and extensive; the clearness and speed of an operation may either attain to a high grade, or else cover a wide field; the 'attention' may be either concentrated or else diffused" (p. 260). Furthermore, he acknowledged the similarity of this contrast to Meumann's attention types, which pit a concentrating or fixating mode of attention against a diffusive or fluctuating mode. However, from analyses of concentrated attention on isolated tasks performed successively versus diffused attention on dual tasks performed simultaneously, Spearman concluded that these do not form separate factors but, rather, represent intensive and extensive aspects of g.

In contrast, Burt (1949) reported a bipolar factor of fixating versus diffusive attention that was related to both perseveration and emotional stability. Although Burt felt that this factor should probably be regarded as temperamental rather than cognitive, he noted its similarity to Spearman's descriptions of the typical perseverator versus oscillator, thereby linking Spearman's additional general factors of perseveration and oscillation to attentional modes. Indeed, such a possibility was also alluded to by Spearman (1927) as a way that "wheels into general line the prolific suggestions of Meumann" (p. 292). As we shall see, Meumann's attention types and Burt's bipolar attention factor presage our stylistic dimension of sharp-focus versus broad-focus scanning, which is also related to measures of rigidity and temperament.

On the qualitative side, g entails a combination of noegenetic processes with abstractness (Spearman & Wynn Jones, 1950, p. 190). The noegenetic processes of awareness of experience, eduction of relations, and eduction of correlates underscore the centrality of reasoning in intelligence and continue to be essential in theories of fluid intelligence from Cattell (1971) to Sternberg (1985). Spearman (1927, p. 214) viewed abstraction as the "climax of eduction." By cognizing mental content apart from its context, abstraction greatly facilitates "transfer of ability from the simpler situations to the more complicated ones" (pp. 215–216). Despite the broad range of application deriving from this fluid transferability of reasoning or noegenetic processes, the concept of attention is often assumed to be broader than the concept of intelligence because attentional resources are used in nonintellective information-processing tasks such as signal detection (e.g., Hunt, 1980). However, with Spearman's embracing of awareness of experience as an intellective process, the margins are, at the very least, fuzzy and disputable.

The issues of mental energy and capacity endure in present-day cognitive psychology but with different terminology. By and large, one currently hears little about mental energy as such but, rather, about attention being a heightened state of arousal (Moray, 1969; Posner, 1975) or entailing mental effort (Hasher & Zacks, 1979; Kahneman, 1973). A refreshing exception is Hunt's (1980) contention that the allocation of attentional resources provides the common thread accounting for the ubiquitous positive correlations (or positive manifold) among different cognitive tests: Hunt concluded that studies of dual-task interference "support the argument that there is a pervasive 'mental energy' that underlies a wide variety of cognitive tasks" (p. 470).

Similarly, one hears little nowadays about general mental capacity as such, but rather, about the limitations on working memory resulting in a restricted pool of attentional resources available for cognitive processing. These constraints may take the form, for example, of competition for representation in working memory (Anderson, 1983), competition for limited-capacity processing channels (Broadbent, 1957, 1958), or modulation of processing in otherwise automatic pathways (Cohen, Dunbar, & McClelland, 1990). This allusion to automatic pathways alerts us to the possibility of automatic processes that do not require attention for their execution and that, in effect, represent additional resources beyond working memory. The distinction between automatic and controlled processes is discussed in connection with our subsequent brief review of theories of selective attention.

The prospect of additional automatic-processing resources also broaches the more general issue of whether there is a single pool of shared central resources to meet the processing needs of the entire mental system as opposed to multiple resource pools. Proposed alternatives include Howard Gardner's (1983) eschewal of a central pool in favor of separate resources for each of his modular intelligences and Kahneman's (1973) view of a central resource combined with multiple satellite resources, which are concerned, for example, with motor movements and perceptual mechanisms.

Some evidence bearing on this issue of the centrality of specificity of working memory resources emerges in a factor-analytic study by Kyllonen and Christal (1990). This study primarily addressed the relationship between reasoning ability and working memory capacity, or in Spearman's terms, the relation between the qualitative and quantitative aspects of intelligence. Kyllonen and Christal (1990) administered several tests of reasoning ability along with tasks designed according to Baddeley's (1986, pp. 34–35) definition of working-memory capacity, in that the tasks "require the simultaneous processing and storage of information" and "measure various contents."

They isolated a general working-memory factor cutting across a variety of processing codes and input modalities, which is counter to the notion that working-memory capacity is process- or domain-specific but does not rule out the possibility of additional subsidiary resources.

Kyllonen and Christal (1990) also concluded that reasoning ability and working memory capacity, being correlated in the .80s, are closely related but not identical. Reasoning ability was more highly correlated with general knowledge, whereas working memory capacity was more highly correlated with information-processing speed. The title and tenor of their paper favor the conclusion that individual differences in reasoning ability reflect little more than differences in working-memory capacity. This implies a causal connection from working-memory to reasoning ability, which is fundamentally different from Spearman's more unitary view that reasoning or noegenetic processing is the qualitative aspect and mental span the quantitative aspect of one-and-the-same g. However, Kyllonen and Christal (1990) do allow the contrary causal hypothesis that "working-memory capacity is primarily determined by individual differences in reasoning ability" (p. 428). This latter formulation is consistent with Burt's (1940) appraisal mentioned earlier that attention is an effect or symptom of intelligence rather than the other way around.

Next we consider some of the processes of selective attention that might underlie, in distinctive combinations, the observed individual differences in attentional mode. Before doing this, however, I cannot resist noting that this sketchy review of energy and capacity in mental functioning, if nothing else, should serve to titillate all of the nothing-new-under-the-sun buffs and old-wine-in-new-bottles buffs.

ENHANCEMENT AND INHIBITION
IN SELECTIVE ATTENTION

Almost all theories of selective attention incorporate some notion of capacity or resource limitations. Almost all theories also recognize that, in complex tasks such as reading, or typing, many of the operations occur in concert so that much of the processing likely takes place in parallel outside the normal control of attention. As a consequence, most theories distinguish between controlled or attentional processes, which are voluntary, relatively slow, and require attention for their execution and automatic or inattentive processes, which are fast and do not require attention.

More specifically,

the automatic processes . . . do not much partake of capacity limitations: They can operate in parallel with certain other automatic and attentive

processes without loss and without interference with those other processes. The attentive processes are limited in capacity and tend to
interfere with one another, often leading them to be used successively.
(Shiffrin, 1988, p. 764)

This dichotomy between controlled and automatic processes is
convenient for discussion but simplistic in application because processes vary in degree of automaticity as a function of relative strength
related to practice (Cohen, Dunbar, & McClelland, 1990). There is also
evidence that automatic and controlled processes operate concurrently
and interactively at most stages of processing (Shiffrin, 1988). A
further complication is that attention itself can be automatized, as
when attention is drawn by targets. Hence, the presentation of targets
will elicit attention, utilizing attentional resources and interfering with
other ongoing processes requiring attention (Shiffrin & Schneider,
1977).

A common view of perceptual processing involves some automatic
or parallel processing of primitive stimulus features at an early preat-
tentive stage, followed by a rather strict selective filter that allows only
stimuli relevant to a designated "channel" to pass through for further
processing (Broadbent, 1957, 1958). However, this bottleneck theory of
perception was modified to an attenuation theory by Treisman (1960,
1969) when it became clear that the selective filter served to reduce the
signal-to-noise ratio of unattended messages rather than blocking them
completely. Thus, the attended channel would receive full or enhanced processing while the other channels received attenuated processing. Treisman used a metaphor of an "attention window" having
an aperture of variable size that can be adjusted to select a small or
large group of adjacent items for enhanced processing (e.g., Treisman,
1990).

A similar and popular metaphor likening attention to a spotlight
beam has a long and checkered history. When applied to perusal of
internal fields of memory or imagining, the metaphor usually invokes
the "mind's eye" (e.g., Kosslyn, 1987). For example, James (1890)
discussed attention in terms of the "span of consciousness" and spoke
of the "ideational excitement of the center" compared to the marginal
region. More pointedly, Hernández-Peón (1964) compared attention to
a beam of light in which the central brilliant part represents the focus
surrounded by a less intense fringe. Only the items located in the focus
of attention are distinctly perceived whereas we are less aware of the
objects located in the fringe of attention (p. 167).

However, this rudimentary version has to be elaborated and modified to accommodate new findings and changing theories. For exam-

ple, the focus of the beam is to be characterized by detailed information extraction rather than just high acuity or sensory resolving power (Eriksen & Hoffman, 1973). Furthermore, the span or bandwidth of the attentional beam is variable; it can be either wide or narrow, which affects the range of stimuli processed holistically (Humphreys, 1981). Moreover, the spotlight needs some mechanism for switching between two processes, one being diffuse with parallel processing of multiple items of information and the other more concentrated with serial processing of separate items (Jonides, 1983).

A zoom-lens version has also been proposed having a reciprocal relation between resolving power for discerning information and the size or bandwidth of the field of view (Eriksen & Yeh, 1985). This is reminiscent of Spearman's (1927) trade-off mentioned earlier between "a high grade" and "a wide field" of mental energy. In a two-process zoom-lens version, the narrow focus would process separate items of information serially with high resolving power, while the wide focus would process multiple items in parallel with attenuated resolving power. As discussed later, within the limits of available attentional resources or mental energy, the degree of enhancement or resolving power might also be treated as an independently varying process. Furthermore, the enhancement yielded by the attentional beam may be integrative, providing "the 'glue' which integrates the initially separable features into unitary objects" (Treisman & Gelade, 1980, p. 98) and facilitating the structural analysis of their relationships (Treisman, 1990).

The spotlight metaphor also suggests that the direction of the attentional beam both illuminates the targeted area and withdraws illumination from other areas. Do the selectivity effects derive primarily from facilitation or from suppression, that is, from enhanced processing in the attended area or from attenuated processing in the unattended areas, or both? A developing consensus indicates that attentional selectivity derives from some form of signal enhancement rather than solely from noise suppression or filtering (Eriksen & Hoffman, 1974). Furthermore, there is evidence both for perceptual filtering prior to verbal analysis of distractor material and for response suppression after verbal analysis (Greenwald, 1972). Target enhancement appears to go hand in hand with active inhibition of distractors, but this facilitation and inhibition are separate processes that may be independent yet often work in tandem (Neumann & DeSchepper, 1991; Posner & Snyder, 1975). In sum, "it may be that objects presented in regions of nonfocus will be processed automatically and hence will generate encodings that must be inhibited in order to carry out the requirement of the main task" (Shiffrin, 1988, p. 785).

The facilitative, inhibitory, and integrative aspects of attention are explicitly treated by Pascual-Leone (1969, 1989) as separate processes, each of which exhibits consistent individual differences. In his theory of constructive operators, Pascual-Leone posited a mental energizing or excitatory component and a mental interruption or inhibitory component. The former is referred to as mental attention or mental energy and is quantified as M-capacity or M-power. M-capacity is the maximum number of schemes a person is capable of activating at any one time, schemes being internal representations of task-relevant information. Pascual-Leone distinguished structural M-capacity or M-reserve, which is all the capacity a person possesses, from functional M-capacity, which is the amount actually used in the mental activity. M-reserve is tantamount to working-memory capacity and corresponds to Spearman's mental span and his quantitative aspect of g. Functional M-capacity is typically lower than M-reserve, affording some leeway within those limits for effortful boosting of attentional resources to enhance processing. The inhibitory or I-component provides for separately varying mechanisms or processes of interruption to suppress distracting or misleading schemes.

The M- and I-processes "together constitute the so-called 'beam' of mental attention. The mental energy boosts the activation of relevant schemes to be attended while mental interrupt inhibits those task-irrelevant schemes to which the subject does not intend to attend—thus creating the sharp 'edge' of the 'light' of consciousness which is experiencedphenomenologically" (Pascual-Leone, 1989, p. 45). Pascual-Leone also posited an F-factor for gestalt field effects, which contribute to the integrative nature of attention, for example, by synthesizing stimulus features for object identification as well as categorization and by facilitating figure–ground organization. "By forcing a gestaltist structuring of the . . . activated schemes the F-factor brings about the closing that completes the effect of an attentional flashlight 'beam'" (p. 61).

However, sometimes the F-factor yields compelling configurations that are perceptually misleading with respect to task demands, as in Witkin's embedded-figures and rod-and-frame tests. In the former, a simple figure must be isolated from overlapping configurations of which it is a part, and in the latter a luminous rod surrounded by a luminous tilted frame is to be set to the true vertical in an otherwise darkened room (Witkin & Goodenough, 1981). Thus, respondents are faced with a conflict between the effects of the F-factor and task requirements to overcome the misleading features, that is, to utilize M- and I-resources for restructuring. Ability or competence contributes to task performance in terms of individual differences in M-power.

Cognitive styles contribute in terms of consistent strategic differences in mobilizing and allocating M- and I-resources.

The intent of this brief review of theory and research on selective attention was to expose the rich array of process variables from cognitive psychology that might exhibit consistent individual differences, thereby potentially contributing to stylistic dimensions of attention deployment. We have seen that individual differences might occur independently in facilitative, inhibitory, and integrative processes of attention; in the width or narrowness of the attentional focus; in the degree of resolving power for information extraction; in the extent to which resolving power and bandwidth are reciprocal; and, in the tendency for attentional processes to occur serially over successive items of information or in parallel over multiple items simultaneously.

Varied as these possibilities are, they do not exhaust the multiplicity of individual differences in attentional behavior observed in studies of eye movements, memory retrieval, and perceptual task performance. For example, we must refine the distinction between intensity and extensity of attention in terms of focusing versus nonfocusing and scanning versus nonscanning. Focusing versus nonfocusing refers to the width of the attentional beam and to its two reciprocal tendencies; that is, as the beam widens, it may become relatively diffuse and unfocused with attenuated processing, or it may become more integrative of multiple items and relationships through parallel processing. Extensive versus limited scanning refers to the movement of the beam, whatever its size and intensity.

As a consequence, there is more than one kind of broad as well as of narrow attention (Wachtel, 1967). Broad attention can refer either to extensive scanning of the stimulus field or else to perusal with a broad attentional bandwidth, which might be either unfocused or integrative. The extensive scanning may be marked by high scatter or dispersion of attentional fixations or by large jumps from one fixation to the next, or both (Luborsky, Blinder, & Schimek, 1965). Furthermore, extensive scanning may reflect unsystematic or anxious roaming of the stimulus field, systematic or planful coverage, or flexibly controlled deployment of attention to multiple information sources.

In contrast, narrow attention can refer either to limited scanning of the stimulus field or else to perusal with a narrow attentional bandwidth. The narrow attentional beam may represent enhanced perception of successive details or selective perception that reduces responsiveness to compelling irrelevancies, or both. The limited scanning may be marked by low scatter of fixations or by small track lengths between fixations, or both. Furthermore, limited scanning may reflect meticulous or repeated examination of details, cautious adherence to central or salient features, or defensive avoidance of the threatening or unknown.

Whether the scanning is extensive or limited with either broad or narrow bandwidth, the attentional behavior may in addition exhibit consistent individual differences in speed. Moreover, rapid scanning as well as slow scanning may be in the service of precision and comprehensiveness. On the other hand, either may instead be reflective of defensiveness, the slow scanner avoiding attention to potentially threatening aspects of the field by only hesitantly venturing to look around and the fast scanner distracting attention from potential threats by looking rapidly everywhere (Luborsky et al., 1965). Finally, all of these aspects of attention, in whatever combination, may apply not only to external perceptual fields but also to perusal of internal fields of memory, meaning, and knowledge.

SHARP-FOCUS VERSUS BROAD-FOCUS AND SERIAL VERSUS PARALLEL SCANNING

Let us now turn to the two attentional modes or cognitive styles of sharp-focus versus broad-focus scanning and signal versus information scanning that emerged as second–order factors in separate analyses of male and female samples (Messick, 1989). Although these two second-order dimensions appear to be comparable in the two sexes, the contributing first-order structures as well as some personality correlates are divergent, suggesting differential underlying dynamics as a function of gender.

In addition to marker tests for verbal and quantitative ability, the battery included measures of perceptual speed and closure, breadth of categorizing, inkblot perception, and a variety of personality scales. Measures were also included for facility in detecting stimuli or stimulus classes both in unorganized or randomly structured fields (such as locating four-letter words in arrays of letters, or finding misspelled words or words containing the letter a in long lists of words) as well as in organized fields (such as finding a simple pattern embedded in a complex figure or locating faces camouflaged in pictorial scenes). Many of the tests were scored not only for the number of correct responses but also for the number of wrong and omitted responses.

In the variety of search tasks employed, the signals ranged in specificity from a unique target (such as the letter a or a standard pattern) to instances of a circumscribed class (such as four-letter words, round things, or blue things) to instances of more open classes (such as faces or misspelled words). Given that scanning propensities may be reflected in memory retrieval as well as in perceptual search—that is, in the manner in which internal fields of memory, meaning, and knowledge are surveyed—measures were also included for remoteness of word association as well as for fluency in ideational production of class instances.

A concerted effort was made to differentiate between two possible modes of attention, namely, serial scanning for signal detection and parallel-process scanning that apprehends incidental information in the field. This was attempted using perceptual search tasks in which the respondent was required to find stimuli or signals embedded in meaningfully organized visual fields—for example, to locate faces camouflaged in pictorial scenes. Two scores were obtained, one for the number of good or keyed hidden faces located and another for the number of areas circled that did not contain a keyed face, that is, the number of "fabulated" faces (Smith & Klein, 1953).

The distinction here is between good form appropriateness as opposed to poor form appropriateness of figures identified as "faces," a distinction supported by confirming loadings for inkblot measures of form appropriateness and form definiteness on the same factors. On completion of the search task, the stimulus materials were removed, and the respondents were then asked specific questions about the content of the pictorial scenes. Persons who take in incidental information about the field in the process of scanning could thus be differentiated from those whose attention is apparently limited selectively to detecting the hidden signals.

Also pertinent to the distinction between signal and information scanning is the Stroop Color–Word Test, which taps susceptibility to cognitive interference or degree of responsiveness to compelling irrelevant stimuli (MacLeod, 1991). The Stroop task consists of color names printed in differently colored inks; respondents must name the ink colors as quickly as possible and not read the words. Resistance to color–word interference is thought to be a function of two processes: One is selective deployment of attention successively to the appropriate aspects of the stimulus and the response, namely, to the color of the ink and its corresponding color name; the other is flexible control of both inhibition and facilitation of response in dealing with successive color–word stimuli, that is, active inhibition of the printed color name and simultaneous (or successive) facilitation of the name of the contrasting colored ink in which it is printed (Gardner et al., 1959; Klein, 1964; Rand, Wapner, Werner, & McFarland, 1963). There are consistent individual differences in each process as well as in the relative balance with which they occur in concert; in the extreme, some individuals may rely on only one or the other.

The conjecture here is that those individuals who rely relatively more on the first process of selective attention on the Stroop test would also tend to deploy selective attention serially as a strategy (or perhaps a style) of signal detection. In contrast, those tending toward parallel processing would automatically develop multiple encodings of incidental information, some of which (like the color words on the Stroop test) interfere with task performance and need to be actively inhibited, thereby leading these parallel processors to rely relatively more on the second Stroop process of response inhibition and flexible control.

Indeed, two of the first-order factors in our scanning study were consistent with this view: One involved signal scanning for both unique targets via perceptual search and class instances via memory search; the other involved information scanning, with loadings for incidental knowledge of the pictorial scenes as well as other tasks facilitated by multiple encodings. Furthermore, the Stroop interference score loaded substantially on both factors, which is consistent with the view that signal scanning implicates one of the two Stroop processes (namely, serial selective attention) whereas information scanning implicates the other (namely, active inhibition of the intrusive effects of parallel processing). These two first-order factors were negatively correlated and, along with some other first-order factors, generated a bipolar second-order dimension of signal versus information scanning that is reflective, as we have seen, of serial versus parallel processing.

The structure just described was for the male sample. In the female sample, the corresponding bipolar second-order factor is quite comparable, with similar tests loading it in a hierarchical analysis, but the contributing first-order factors were somewhat different. For example, the Stroop interference score loads only the signal-scanning factor in the female sample, which suggests that females either rely primarily on selective attention in Stroop test performance or else use both selective attention and response inhibition in relative balance.

The other bipolar second-order factor is interpretable as sharp-focus versus broad-focus scanning in both male and female samples. At the test level, one of the major contrasts is between finding good faces in pictorial scenes as opposed to having such a broad view of faces that many fabulated versions are accepted. In males, the broad bandwidth appears to involve attenuated processing because several wrong and omits scores on closure tests load in this direction, as do measures of rigidity and authoritarianism. The first-order factors loading in the broad bandwidth direction involve quick closure via broad estimation, which is facilitative on tasks where approximations are adaptive but in other instances also carries the maladaptive baggage of premature closure. Hence, this cognitive style might be better characterized for males as sharp-focus versus loose-focus scanning or focused versus unfocused scanning.

In contrast, the broad bandwidth pole in females appears more integrative: it was negatively correlated with rigidity and authoritarianism and positively correlated with self-sufficiency and affective interests. These correlates suggest that this factor might be better characterized for females by something like tight-focus versus open-focus scanning. Another difference between males and females is that all but one first-order factor for females cut across both perception and memory, whereas for males there are separate factors for scanning external perceptual fields and internal memory fields, mediated by the isolation of affect.

By invoking process concepts such as inhibition as well as aspects of personality such as rigidity and orientation toward affect in the interpretation of these stylistic attentional modes, we hark back once again to Spearman's fertile conjectures. In speaking of the conative control of attention, he noted

> that another important problem still unsettled is as to whether the conative influence is always primarily enhansive, or can also be (directly) inhibitive. Yet another moot point is as to whether not only conation, but also affection, possesses such immediate influence in the regulating of cognitive intensity. (Spearman, 1923, p. 136)

STYLE IN THE EXPRESSION AND DEVELOPMENT OF COMPETENCE

Given the close association historically between intelligence and attention, it is important to explore potential relationships between human abilities and such stylistic attentional modes as sharp-focus versus broad-focus scanning and signal versus information scanning. These and other cognitive styles, such as field independence versus field dependence and reflection versus impulsivity, reflect consistent individual differences in the manner or form of cognition as distinct from the content or level of cognition (Messick, 1984). As such, cognitive styles are often viewed as *performance* variables rather than *competence* variables (Globerson, 1989; Neimark, 1981).

From this perspective, cognitive styles reflect not competence per se but, rather, the utilization of competence, that is, they moderate access to competence as well as its strategic deployment in meeting task requirements (Neimark, 1985). Indeed, Pascual-Leone's (1969) theory of constructive operators is tantamount to a performance model overlaid on the competence model of Piaget. His M-power, along with operators for content knowledge (C) and procedural learning (L), represent competence; his I- and F-factors, along with operators for affect and motivation (A) as well as for biases and beliefs (B), relate to performance.

As a case in point, Neimark (1981) argued that low success rates of field-dependent persons on Piaget's formal operational tasks, which by their nature are ambiguous and unstructured, do not reflect deficiencies in formal thinking but rather a performance artifact due to misleading field effects. Others who agree with the performance-artifact explanation emphasize differences in strategy or cue selection as well as the propensity of field-dependants to underutilize their repertoire of executive planning schemes (Globerson, 1989; Linn, 1978; de Ribaupierre & Pascual-Leone, 1979).

However, because competence is inferred from task performance in the assessment of human abilities and because styles influence performance apart from competence, the effects of styles constitute contaminants in the assessment of abilities. Somehow styles and abilities need to be disentangled to improve the valid measurement of each. This might be accomplished, for example, by developing refined task materials and experimental controls, convergent and discriminant evidence via multitrait–multimethod designs, effective factor-analytic techniques, and style-appropriate training of strategy selection and use so as to reveal competence optimally.

Nevertheless, separating the contributions of styles from abilities in performance appears to be both difficult and daunting. This is so because their interplay occurs not only at the level of outcomes but also at the level of processes. Stylistic attentional modes influence the nature and quality of stimulus information available for thinking and problem solving (Zelniker, 1989), thereby affecting not just the manner but the material of cognition. These style-based differences in the substance of cognition shape the nature of ability and knowledge structures that are formed as well as their higher-order organization. Thus, cognitive styles are both performance and competence variables combined: styles influence not only the utilization of cognitive structures but also their development (Brodzinsky, 1985; Messick, 1984, 1987). Once again, however, this is not a new perspective. In 1960, as an instance, Riley Gardner and his colleagues interpreted their factor-analytic results linking cognitive controls and intellective abilities on the same factors in these words:

It seems possible that . . . mutual 'feedback' . . . occurs in the developmental emergence of cognitive controls and abilities. For example, generalized facility in selective attention may provide a necessary condition for the differentiation of several linked abilities . . . [In turn] specific abilities may contribute to the differentiation of the control. (Gardner et al., 1960, p. 117)

Hence, stylistic modes of attention, by influencing both the expression and the development of competence, pose both a problem and a challenge for the theory and measurement of human abilities. Stylistic consistencies in cognition pose a problem precisely because they bear on both performance and competence. As performance variables their contaminating effects must be taken into account in the measurement of abilities. As competence variables their role in the development and structuring of abilities and knowledge requires an intricate theoretical rationale relating intelligence and personality. Finally, as bridging variables between cognition and personality, styles offer a challenge because stylistic self-consistency may afford an elucidative purview for addressing both the richness and the individuality of human intellect.

ACKNOWLEDGMENTS

Thanks are gratefully acknowledged to Isaac Bejar, Walter Emmerich, and Irving Sigel for their reviews of the manuscript and to Ann Jungeblut for her comments and support throughout the course of the writing.

REFERENCES

Anderson, J. R. (1983). *The architecture of cognition.* Cambridge, MA: Harvard University Press.

Baddeley, A. D. (1986). *Working memory.* Oxford, England: Clarendon.

Broadbent, D. E. (1957). A mechanical model for human attention and memory span. *Psychological Review, 64,* 205–215.

Broadbent, D. E. (1958). *Perception and communication.* London: Pergamon.

Brodzinsky, D. M. (1985). On the relationship between cognitive styles and cognitive structures. In E. D. Neimark, R. De Lisi, & J. L. Newman (Eds.), *Moderators of competence* (pp. 147–174). Hillsdale, NJ: Lawrence Erlbaum Associates.

Broverman, D. M. (1960a). Cognitive style and intraindividual variation in abilities. *Journal of Personality, 28,* 240–256.

Broverman, D. M. (1960b). Dimensions of cognitive style. *Journal of Personality, 28,* 167–185.

Burt, C. B. (1940). *The factors of the mind.* London: University of London Press.

Burt, C. (1949). The structure of the mind: A review of the results of factor analysis. *British Journal of Educational Psychology, 19,* 100–111, 176–199.

Cattell, R. B. (1946a). The riddle of perseveration: I. Creative effort and disposition rigidity. *Journal of Personality, 14*, 229–238.

Cattell, R. B. (1946b). The riddle of perserveration: II. Solution in terms of personality structure. *Journal of Personality, 14*, 239–267.

Cattell, R. B. (1971). *Abilities: Their structure, growth and action*. Boston: Houghton Mifflin.

Cohen, J. D., Dunbar, K., & McClelland, J. L. (1990). On the control of automatic processes: A parallel distributed processing account of the Stroop effect. *Psychological Review, 97*, 332–361.

de Ribaupierre, A., & Pascual-Leone, J. (1979). Formal operations and M power: A neo-Piagetian investigation. In D. Kuhn (Ed.), *Intellectual development beyond childhood* (pp. 1–44). San Francisco: Jossey-Bass.

Eriksen, C. W., & Hoffman, J. E. (1973). The extent of processing of noise elements during selective encoding from visual displays. *Perception & Psychophysics, 14*, 155–160.

Eriksen, C. W., & Hoffman, J. E. (1974). Selective attention: Noise suppression or signal enhancement? *Bulletin of the Psychonomic Society, 4*, 587–598.

Eriksen, C. W., & Yeh, Y. Y. (1985). Allocation of attention in the visual field. *Journal of Experimental Psychology: Human Perception and Performance, 11*, 583–597.

Frick, J. W., Guilford, J. P., Christensen, P. R., & Merrifield, P. R. (1959). A factor-analytic study of flexibility of thinking. *Educational and Psychological Measurement, 19*, 469–496.

Gardner, H. (1983). *Frames of mind: The theory of multiple intelligences*. New York: Basic Books.

Gardner, R. W., Holzman, P. S., Klein, G. S., Linton, H. B., & Spence, D. P. (1959). Cognitive control: A study of individual consistencies in cognitive behavior. *Psychological Issues, 1*, Monograph 4.

Gardner, R. W., Jackson, D. N., & Messick, S. (1960). Personality organization in cognitive controls and intellectual abilities. *Psychological Issues, 2*, Monograph 8.

Globerson, T. (1989). What is the relationship between cognitive style and cognitive development? In T. Globerson & T. Zelniker (Eds.), *Cognitive style and cognitive development* (pp. 71–85). Norwood, NJ: Ablex.

Globerson, T., & Zelniker, T. (1989). *Cognitive style and cognitive development*. Norwood, NJ: Ablex.

Greenwald, A. G. (1972). Evidence of both perceptual filtering and response suppression for rejected messages in selective attention. *Journal of Experimental Psychology, 94*, 55–67.

Hasher, L., & Zacks, R. T. (1979). Automatic and effortful processes in memory. *Journal of Experimental Psychology: General, 106*, 356–388.

Hernández-Peón, R. (1964). Psychiatric implications of neurophysiological research. *Bulletin of the Menninger Clinic, 28*, 165–185.

Humphreys, G. W. (1981). On varying the span of visual attention: Evidence for two modes of spatial attention. *Quarterly Journal of Experimental Psychology, 33A*, 17–31.

Hunt, E. (1980). Intelligence as an information-processing concept. *British Journal of Psychology, 71*, 449–474.

James, W. (1890). *The principles of psychology*. New York: Holt.

Jonides, J. (1983). Further toward a model of the mind's eye's movement. *Bulletin of Psychonomic Society, 21*, 247–250.

Kahneman, D. (1973). *Attention and effort*. Englewood Cliffs, NJ: Prentice-Hall.

Klein, G. S. (1958). Cognitive control and motivation. In G. Lindzey (Ed.), *Assessment of human motives* (pp. 87–118). New York: Holt, Rinehart & Winston.

Klein, G. S. (1964). Semantic power measured through the interference of words with color-naming. *American Journal of Psychology, 77*, 576–588.

Kosslyn, S. M. (1987). Seeing and imagining in the cerebral hemispheres: A computational approach. *Psychological Review, 94*, 148–175.

Kyllonen, P. C., & Christal, R. E. (1990). Reasoning ability is (little more than) working-memory capacity?! *Intelligence, 14*, 389–433.

Linn, M. C. (1978). Influence of cognitive style and training on tasks requiring the separation of variables schema. *Child Development, 49*, 874–877.

Luborsky, L., Blinder, B., & Schimek, J. (1965). Looking, recalling, and GSR as a function of defense. *Journal of Abnormal Psychology, 70*, 270–280.

MacLeod, C. M. (1991). Half a century of research on the Stroop effect: An integrative review. *Psychological Bulletin, 109*, 163–203.

Messick, S. (1984). The nature of cognitive styles: Problems and promise in educational practice. *Educational Psychologist, 19*, 59–74.

Messick, S. (1987). Structural relationships across cognition, personality and style. In R. E. Snow & M. J. Farr (Eds.), *Aptitude, learning, and instruction: Vol. 3. Conative and affective process analyses* (pp. 35–75). Hillsdale, NJ: Lawrence Erlbaum Associates.

Messick, S. (1989). *Cognitive style and personality: Scanning and orientation toward affect* (RR-89-16). Princeton, NJ: Educational Testing Service.

Messick, S. (1992). Multiple intelligences or multilevel intelligence? Selective emphasis on distinctive properties of hierarchy: On Gardner's *Frames of Mind* and Sternberg's *Beyond IQ* in the context of theory and research on the structure of human abilities. *Psychological Inquiry, 3*, 365–384.

Moray, N. (1969). *Attention: Selective processes in vision and hearing.* London: Hutchinson Educational.

Neimark, E. D. (1981). Confounding with cognitive style factors: An artifact explanation for the apparent nonuniversal incidence of formal operations. In I. E. Sigel, D. M. Brodzinsky, & R. M. Golinkoff (Eds.), *New directions in Piagetian theory and practice* (pp. 177–189). Hillsdale, NJ: Lawrence Erlbaum Associates.

Neimark, E. D. (1985). Moderators of competence: Challenges to the universality of Piagetian theory. In E. D. Neimark, R. De Lisi, & J. L. Newman (Eds.), *Moderators of competence* (pp. 1–14). Hillsdale, NJ: Lawrence Erlbaum Associates.

Neumann, E., & DeSchepper, B. G. (1991). Costs and benefits of target activation and distractor inhibition in selective attention. *Journal of Experimental Psychology: Learning, Memory and Cognition, 17*, 1136–1145.

Pascual-Leone, J. (1969). *Cognitive development and cognitive style: A general psychological integration.* Unpublished doctoral dissertation, University of Geneva, Switzerland.

Pascual-Leone, J. (1989). An organismic process model of Witkin's field-dependence—independence. In T. Globerson & T. Zelniker (Eds.), *Cognitive style and cognitive development* (pp. 36–70). Norwood, NJ: Ablex.

Posner, M.I. (1975). Psychobiology of attention. In M. S. Gazzaniga & C. Blakemore (Eds.), *Handbook of psychobiology* (pp. 441–480). New York: Academic Press.

Posner, M. I., & Snyder, C. R. R. (1975). Facilitation and inhibition in the processing of signals. In P. M. A. Rabbitt & S. Dornic (Eds.), *Attention and performance* (Vol. 5, pp. 669–692). New York: Academic Press.

Rand, G., Wapner, S., Werner, H., & McFarland, J. H. (1963). Age differences in performance on the Stroop Color-Word test. *Journal of Personality, 31*, 534–558.

Shiffrin, R. M. (1988). Attention. In R. C. Atkinson, R. J. Herrnstein, G. Lindzey, & R. D. Luce (Eds.), *Stevens' handbook of experimental psychology* (Vol. 2, 2nd ed., pp. 739–811). New York: Wiley.

Shiffrin, R. M., & Schneider, W. (1977). Controlled and automatic human information processing: II. Perceptual learning, automatic attending and general theory. *Psychological Review, 84*, 127–190.

Smith, G. J. W., & Klein, G. S. (1953). Cognitive controls in serial behavior patterns. *Journal of Personality, 22*, 354–374.

Spearman, C. (1923). *The nature of intelligence and the principles of cognition.* London: Macmillan.

Spearman, C. (1927). *The abilities of man.* New York: Macmillan.

Spearman, C., & Wynn Jones, L. (1950). *Human ability.* London: Macmillan.

Sternberg, R. J. (1985). *Beyond IQ.* New York: Cambridge University Press.

Treisman, A. M. (1960). Contextual cues in selective listening. *Quarterly Journal of Experimental Psychology, 12*, 242–248.

Treisman, A. M. (1969). Strategies and models of selective attention. *Psychological Review, 76*, 282–299.

Treisman, A. (1990). Variations on the theme of feature integration: Reply to Navon (1990). *Psychological Review, 97*, 460–463.

Treisman, A., & Gelade, G. (1980). A feature integration theory of attention. *Cognitive Psychology, 12*, 97–136.

Wachtel, P. L. (1967). Conceptions of broad and narrow attention. *Psychological Bulletin, 68*, 417–429.

Witkin, H. A., & Goodenough, D. R. (1981). *Cognitive styles: Essence and origins—Field dependence and field independence.* New York: International Universities Press.

Zelniker, T. (1989). Cognitive style and dimensions of information processing. In T. Globerson & T. Zelniker (Eds.), *Cognitive style and cognitive development* (pp. 172–191). Norwood, NJ: Ablex.

CHAPTER 6

Spatial Ability and g

David F. Lohman
The University of Iowa

Spatial abilities have long been relegated to a secondary status in accounts of human intelligence. Tests of spatial abilities are often viewed as measures of practical and mechanical abilities that are useful in predicting success in technical occupations, but not as measures of abstract reasoning abilities (Smith, 1964). This conflicts with the important role afforded to spatial imagery in accounts of creative thinking (Shepard, 1978), and with the observed correlations between spatial tests and other measures of intelligence. In fact, Spearman (see Spearman & Wynn Jones, 1950) considered spatial tests merely as unreliable measures of g. Hierarchical factor analyses generally support Spearman's conclusion, especially for complex spatial tests. Such tests are primarily measures of g, secondarily measures of something task-specific, and thirdly measures of something that covaries uniquely with performance on other spatial tasks (Lohman, 1988). Simpler, speeded spatial tasks show lower g loadings, higher task-specific loadings, and higher spatial factor loadings. In this chapter, I first summarize and then attempt to explain these findings. The relationship between spatial task performance and g may reflect both statistical artifacts and psychological factors. Psychological factors include the attentional demands of maintaining and transforming images in working memory (Kyllonen & Christal, 1990) and the importance of mental models in reasoning (Johnson-Laird, 1983). Indeed, one can turn Spearman's conclusion around and with equal conviction conclude that measures of g are, by and large, unreliable measures of the ability to generate and coordinate different types of mental models in working memory. Evidence that supports and challenges such a conclusion is reviewed.

INTRODUCTION

There is a paradox in the literature on human spatial abilities. Indeed, many of those who have studied spatial abilities have noted it with reactions that range from amusement to annoyance (Paivio, 1971; Smith, 1964). It is this: On the one hand, tests of spatial abilities—especially performance tests that use blocks or form boards or pieces of paper that must be folded and unfolded—such tests are among the best measures of g (or Gf). Furthermore, spatial abilities are routinely implicated in accounts of creative and higher order thinking in science and mathematics (Shepard, 1978; West, 1991). On the other hand, spatial abilities are often equated with concrete, lower level thinking. Thus, they are used to predict success in various practical and technical occupations, such as carpentry, auto mechanics, and the like.

The source of the paradox is this. Hierarchical models of human abilities and the cannon of parsimony give g logical and statistical priority over measures of spatial ability. Therefore, we first account for the effects of g, and then examine correlations between residual scores and other variables. To be sure, there is something left. But the majority of the systematic variance is gone. It has already "been accounted for" by g. Or has it? Is g a psychological entity? Or is it primarily a statistical dimension? Modern theories of cognition can contribute usefully to a reexamination of the debate between Spearman and Thorndike, a debate later joined by Thomson and Thurstone on Thorndike's side, and by Burt and Vernon on Spearman's side (see Thorndike & Lohman, 1990). I believe that we know some things now that Spearman, Thomson, and Thorndike did not know that may allow us to see this controversy in a new light.

IMPORTANCE OF SPATIAL ABILITIES

Spatial ability may be defined as the ability to generate, retain, retrieve, and transform well-structured visual images. It is not a unitary construct. There are, in fact, several spatial abilities, each emphasizing different aspects of the process of image generation, storage, retrieval, and transformation. Spatial abilities are pivotal constructs of all models of human abilities. For example, Guilford (1967) devoted one slice of his Structure of the Intellect model to them. Hierarchical models (e.g., Vernon, 1950) place broad verbal-educational and spatial-visualization factors immediately below general ability because after general ability, the verbal-spatial dimension captures more variance than any other dimension in large, representative batteries of ability tests (see e.g., Eysenck's 1939 reanalysis of Thurstone's 1938 data). Similarly, research on hemispheric specialization suggests that the difference between verbal-sequential processing and spatial-analog processing is a fundamental dichotomy in human cognition. Paivio (1971) long argued for a dual code theory of memory in which verbal and spatial information are stored in different codes. More recently Anderson (1983), a long-standing opponent of this view, proposed a multicode theory of memory, with separate codes for temporarily ordered strings, spatial images, and abstract propositions.

High levels of spatial ability have frequently been linked to creativity, not only in the arts, but in science and mathematics as well (Shepard, 1978; West, 1991). For example, on several occasions Albert Einstein reported that verbal processes seemed not to play a role in his creative thought. Rather, he claimed to achieve insights by means of thought experiments on visualized systems of waves and physical bodies in states of relative motion. Other physicists (such as James Clerk Maxwell, Michael Faraday, and Herman Von Helmholtz), inventors (such as Nikola Tesla and James Watt), and generalists (such as Benjamin Franklin, John Herschel, Francis Galton, and James Watson) also displayed high levels of spatial abilities and reported that they played an important role in their most creative accomplishments.

In psychology, Shepard (1978, 1990) has given particularly lucid accounts of the role of spatial imagery in his own thinking. Involuntary dream images were the source of many of his most creative and influential contributions, including the idea for his experiment with Metzler on mental rotation, the first method of nonmetric multidimensional scaling, and the computer algorithm underlying additive non-hierarchical cluster analysis.

However, in spite of the prominent role of spatial abilities both in models of human abilities and in models of cognition, tests of spatial abilities are not widely used, except as tests of "performance" or "nonverbal" intelligence, a role they have fulfilled since the introduction of the Army Beta exam during World War I. Smith (1964) and Ghiselli (1973) summarized studies in which spatial tests have been used to predict job performance. Spatial tests add little to the prediction of success in traditional school subjects, even geometry, after general ability has been entered into the regression (Bennett, Seashore,

& Wesman, 1974; McNemar, 1964). Predictive validities are somewhat higher for trade school courses (Bennett et al., 1974; Newman, 1945) and engineering school courses, particularly engineering drawing (e.g., Holliday, 1943). Tests of spatial and mechanical abilities are the best predictors of successful completion of training for machine workers and bench workers (Ghiselli, 1973) and for success in training courses for air crew positions (Guilford & Lacey, 1947). Vernon (1950) noted that validities are generally higher for younger and female populations than for older and male populations.

Combining Vernon's (1950) suggestion that the predictive value of spatial tests depends on other characteristics of subjects with the general finding that spatial abilities are more predictive in some courses of instruction than in others, leads to the sort of hypothesis common in the Aptitude × Treatment Interaction (ATI) literature. The hypothesis that "verbalizers" and "visualizers" would profit from different instructional methods stretches from Galton (1880) to the present. It has been one of the most popular, yet one of the most elusive ATI hypotheses. Interactions between verbal and spatial abilities and instructional methods designed to require differential amounts of verbal and spatial processing are few, usually small, and inconsistent (Cronbach & Snow, 1977; Gustafsson, 1976), for both statistical (Gustafsson, 1989) and psychological reasons (Cronbach & Snow, 1977).

There are several possible reasons for the gulf between the theoretical importance of spatial abilities and their practical utility in predictive studies or in ATI studies. First, it may be that, beyond some minimum level of competence, spatial abilities are simply not that important for success in school or work. Second, the strength of spatial ability relative to other abilities, particularly verbal and phonemic fluency abilities, may be more important for predicting how problems are represented and solved rather than whether they can be solved. Third, the criterion measures used in most studies may be biased in favor of other abilities, such as verbal or reasoning skills. Fourth, existing tests may not be very good measures of spatial abilities. Fifth, the practice of first entering g into the regression may distort more than it reveals. In other words, the epistemological decision to give parsimony priority over psychological meaningfulness may leave us trying to explain a dimension that is statistically optimal, but psychologically obscure. This last argument will be a major focus of this chapter. Before embarking on that discussion, however, it may be helpful briefly to review what is included under the heading of "spatial abilities," beginning with how these abilities are measured.

MEASURING SPATIAL ABILITIES

Spatial abilities have been measured using four different types of tests: performance tests, paper-and-pencil tests, verbal tests, and film or dynamic computer-based tests.

Performance tests were the earliest. Form board, block manipulation, and paper-folding tasks were among the items Binet and Simon (1916) used to measure the intelligence of children. Others created entire tests of a particular item type, such as form boards (Itard, 1801, cited in Spearman & Wynn Jones, 1950; Paterson, Elliot, Anderson, Toops, & Heidbreder, 1930) or blocks (Kohs, 1923). Many of these tasks are used in contemporary intelligence tests as measures of performance or nonverbal intelligence (e.g., Wechsler, 1955). Another type of performance test seeks to estimate the ability to function in large-scale space. However, measures of the ability to orient oneself, to find efficient routes between locations, and so on, show at best moderate correlations with other measures of spatial abilities (Allen, 1982; Lorenz & Neisser, 1986), perhaps in part because such tasks may be solved in ways that do not demand analog processing.

Paper-and-pencil tests of spatial abilities have an even more extensive history. Many such tests have been devised over the years. Eliot and Smith (1983) assembled directions and example items for 392 spatial tests, most of which were used in factorial investigations of abilities. Early factor analyses sought to demonstrate the existence of one or more spatial factors (El Koussy, 1935; Kelley, 1928). Some researchers, particularly those in Britain, were satisfied when they showed that a single spatial factor could be identified in the correlations among spatial tests once the general factor had been removed. These researchers tended to construct tests of spatial abilities that contained several different types of items and to study young, age-heterogeneous samples. American researchers used different methods of factor analysis, more homogeneous tests, and older, more homogeneous subject samples, and therefore, identified many different spatial factors. French (1951) made an early attempt to catalog these factors. Others (Eysenck, 1967; Guilford, 1967) proposed rational models that classified existing factors and suggested how new factors might be identified. Recent efforts to understand the dimensions of spatial abilities have moved away from these rational schemes and have sought instead to reanalyze old data sets using modern factor-analytic methods and a hierarchical factor model in which factors are organized according to breadth from g, to broad group factors, to narrow group factors, to specifics (Carroll, 1993; Lohman, 1979). Table 6.1 lists the

TABLE 6.1

Major Spatial Factors, Definitions, and a Representative Test for Each

Factor	Definition[a]	Example Test[b]
Visualization	Ability in manipulating visual patterns, as indicated by level of difficulty and complexity in visual stimulus material that can be handled successfully, without regard to the speed of task solution.	Paper Folding
Speeded Rotation	Speed in manipulating relatively simple visual patterns, by whatever means (mental rotation, transformation or otherwise).	Cards
Closure Speed	Speed in apprehending and identifying a visual pattern, without knowing in advance what the pattern is, when the pattern is disguised or obscured in some way.	Street Gestalt
Closure Flexibility	Speed in finding, apprehending and identifying a visual pattern, knowing in advance what is to be apprehended, when the pattern is disguised or obscured in some way.	Concealed Figures
Perceptual Speed	Speed in finding a known visual pattern, or in accurately comparing one or more patterns, in a visual field such that the patterns are not disguised or obscured.	Identical Pictures

[a]From Carroll (1993, pp. 362–363).
[b]See Eliot and Smith (1983).

five major spatial factors identified in these reviews, a brief definition of each, and the name of a test that commonly loads in the factor. However, the specific variance in such tests is large, and so attempts to measure these abilities should always employ multiple tests for each factor (see Carroll, 1993, and Lohman, Pellegrino, Alderton, & Regian, 1987, for additional recommendations on tests, and Eliot & Smith, 1983, for examples of test items).

Verbal tests of spatial abilities have received much less attention, despite the fact that they often show high correlations with other spatial tests and various criterion measures (Ackerman & Kanfer, 1993; Guilford & Lacey, 1947). In this type of test, examinees must listen to a problem, presumably one that requires construction of a mental image, and then answer one or more questions. For example, "Imagine that you walk north for a while then take a right turn, then walk further and take another right turn. In what direction are you facing?" Such tests require subjects to use spatial abilities in a way that is probably more representative of the manner in which such abilities are used in everyday life than do the items on most paper-and-pencil tests. Many cognitive tasks often require—or at least benefit from—the ability to construct a mental image that can be coordinated with linguistic inputs (Baddeley, 1986; Johnson-Laird, 1983; Kintsch, 1986).

Although spatial tests may require subjects to transform objects, such as by rotating or transposing them mentally, they typically present static objects. Some theorists have hypothesized that the perception of dynamic spatial relationships involves different abilities. Gibson (1947) and later Seibert and Snow (1965) developed a variety of motion picture tests that were designed to measure these *dynamic spatial abilities*. However, individual differences on most dynamic spatial tasks appear to be well accounted for by performance on factors defined by paper-and-pencil tests. One exception is an ability factor called Serial Integration that appeared in several studies. Tests defining this factor require subjects to identify a common object from a series of incomplete pictures presented successively. More recently, Pellegrino and Hunt (1989) devised several computer-administered tests of dynamic spatial abilities. Results to date show that individual differences in the ability to predict object trajectories and arrival times can be reliably measured and load on different factors than performance on paper-and-pencil tests.

Response Mode and Speededness

In addition to differences in presentation format (e.g., performance, paper-and-pencil, verbal, dynamic), spatial tests also differ in the type of response required (such as the selection of an alternative, construction of a response, or a verbal statement). For paper-and-pencil tests, there is some evidence that constructed-response tests are somewhat better measures of spatial ability (Lohman, 1988), and for this reason have long been preferred by British psychometricians (Eliot & Smith, 1983). Smith (1964) argued that spatial ability is best measured when subjects are required to maintain an image in its correct proportions. This is often done by presenting well-structured but fairly simple geometric designs that subjects must remember and then reproduce. As with all constructed-response tests, however, scoring is more difficult than when multiple-choice tests are used. On the other hand, much additional information about subjects' abilities and test strategies can be had from a careful analysis of the type errors they make in drawing or constructing their answers (e.g., Kyllonen, 1984).

Another important aspect of spatial tests is the relative emphasis placed on speed versus level. Tests administered under highly speeded conditions tend to measure more specific aspects of spatial ability than do tests administered under relatively unspeeded conditions. Altering the complexity of test items generally results in a change in the factorial loading of a test. Simple items must be administered under speed conditions in order to generate individual differences, and so changes in task complexity usually mean a change in test speededness as well. Computer-based tests offer the opportunity to gather both error and latency scores, which can then be combined to predict criterion performances with greater precision than from either measure considered separately (Ackerman & Lohman, 1990). However, performance on such tests is more influenced by the speed or accuracy emphasis subjects adopt than is performance on time-limited tests.

Practice and Training Effects

Spatial tests often show substantial practice effects. Retest gains range from .2 to 1.2 SD, effects being somewhat large for simpler tests, shorter retest intervals, and subjects who are given feedback (Krumboltz & Christal, 1960; Lohman, 1988, 1993). Effects of this magnitude can seriously compromise interpretation of test scores if examinees are differentially familiar with test problems. However, transfer to nonpracticed tests that load on the same spatial factor is typically much smaller, often nonexistent. Several studies now suggest that the key variable in predicting transfer is similarity of procedures employed rather than of stimuli used, at least when the subjects are young adults and the stimuli are regular polygons (Lohman, 1993).

Spatial abilities can be improved with practice and training, even though particular courses of instruction (such as engineering drawing) have inconsistent effects. This may in part reflect the fact that treatments designed to improve performance on spatial tasks often are disruptive for high verbal ability subjects. One possibility is that these treatments impose or induce external regulation of performance. External regulation may compensate for the inadequate self-regulation activities of low verbal subjects, but interfere with the self-regulation activities of high verbal subjects (Lohman, 1986a).

Although short-term studies often produce small or conflicting findings, Balke-Aurell's (1982) investigation of the effects of tracking in the Swedish secondary school system suggests that the cumulative effects of differential educational and work experiences can be quite large. Students educated in schools using a verbally oriented curriculum showed greater growth in verbal abilities than spatial abilities, whereas those educated in schools using a technical curriculum showed greater growth in spatial abilities.

Personality Correlates

The relative ease with which individuals can create imagistic versus semantic elaborations also correlates with personality constructs (Smith, 1964). One of the clearest demonstrations of this comes from the work of Riding (1983). Riding was interested in children's habitual modes of thinking. He developed a task in which he read a short story to a child and then asked a series of questions about the passage, all of which required some inference. Questions were of two types, those that depended on imagery and those that depended on semantic elaboration. For example, the story may have mentioned the fact that someone knocked on the door of a cottage. The question might be, "What color was the door"? Of course, there was no right answer, because color of the door was not specified. Response latency was recorded. However, the dependent variable of interest was an ipsative score that compared latencies on semantic and imagery questions. The idea was to identify children who were much quicker to answer one type of question than the other. Correlations were then computed between this ipsative score and a personality scale. Children who showed a preference for imagistic processing were much more likely to be introverted, whereas those who showed a preference for verbal elaboration were more likely to be extroverted.

CONTRIBUTIONS OF COGNITIVE RESEARCH

Spatial Cognition

Cognitive psychology has contributed importantly to our under-standing of how subjects encode, remember, and transform visual images, and thus to what spatial abilities might be. Seminal research here was that of Shepard and his students. Shepard (1978) posed an interesting challenge to cognitive scientists:

> Suppose that we do not start by asking what kinds of thought processes are most accessible to empirical study, are most conveniently external-ized in the form of discrete symbols, words, or sentences, or are most readily described by existing models imported into cognitive psychology from linguistics or computer science. Suppose, instead, that we first ask what sorts of thought processes underlie human creative acts of the highest and most original order. Perhaps we shall come to be less than fully satisfied with research that is exclusively motivated by current

theories of linear sequential processing of discrete symbolic or propositional structures. (p. 134)

The challenge to propositional theories of cognition was made most
forcefully in an early series of experiments on mental rotation (see
Shepard & Cooper, 1982, for a summary). The basic finding was that
the time required to determine whether two figures could be rotated
into congruence was a linear function of the amount of rotation
required. On the basis of this and other evidence, Shepard claimed that
mental rotation was an analog process that showed a one-to-one
correspondence with physical rotation. The second claim was that this
rotation process was performed on a mental representation that
somehow preserved information about structure at all points during
the rotation transformation.

Others have been more explicit about the nature of the representation. Most agree that spatial knowledge can be represented in more
than one way. One representation (sometimes called an image code) is
thought to be more literal (Kosslyn, 1980) or at least more structure- or
configuration-preserving (Anderson, 1983). Another representation is
more abstract and is more meaning- or interpretation-preserving (Anderson, 1983; Kosslyn, 1980; Palmer, 1977) and is usually modeled by
the same propositional structures used to represent meaningful verbal
knowledge. Much of the confusion in understanding spatial abilities
can be traced to whether spatial abilities are restricted to image-coded
memories and the analog processes that operate on them or whether
proposition-coded memories and the general procedural knowledge
that operate on them are also considered part of the term. In other
words, much of the confusion lies in whether abilities are defined by
performance on a certain class of tasks or by skill in executing certain
types of mental processes.

Individual Differences in Spatial Cognition

Although research and theory in cognitive psychology and artificial
intelligence suggest much about the nature of spatial knowledge and
processes, it does not explicitly address the source of individual
differences in spatial processing. Research on this question has followed four hypotheses: that spatial abilities may be explained by
individual differences in (a) speed of performing analog transformations, (b) skill in generating and retaining mental representations that
preserve configural information, (c) the amount of visual-spatial information that can be maintained in an active state, or (d) the sophistica-
tion and flexibility of strategies available for solving such tasks.

Transformation Hypothesis

The most popular hypothesis has been that spatial abilities may be explained by individual differences in the speed with which subjects can accurately perform analog mental transformations, particularly rotation. However, correlations between rate of rotation (estimated by the slope of the regression of latency on angular separation) and spatial ability vary from highly negative (e.g., Lansman, 1981) to moderately positive (e.g., Poltrock & Brown, 1984). Correlations are generally higher for three-dimensional rotation problems than for two-dimensional problems (Cooper & Regan, 1982; Pellegrino & Kail, 1982), and for practiced than for nonpracticed subjects (Lohman & Nichols, 1990). However, even moderate correlations between the slope measure and other variables are difficult to interpret. The slope is heavily influenced by the amount of time taken on trials requiring the most rotation. It may, thus, better reflect the number of attempts made to solve the problem or simply the time taken to solve these most difficult problems, not rate of rotation. More importantly, it can be shown that slopes and other component scores are incapable of explaining individual differences that are consistent across trials. Instead, these individual differences are captured in individual mean or intercept scores (Lohman, 1994). On the other hand, correlations between overall error rates and spatial reference tests are often quite high. Indeed, although rate of information processing on rotation tasks and accuracy levels achieved under liberal time allotments are necessarily confounded, differences between high and low spatial subjects are much greater on the accuracy score than on a rate of information processing score (Lohman, 1986b). One interpretation of this finding is that the amount of information that can be maintained in an active state of working memory is more important than rate of processing that information in accounting for individual differences in spatial ability.

Superior Spatial Working Memory

Baddeley's (1986) model of working memory hypothesizes a central executive and two slave systems: an articulatory loop and a visual-spatial scratch pad. Perhaps high spatial subjects can maintain more image-coded information in this scratch pad. Kyllonen's (1984) study of ability differences in types and number of errors made on a paper folding task supported this hypothesis. His study showed that high and low spatial subjects differed not so much in the type of error committed but in the number of errors committed. Because of this, Kyllonen

(1984) concluded that the main difference between the performance of high- and low-spatials was that lows were more likely to forget a fold and then either not perform it or substitute an incorrect fold for the forgotten one. Other theorists (e.g., Just & Carpenter, 1992) emphasize the trade-off between storage and transformation functions in a unitary working memory system. By this account, mental rotation problems are good measures of spatial ability because they place substantial demands on both storage and transformation functions, and require subjects to manage the trade-off between them. Other evidence in support of this view comes from verbal problems that require imagery for their solution, such as Binet's "It is 12:15. If we switch the hands on the clock, what time will it be"? Tests constructed of such problems often show high predictive validities, but are not factorially pure (Ackerman & Kanfer, 1993).

Nature of the Representation

Several investigators have sought to determine whether high and low spatial subjects differ in the type of mental representations they create (see e.g., Cooper, 1982; Lohman, 1988). Individual differences in memory for random forms shows no relationship with performance on other spatial tests (Christal, 1958). Thus, it is not so much the ability to remember figural stimuli but the ability to remember systematically structured figural stimuli that distinguishes between subjects high and low in spatial ability. Low spatial subjects seem to have particular difficulty in constructing systematically structured images. High spatial subjects appear to be able to construct images that can be compared holistically with test stimuli. Differences between high and medium spatial subjects are often small in this respect. It is the very low spatial subjects who appear qualitatively different (Lohman, 1988; Pellegrino & Kail, 1982).

Strategies

It has long been noted that spatial tasks may be solved in more than one way, with some strategies placing greater demands on analog processing than others. Several studies have now shown that the strategies subjects employ on form-board type tasks are systematically related to their ability profiles (Kyllonen, Lohman, & Woltz, 1984; Lohman, 1988). The major distinction is between spatial and nonspatial strategies. Subjects using the spatial strategy remember complex polygons by decomposing them into simpler geometric shapes. When required to assemble figures mentally, their performance is more influenced by the characteristics of the to-be-assembled figure than by that of the component figures. Time to perform this assembly operation is usually negatively correlated with reference spatial tests. On the other hand, subjects using the nonspatial strategy try to remember complex polygons by associating the figure with another concrete, easily labeled object. When asked to assemble figures mentally, their performance is strongly influenced by the complexity of the component figures rather than the to-be-assembled figure. Further, time to perform the assembly often shows higher correlations with tests of verbal ability than with tests of spatial ability.

Rotation tasks are also solved in different ways by different subjects. Bethell-Fox and Shepard (1988) found that rotation times for unfamiliar stimuli were generally influenced by the complexity of the stimulus. With practice, most subjects learned to rotate all stimuli at the same rate. However, some subjects continued to show effects for stimulus complexity even after much practice. Bethell-Fox and Shepard (1988) argued that these subjects rotated stimuli piece by piece whereas after practice others rotated them holistically. Carpenter and Just (1978) argued that even practiced subjects do not rotate an image of an entire three-dimensional object, but rather only a skeletal representation of it. In experiments on a cube rotation task, they found that subjects used different strategies, presumably related to the coordinate system the subject adopted. Low spatial subjects appeared to rotate the cube iteratively along standard axes whereas high spatial subjects were able to use the shorter trajectory defined by a single transformation through both axes (Just & Carpenter, 1985).

Thus, subjects of different ability levels and profiles often solve spatial tests in predictably different ways. However, flexibility of strategy in solving such tasks seems to be more related to g or Gf than to spatial ability (Kyllonen et al., 1984). Indeed, subjects high in spatial but low in verbal abilities have been found to apply the same "spatial" strategy to all problems. Perhaps they have no need to switch to other strategies.

Spatial Ability g

Factorial studies of spatial ability routinely show that spatial tests are good measures of g. Investigations of individual differences in spatial processing suggested that the major reason for overlap is that spatial tests place extraordinary demands on working memory. If Kyllonen and Christal (1990) are correct, then this would explain the high correlation between them.

It is useful to extend this reasoning further. Although individuals are sometimes required to solve the sorts of problems presented on tests (particularly paper-and-pencil tests) of spatial abilities, everyday thinking for the most part requires a different use of spatial abilities. One example comes from research on reading comprehension. For years, reading comprehension was modeled as the process of creating an internal model of the text that mimicked its logical structure. In other words, to comprehend something meant to construct an internal outline or summary of it. Then Kintsch and Greeno (1985) joined forces to understand how children solve—or better, why they fail to solve—word problems in mathematics. What they discovered was that a text model was not enough. Children needed also to construct a visual mental model that could be coordinated with the text model. Further, the visual model (or analog) became increasingly important as problem complexity increased. It provided a way to integrate and coordinate concepts and the relationships among them. A good example of what this means for comprehension comes from the experience of assembling a toy from printed directions that only look like English. I can read the words, ''Put hex nut K and lockwasher Q on spindle d–1, and tighten loosely.'' I may be able to repeat them, to paraphrase them, even to summarize them. But if I cannot visualize what I must do, then I do not understand. Similarly, children need pictures to help them understand stories. Indeed, the first text without pictures they read is an important milestone. Thus, by this theory, understanding means using linguistic clues to construct a text model and imagery clues (or analogy or metaphor) to construct an image model, and then coordinating the two. These two aspects of working memory are nicely depicted in Baddeley's (1986) theory. Baddeley claimed that working memory contains a central executive (whose functioning remains somewhat mysterious: In fact, he called it ''the area of residual ignorance'') and two slave systems: a phonological loop and a visual-spatial scratch pad. As I see it, the most important function of imagery in the visual-spatial scratch pad is simply to help us keep track of what we are doing, to see relationships among concepts we have represented either literally or metaphorically by our images. Thought without imagery would be like prose without metaphor. Indeed, one indication of the importance of these models in our thought is the pervasiveness of metaphor in our speech.

Thus, one can turn Spearman's conclusion around (to use a spatial metaphor) and, with equal conviction, conclude that measures of g are largely unreliable measures of the ability to generate and transform different types of mental models in working memory. Alternatively, g may represent the crucial but poorly understood process of coordinating different types of mental models represented in linguistic and imagistic slave systems. It would, to use Baddeley's (1986) words, represent the "area of residual ignorance," or what he also called the Supervisory Attentional System.

Although the mental models view of Johnson-Laird (1983) and Kintsch and Greeno (1985) is useful, another perspective is provided by Anderson's (1983) ACT* theory. Here the crucial distinction is between different types of memory codes. The first set of memory codes contains several perception-based codes (such as the image code and the linear-order code) that preserve important structural aspects of a percept, such as the configuration of its elements (image) or their temporal sequence (linear-order). Interestingly, these two codes correspond rather nicely to Baddeley's two slave systems. The second type of code—called the abstract proposition—is not tied to any particular perceptual process. Rather, it is said to preserve meaning, which may be extracted from perception-based codes or from other proposition-coded memories. I believe that evidence for the separability of meaning-based and perception-based codes is compelling. Anderson (1983) reviewed some of it. Other evidence comes from differential psychology, particularly studies of savants. Indeed, the most striking characteristic of most savants is their remarkable ability to retain and manipulate information in a perception-based code without being able to extract more abstract meanings from these perceptual experiences.

On this view, then, particular abilities represent the effectiveness (relative to other individuals) with which an individual can create, transform, and retain different types of mental codes. The dominance of g would reflect the importance of the abstract proposition code in human cognition, that is, with individual differences in the ability to discover and retain meaningful relationships. Particular verbal and spatial abilities would be relegated to a secondary status, although one would expect them to be more important early in development, as some have hypothesized. For example, Bruner (1973) hypothesized such a role for imagery abilities. Both Janet and Vygotsky noted a similar phenomenon in children's acquisition of language. Wertsch and Stone (1985) summarized Vygotsky's adaptation of Janet in the following way:

> One of the mechanisms that makes possible the cognitive development and general acculturation of the child is the process of coming to recognize the significance of the external sign forms [e.g., words] that he or she has already been using in social interaction. [In other words] children can say more than they realize and it is through coming to

understand what is meant by what is said that their cognitive skills develop. (p. 167)

The suggestion that g is closely tied to the ability to create, transform, and retain meaning-coded memories may in fact overlap with the mental models view. Perhaps what was earlier called the Supervisory Attentional System, that is, the ability to choose among different mental models and especially, to coordinate linguistic-based (or what Kintsch, 1986, called the text-based model) and image-based models; perhaps this is the function and meaning of general intellectual ability.

I hasten to add, however, that the psychological basis of a general cognitive function has no necessary relationship with a general dimension of individual differences. The former refers to generalization across cognitive functions or tasks, whereas the latter refers to generalization across individuals. Just as printers must learn not to confuse the ps and qs, so too, must we learn not to confuse generalization across the rows and columns of our data matrices. In other words, even though the ability to create, transform, and retain meaning-based memories may be the most important source of cross-task consistency for a particular individual, individual differences may derive only in part from this process. Indeed, the literature I reviewed earlier suggests that general working memory or attentional resources may account for even more of the individual difference variance.

CONCLUSIONS

Spatial ability may be defined as the ability to generate, retain, retrieve, and transform well-structured visual images. Distinguishably different aspects of spatial ability can thus be measured by constructing tests that emphasize different aspects of this process. Once relegated to lower order processing and concrete thought, spatial abilities are now understood as important for higher order thinking in science and mathematics, for the ability to generate and appreciate metaphor in language, and for creativity in many domains. The ability to generate visual-spatial models that can be coordinated with linguistic inputs has a pervasive impact on all of cognition. Individuals who excel in the ability to create and manipulate such models are not only more likely to succeed in occupations that require spatial abilities, but are also more likely to generate such models spontaneously when thinking and, especially when verbal fluency abilities are relatively low, to be more introverted. Spatial transformations place heavy demands on working memory and so spatial tests often show high correlations with tests of general fluid ability.

REFERENCES

Ackerman, P. L., & Kanfer, R. (1993). Integrating laboratory and field study for improving selection. Development of a battery for predicting air traffic controller success. *Journal of Applied Psychology, 78*, 413–432.

Ackerman, P. L., & Lohman, D. F. (1990). *An investigation of the effect of practice on the validity of spatial tests.* (Final report, NPRDC Contract N66001-88C-0291). Minneapolis, MN: Personnel Decisions Research Institute.

Allen, G. L. (1982). *Assessment of visuospatial abilities using complex cognitive tasks.* Norfolk, VA: Old Dominion University, Department of Psychology.

Anderson, J. R. (1983). *The architecture of cognition.* Cambridge, MA: Harvard University Press.

Baddeley, A. (1986). *Working memory.* Oxford, England: Clarendon.

Balke-Aurell, G. (1982). *Changes in ability as related to educational and occupational experience.* Goteborg, Sweden: Acta Universitatis Gothoburgensis.

Bennett, G. K., Seashore, H. G., & Wesman, A. G. (1974). *Manual for the Differential Aptitude Test* (5th ed.). New York: Psychological Corporation.

Bethell-Fox, C. E., & Shepard, R. N. (1988). Mental rotation: Effects of stimulus complexity, familiarity and individual differences. *Journal of Experimental Psychology: Human Perception and Performance, 14*, 12–23.

Binet, A., & Simon, T. (1916). *The development of intelligence in children* (E. S. Kite, Trans.). Baltimore: Williams & Wilkins.

Bruner, J. S. (1973). *Beyond the information given.* New York: Norton.

Carpenter, P. A., & Just, M. A. (1978). Eye fixations during mental rotation. In. J. W. Senders, D. F. Fisher, & R. A. Monty (Eds.), *Eye movements and the higher psychological functions* (pp. 115–133). Hillsdale, NJ: Lawrence Erlbaum Associates.

Carroll, J. B. (1993). *Human cognitive abilities: A survey of factor-analytic studies.* New York: Cambridge University Press.

Christal, R. E. (1958). Factor analytic study of visual memory. *Psychological Monographs, 72* (13, Whole No. 466).

Cooper, L. A. (1982). Strategies for visual comparison and representation: Individual differences. In R. J. Sternberg (Ed.), *Advances in the psychology of human intelligence* (Vol. 1, pp. 77–124). Hillsdale, NJ: Lawrence Erlbaum Associates.

Cooper, L. A., & Regan, D. T. (1982). Attention, perception and intelligence. In R. J. Sternberg (Ed.), *Handbook of human intelligence* (pp. 123–169). Cambridge, England: Cambridge University Press.

Cronbach, L. J., & Snow, R. E. (1977). *Aptitudes and instructional methods: A handbook for research on interactions.* New York: Irvington.

Eliot, J. C., & Smith, I. M. (1983). *An international directory of spatial tests.* Windsor, England: NFER-Nelson.

Eysenck, H. J. (1939). Review of *Primary mental abilities* by L. L. Thurstone. *British Journal of Psychology, 9*, 270–275.

Eysenck, H. J. (1967). Intellectual assessment: A theoretical and experimental approach. *British Journal of Educational Psychology, 37*, 81–98.

French, J. W. (1951). The description of aptitude and achievement tests in terms of rotated factors. *Psychometric Monographs*, No. 5.

Galton, F. (1880). Statistics of mental imagery. *Mind, 5*, 300–318.

Ghiselli, E. E. (1973). The validity of aptitude tests in personnel selection. *Personnel Psychology, 26*, 461–477.

Gibson, J. J. (Ed.). (1947). Motion picture testing and research. *Army Air Force aviation psychology program* (Rep. No. 7). Washington DC: U.S. Government Printing Office.

Guilford, J. P. (1967). *The nature of human intelligence*. New York: McGraw-Hill.

Guilford, J. P., & Lacey, J. I. (Eds.). (1947). Printed classification tests. *Army Air Force aviation psychology research program* (Rep. No. 5). Washington DC: U.S. Government Printing Office.

Gustafsson, J. E. (1976). Verbal and figural aptitudes in relation to instructional methods: Studies in aptitude-treatment interaction. *Gotenborg Studies in Education Sciences, 17*.

Gustafsson, J. E. (1989). Broad and narrow abilities in research on learning and instruction. In R. Kanfer, P. L. Ackerman, & R. Cudeck (Eds.), *Abilities, motivation and methodology: The Minnesota Symposium on learning and individual differences* (pp. 203–237). Hillsdale, NJ: Lawrence Erlbaum Associates.

Holliday, F. (1943). The relations between psychological test scores and subsequent proficiency of apprentices in the engineering industry. *Occupational Psychology, 17*, 168–185.

Johnson-Laird, P. N. (1983). *Mental models: Towards a cognitive science of language, inference and consciousness*. Cambridge, MA: Harvard University Press.

Just, M. A., & Carpenter, P. A. (1985). Cognitive coordinate systems: Accounts of mental rotation and individual differences in spatial ability. *Psychological Review, 92*, 137–172.

Just, M. A., & Carpenter, P. A. (1992). A capacity theory of comprehension: Individual differences in working memory. *Psychological Review, 99*, 122–149.

Kelley, T. L. (1928). *Crossroads in the mind of man*. Stanford, CA: Stanford University Press.

Kintsch, W. (1986). Learning from text. *Cognition and Instruction, 3*, 87–108.

Kintsch, W., & Greeno, J. G. (1985). Understanding and solving word arithmetic problems. *Psychological Review, 92*, 109–129.

Kohs, S. C. (1923). *Intelligence measurement: A psychological and statistical study based upon the block designs test*. New York: Macmillan.

Kosslyn, S. M. (1980). *Image and mind*. Cambridge, MA: Harvard University Press.

Koussy, A. A. H. El. (1935). The visual perception of space. *British Journal of Psychology, 20* (Monograph Suppl.).

Krumboltz, J. D., & Christal, R. E. (1960). Short-term practice effects in tests of spatial aptitude. *Personnel and Guidance Journal, 38*, 384–391.

Kyllonen, P. C. (1984). Information processing analysis of spatial ability. (Doctoral dissertation, Stanford University, 1984). *Dissertation Abstracts International, 45*, 819A.

Kyllonen, P. C., & Christal, R. E. (1990). Reasoning ability is (little more than) working memory capacity?! *Intelligence, 14*, 389–433.

Kyllonen, P. C., Lohman, D. F., & Woltz, D. J. (1984). Componential modeling of alternative strategies for performing spatial tasks. *Journal of Educational Psychology, 76*, 1325–1345.

Lansman, M. (1981). Ability factors and the speed of information processing. In M. P. Friedman, J. P. Das, & N. O'Connor (Eds.), *Intelligence and learning* (pp. 441–457). New York: Plenum.

Lohman, D. F. (1979). *Spatial ability: A review and reanalysis of the correlational literature* (Tech. Rep. No.8). Stanford, CA: Stanford University, Aptitude Research Project, School of Education. (NTIS NO. AD-A075 972).

Lohman, D. F. (1986a). Predicting mathemathical effects in the teaching of higher order thinking skills. *Educational Psychologist, 21*, 191–208.

Lohman, D. F. (1986b). The effect of speed-accuracy tradeoff on sex differences in mental rotation. *Perception and Psychophysics, 39*, 427–436.

Lohman, D. F. (1988). Spatial abilities as traits, processes and knowledge. In R. J.

Sternberg (Ed.), *Advances in the psychology of human intelligence* (Vol. 40, pp. 181–248). Hillsdale, NJ: Lawrence Erlbaum Associates.

Lohman, D. F. (1993). *Effects of practice and training on the acquisition and transfer of spatial skills: Two speed-accuracy studies* (Final Report Grant AFOSR-91-9367). Iowa City, IA: Lindquist Center for Measurement.

Lohman, D. F. (1994). Component scores as residual variation (or why the intercept correlates best). *Intelligence, 19,* 1–11.

Lohman, D. F., & Nichols, P. D. (1990). Training spatial abilities: Effects of practice on rotation and synthesis tasks. *Learning and Individual Differences, 2,* 69–95.

Lohman, D. F., Pellegrino, J. W., Alderton, D. L., & Regian, J. W. (1987). Dimensions and components of individual differences in spatial abilities. In S. H. Irvine & S. N. Newstead (Eds.), *Intelligence and cognition: Contemporary frames of reference* (pp. 253–312). Dordrecht, Netherlands: Martinus Nijhoff.

Lorenz, C. A., & Neisser, U. (1986). *Ecological and psychometric dimensions of spatial ability* (Tech. Rep. No. 10). Atlanta, GA: Emory University, Department of Psychology.

McNemar, Q. (1964). Lost: Our intelligence? Why? *American Psychologist, 19,* 871–882.

Newman, J. (1945). The prediction of shopwork performance in an adult rehabilitation program: The Kent-Shakow Industrial Formboard Series. *Psychological Record, 5,* 343–352.

Paivio, A. (1971). *Imagery and verbal processes.* New York: Holt, Rinehart & Winston.

Palmer, S. E. (1977). Hierarchical structure in perceptual representation. *Cognitive Psychology, 9,* 441–474.

Paterson, D. G., Elliot, R. M., Anderson, L. D., Toops, H. A., & Heidbreder, E. (1930). *Minnesota mechanical ability tests.* Minneapolis: University of Minnesota Press.

Pellegrino, J. W., & Hunt, E. B. (1989). Computer-controlled assessment of static on dynamic spatial reasoning. In R. F. Dillon & J. W. Pellegrino (Eds.), *Testing: Theoretical and applied perspectives* (pp. 174–198). New York: Praeger.

Pellegrino, J. W., & Kail, R. (1982). Process analyses of spatial aptitude. In R. J. Sternberg (Ed.), *Advances in the psychology of human intelligence* (Vol. 1, pp. 311–366). Hillsdale, NJ: Lawrence Erlbaum Associates.

Poltrock, S. E., & Brown, P. (1984). Individual differences in visual imagery and spatial ability. *Intelligence, 8,* 93–138.

Riding, R. J. (1983). Extraversion, field independence and performance on cognitive tasks in 12-year-old children. *Research in Education, 29,* 1–9.

Seibert, W. F., & Snow, R. E. (1965). *Studies in cine-psychometry I: Preliminary factor analysis of visual cognition and memory.* Lafayette, IN: Purdue University, Audio Visual Center.

Shepard, R. N. (1978). Externalization of mental images and the act of creation. In B. S. Randhawa & W. E. Coffman (Eds.), *Visual learning, thinking and communication* (pp. 133–190). New York: Academic Press.

Shepard, R. N. (1990). *Mind sights.* San Francisco: Freeman.

Shepard, R. N., & Cooper, L. A. (1982). *Mental images and their transformations.* Cambridge, MA: MIT Press.

Smith, I. M. (1964). *Spatial ability.* San Diego: Knapp.

Spearman, C., & Wynn Jones, L. L. (1950). *Human ability.* London: Macmillan.

Thorndike, R. M., & Lohman, D. F. (1990). *A century of ability testing.* Chicago: Riverside.

Thurstone, L. L. (1938). Primary mental abilities. *Psychometric Monographs, 1.*

Vernon, P. E. (1950). *The structure of human abilities.* London: Methuen.

Wechsler, D. (1955). *Wechsler adult intelligence scale.* New York: Psychological Corporation.

Wertsch, J. V., & Stone, C. A. (1985). The concept of internalization in Vygotsky's account of the genesis of higher mental functions. In J. V. Wertsch (Ed.), *Culture, communication and cognition: Vygotskian perspectives* (pp.162–179). Cambridge, England: Cambridge University Press.

West, T. G. (1991). *In the mind's eye.* Buffalo, NY: Prometheus.

CHAPTER 7

Multidimensional Latent Trait Models in Measuring Fundamental Aspects of Intelligence

Susan E. Embretson
University of Kansas

Latent trait models have several theoretical advantages over classical test theory for measuring traits. These theoretical advantages include justifiable scaling at the interval level, invariant parameter estimates, and common scaling of items and persons (see Hambleton, Swaminathan, & Rogers (1991); Embretson & DeBoeck, 1994). Common scaling results from the additivity between item difficulties and person abilities. The special form of additivity in the Rasch model has often been taken as evidence for fundamental measurement (Andrich, 1988; Embretson & DeBoeck, 1994).

However, latent trait models have another theoretical advantage; they interface well with contemporary methods to understand the basis of task performance. Mathematical modeling of item difficulty and response time is a major method for studying the information processes in task performance. Because item response theory (IRT) is model-based measurement, it is possible to build models that combine mathematical modeling information processing with measurement. Or, stated another way, IRT models can be developed that permit measurement in the context of a substantive model of performance on the measuring task (i.e., items).

Contemporary theories of task performance typically emphasize the multiple processes that contribute to responses. For example, Sternberg's (1985) componential theory of intelligence contains multiple processes, metacomponents, and so forth, that contribute to task difficulty and individual differences. Similarly, multiple processes have also been attributed to personality and attitude tasks (Cliff, 1977; DeBoeck, 1981). Thus, building an adequate model for a measuring task, either cognitive or affective, will require capability for multiple sources of item and person differences.

Multidimensional models also may be required for measuring designs in which task presentation conditions are changing. Results from contemporary studies on information processing theories indicate that performance is modifiable over conditions. Systematically manipulating conditions that accompany task performance provides important results for testing competing theoretical explanations in these information-processing studies. The manipulations may be presented either prior to or concurrently with the task. For example, concurrent manipulations include masking stimuli, imposing short time limits, supplying cues or more general structural aids. Prior manipulations include practice, instruction, and so forth.

Although such manipulations are usually associated with theoretically oriented studies, they also can be employed in a measuring design. For example, in dynamic testing, both prior and concurrent manipulations are employed to measure learning potential, as separate from static ability (e.g., Brown, 1978; Feuerstein, 1979; Guthke, 1992).

The current chapter presents two multidimensional latent trait models that are specifically structured to incorporate theoretical variables from contemporary information-processing studies. First, the multicomponent latent trait model (MLTM; Embretson, 1980) and its generalized version (GLTM; 1984) are described. Both MLTM and GLTM contain parameters for measuring person and item differences on processing components and strategies that underlie task performance. GLTM is illustrated by an application to a measure of fluid intelligence. Two different latent variables, general control processing and working memory capacity, have been postulated as primary in the construct validity of fluid intelligence. Their relative strength in the construct validity of fluid intelligence is compared with GLTM estimates from the measuring task of progressive matrices. Second, the multidimensional Rasch model for learning and change (MRMLC, Embretson, 1991) and its generalization (MRMLC+; Embretson, 1995a) is described. Both MRMLC and MRMLC+ contain parameters to measure individual differences in modifiability over task presentation conditions. MRMLC+ is illustrated by an application to an intervention study for mathematical reasoning. It should be noted that the generalized version of both models, GLTM and MRMLC+, additionally can link task difficulty to stimulus features that influence processing.

MULTICOMPONENT LATENT TRAIT MODELS

The Model

Both MLTM and GLTM measure persons and items on underlying components that are involved in solving a task. It is assumed that solving a task requires correct outcomes from two or more underlying components or metacomponents. Thus, the task solution requires conjunctive outcomes. As appropriate for conjunctive outcomes, a multiplicative model is postulated for both MLTM and GLTM. Item response models in which the multiple dimensions are compensatory would not be appropriate for a conjunctive task.

In both MLTM and GLTM, the probability that a person solves the total task, X_{ijT}, is given as the product of the probabilities of passing the underlying components. In turn, the component probabilities are given by Rasch models, in which parameters for component ability and component item difficulty are contained. The general component latent trait model (GLTM) model is given as follows:

$$P(X_{ijT} = 1|\theta_j, \alpha_K, \beta_K) = \delta \Pi_K \frac{\exp(\theta_{jk} - \Sigma_m \beta_{mk} u_{imk} + \alpha_k)}{1 + \exp(\theta_{jk} - \Sigma_m \beta_{mk} u_{imk} + \alpha_k)} \quad (1)$$

Where

θ_{jk} = ability for person j on component k
μ_{imk} = value for item i on stimulus factor m in component k
β_{mk} = weight of stimulus complexity factor m in item difficulty on component k
α_k = normalization constant for component k
δ = strategy application probability

As shown in Equation 1, GLTM also contains cognitive models of the impact of stimulus complexity factors on component difficulties. The variables μ_{imk} are scored for each item. The parameters, β_{mk} are analogous to regression weights for the impact of the stimulus complexity factor on component difficulty. MLTM, in contrast, contains only item difficulties for the components. No model from stimulus factors is possible. As GLTM can include MLTM, it is the generalized version of the model.

The original estimation algorithm for both MLTM and GLTM (see Embretson, 1980, 1984) limited model application in several ways. First, subtask data was required to identify the components. Second, only the subtask data was used to estimate the components. The total task data was used only to check fit and to estimate some population parameters. Third, individual differences in strategy application could not be estimated. Estimates were available only for a population parameter.

However, Maris (1992) developed a general method for estimating latent response models which is based on the Dempster, Laird, and Rubin (1977) EM algorithm. The EM algorithm is appropriate for all kinds of missing data problems, including unobserved latent responses. In the Maris EM algorithm for conjunctive models, the probabilities for components in MLTM, $P(X_{ijk} = 1|\theta_{jk}, \xi_{ik})$ can be estimated directly from the total task. The component responses are treated as unobserved latent responses rather than as observed responses from subtasks. The components that are estimated from the EM algorithm are empirically driven to provide adequate fit of the model to the data. They do not necessarily correspond to any specified theoretical component unless appropriate restrictions are placed on the solution. Thus, a cognitive model of the task must be specified within the item difficulties of a component to fix the ability estimations. GLTM, but not MLTM, is suited for these restrictions.

An Application to Fluid Intelligence

A recent study has examined two competing explanations about the basis of fluid intelligence (Embretson, 1995c) using GLTM. The two competing explanations have arisen from intelligence research from the information-processing paradigm. These explanations are briefly described.

According to one view, the primary basis of fluid intelligence is metacomponent processing, particularly the global processes that are involved in all items. That is, global metacomponents are involved in strategy planning, monitoring, and evaluating over the test items. Many information-processing theories of intelligence place primary emphasis on metacomponents (e.g., Brown, 1978; Sternberg, 1985) and most theories at least include metacomponents.

The most consistent theoretical support for global metacomponents comes from the cognitive training paradigm in which cognitive processing is manipulated by training or by imposing conditions. Early support for metacomponents was given by Belmont and Butterfield (1971). They found that retarded children could performance effectively on a verbal learning task when a strategy was imposed by the experimenter. However, when the strategy was not imposed, the retarded children apparently did not apply it spontaneously. Research on dynamic testing similarly supports global metacomponents. For example, a typical design has the experimenter providing a monitoring role to guide the course of problem solving (e.g., Feuerstein, 1979; Guthke, 1992).

According to the other view, fluid intelligence is primarily due to individual differences in working memory capacity. Under this view, component processing is viewed as resource limited. Research from rather different designs has supported working memory capacity as primary in fluid intelligence. For example, Kyllonen and Christal (1990) used confirmatory factor analysis of working memory tasks and reference abilitiy tests. In a series of studies, they found that the working memory factor correlated in the .80s with general reasoning factor, even when the latter was operationalized by very different tests. Other support comes from cognitive component research. For example, Pellegrino and Glaser (1980) studied the inference process on inductive reasoning tests. They theorize that two major factors contribute to the item difficulty: (a) rule complexity, which depends on working memory capacity, and (b) representational variability, which depends on discovering multiple meanings of stimuli. More recently, Carpenter, Just, and Shell (1990) supported a similar theory on a well-established measure of fluid intelligence, the Raven's Progressive Matrices Test. Using diverse methods, including computer simulations, eye movements, error analysis, and protocol analysis, they found that memory load is a major factor in item difficulty. According to their theory, difficult items have a larger memory load, which in turn requires larger working memory capacity in the person.

Recently, the impact of general control processing versus working memory capacity on the construct validity was compared directly on a measuring task for fluid intelligence (Embretson, 1995b). A large item bank of progressive matrices, generated according to the Carpenter et al. (1990) theory was available. GLTM was applied to estimate abilities according to a postulated model of the processing events. Then, structural equations were applied to test hypothesis about construct validity with respect to some reference tests.

Method. To measure fluid ability, several forms of the Abstract Reasoning Test were used. The Abstract Reasoning Test contains progressive matrix items that were generated according to the Carpenter et al. (1990) theory. Memory load, their primary variable, depends on both the number and level of rules. Several replicate items for each combination of the underlying variables for memory load, number of rules and the level of rules, were available. Thus, memory load scores were available for the items. Further, mathematical modeling of item accuracy and response time (Embretson, 1995b) had supported memory load as the primary source of item difficulty, hypothesized by Carpenter et al. (1990).

Data from a sample of 577 Air Force recruits were available on the Abstract Reasoning Test. The subjects were assigned to a computer station which administered one of four structually equivalent forms of the test. On each form, 51 items had memory load scores available. Additionally, the Armed Services Vocational Aptitude Battery (AS-VAB) scores were available from the recruit's enlistment file. The ASVAB scores provided reference tests for construct validity.

The GLTM model was constructed as the product of two generic latent response variables; strategy application, X_{ij1}, and strategy completion, X_{ij2}. For progressive matrix items, the strategy primarily involved inference of the multiple relationships that the correct answer must fulfill. Thus, the latent response variables are related to the total task X_{ijT} as follows:

$$P(X_{ijT} = 1) = P(X_{ij1})P(X_{ij2}) \qquad (2)$$

After Carpenter et al. (1990), it was assumed that completion of the inference depends on the working memory capacity of the person and the memory load of the item. Thus, indices of memory load for the items were required to model strategy completion. Further, after Sternberg (1978), it was assumed that general control processing is required to an equal extent on all items. Thus, equal item difficulties were specified on general control processing. These specifications are given in the following GLTM model, which identified the variables in Embretson (1995c):

$$P(X_{ijT} = 1|\theta_j,\alpha,\beta) = \frac{\exp(\theta_{j1} - \alpha_1)}{1 + \exp(\theta_{j1} - \alpha_1)} \frac{\exp(\theta_{j2} - \beta_2 u_{i2} - \alpha_2)}{1 + \exp(\theta_{j2} - \beta_2 u_{i2} - \alpha_2)}$$

$$(3)$$

where θ_{j1} is the ability for person j on general control processes, α_1 is an intercept that expresses the (constant) difficulty of items on strategy application, θ_{j2} working memory capacity for person j, μ_{i2} is the score for item i on memory load, β_2 is the weight of memory load in rule inference difficulty and α_2 is an intercept for rule inference difficulty.

Results. Abilities for general control processing and working memory were estimated for the GLTM model in Equation 3, using the Maris EM algorithm. The role of general control processing and working memory capacity was compared by examining their contributions to the construct validity of the Abstract Reasoning Test. Both aspects of construct validity (Embretson, 1983), construct representation, the contribution of the processes to test performance, and nomothetic span, the relationship of the test to other tests, criteria and so forth, were studied.

For construct representation, the squared multiple correlation indicated that the two component abilities accounted for the Abstract Reasoning score quite well, $R^2 = .96$. However, general control processes were more important than working memory capacity (r^2's $= .71$ and $.48$). Further, general control processes were relatively unrelated to working memory capacity ($r^2 = .06$).

For nomothetic span, the components accounted well for the validity of the Abstract Reasoning Test with respect to the ASVAB reference tests. Thus, mediated validity was supported. Both general control processing and working memory capacity had independent contributions to the two central ASVAB factors, quantitative and verbal. In the context of other measures, Kyllonen and Christal (1990) supported these two factors as measuring general reasoning and general knowledge, respectively. However, unlike the Kyllonen and Christal (1990) results, working memory capacity was rather weakly related to the reasoning factor; and further, general control processing was more strongly related to the reasoning factor. Similarly, general control processing was more important than working memory capacity for the verbal factor. Some unique relationships also were indicated. Only working memory capacity correlated with the processing speed factor whereas only general control processing correlated with the technical knowledge factor.

Figure 7.1 presents the final structural equation model that summarizes these findings. In summary, general control processing is supported as more important than working memory capacity for both construct representation and nomothetic span. Embretson (1995c) discussed the implications of these findings with respect to other research and theories.

Multidimensional Rasch Model for Learning and Change

As noted earlier, contemporary cognitive research on intelligence supports the modifiability of performance over changing conditions. Measuring individual modifiability on intelligence tests has been the direct concern of dynamic testing and also lifespan development. However, the measurement of individual change has been a challenging psychometric problem. Classical test theory approaches to measuring change have not led to satisfactory solutions (see Cronbach

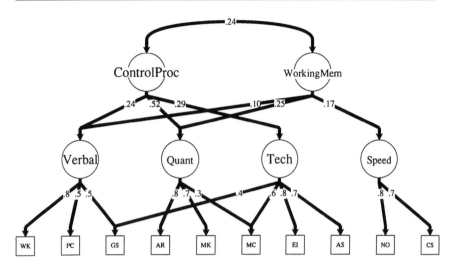

FIG. 7.1. Structural equation model of working memory and general control processes with reference tests.

& Furby, 1970). As summarized by Bereiter (1963), three problems result from measuring change by raw gain scores: (a) a reliability paradox, such that reliable gain scores require low test–retest correlations, (b) the meaning of change may depend on initial level; for example, the same change score may imply greater modifiability if the initial score is high than if it is low, and (c) change has a spurious negative relationship with initial status, due to common errors.

Recently, an IRT model for measuring change has been developed (Embretson, 1991). The MRMLC was developed to reflect the psychological nature of change, rather than provide theoretically dubious calculations on data, as in raw gain scores. Several empirical findings on complex abilities measured repeatedly include increasing performance levels, increasing variabilities, and a simplex pattern of correlations between occasions. The simplex pattern is characterized by successively decreasing correlations between tests with the number of intervening occasions. A plausible structure for data with this empirical characteristic is a Wiener process model, which has been used to model the covariances of tests across occasions (see Jöreskog, 1970).

MRMLC embeds a Wiener process structure in the measurement model to define the role of initial abilities and one or more modifiabilities in test performance on successive occasions. The Wiener process structure adds a new factor at each successive occasion. For the first occasion, only initial ability is involved. For the second occasion, both initial ability and the first modifiability are involved in performance. For the third occasion, initial ability and two modifiabilities are involved, and so forth. Like MLTM, MRMLC contains only item difficulties in the model. However, like GLTM, MRMLC+ permitsstimulus features of items to be linked to item difficulty. Thus, a cognitive model may be embedded in MRMLC+, which may be written as follows:

$$P(X_{i(k)j} = 1) = \frac{\exp(\Sigma_{m=1}\theta_{jm} - \Sigma_m\beta_m u_{im} - \alpha)}{1 + \exp(\Sigma_{m=1}\theta_{jm} - \Sigma_m\beta_m u_{im} - \alpha)} \qquad (4)$$

Where

θ_{j1} = Initial ability
$\theta_{j2} , \ldots , \theta_{jK}$ = modifiabilities.
β_m = weight of stimulus factor m in item difficulty
μ_{im} = value of item i on stimulus factor m
α = a normalization constant.

MRMLC allows for both quantitative change (i.e., performance levels) and qualitative change (i.e., the factors that are involved).

It should be noted that MRMLC and MRMLC+ solve two of Bereiter's issues, and make progress toward the third. The reliability paradox does not exist because changing correlations over occasions are directly expected. That is, the Wiener process structure produces a simplex pattern of correlations over occasions. Thus, the lower test to retest correlations are expected directly from the model, due to the changing factorial composition. Second, the meaning of modifiability for performance changes does depend on different initial levels. Embretson (1991) showed how different raw gains are associated with the same modifiability, depending on initial level. Third, MRMLC and MRMLC+ resolve the spurious negative correlation between initial ability and change to the extent that it results from scaling factors. However, substantive reasons that contribute to unreliability at the initial measure, like temporal conditions for the person, are not resolved.

Application to the Modifiability
of Mathematical Reasoning

Linking individual learning to changes in specific processes and knowledge is a major issue in contemporary instruction (Glaser & Bassock, 1989). Not only is an adequate theory of the task required, but a measurement model that can link modifiability to substantive changes also is required.

Mathematical problem solving, particularly as measured by word problems, is an important area to measure learning. Embretson (1995a) applied MRMLC+ to study the impact of a short instructional sequence on mathematical problem solving. The instruction focused on elaborating the problem schema. The primary purpose of the study was to determine the extent and meaning of individual differences in learning from instruction. Interpreting the meaning of individual learning requires not only an adequate means to scale items and persons, but also a plausible theory of mathematical problem solving.

Mayer, Larkin, and Kadane's (1984) theory of mathematical reasoning provides an good framework for studying mathematical learning because it includes both processes and knowledge. Mayer et al. postulated four major processes in mathematical reasoning, each of which requires different knowledge for successful completion. The processes, and their associated knowledge structures, are as follows: (a) problem translation process requires linguistic and factual knowledge, such as encoding word meanings and knowing quantity conversions, (b) problem integration requires schematic knowledge, such as how the variables may be placed in equations, (c) problem planning requires strategic knowledge, such as how to isolate unknowns, and (d) problem execution requires algoritmic knowledge, such as arithmetic and algebraic manipulations.

Method. A set of word problems was developed to be appropriate for young adults. The Mayer et al. knowledge variables were operationalized by eight variables that could be scored on mathematical word problems (see Table 7.1). The Scholastic Aptitude Test items were taken as a model with respect to knowledge requirements, as defined

TABLE 7.1
Characteristics of Mathematical Word Problems on Stimulus Complexity Factors for Three Types of Knowledge

Knowledge Type	Mean	SD	r_{Rasch}	η_{model}
Factual/Linguistics				
Number of words	31.30	9.23	.61	.038
Flesch-Kincaid reading level	6.78	3.17	.45	.117
Conversions of units	.15	.36	−.03	—
Metric systems	.20	.40	.19	—
Schematic				
Number of equations	1.85	.75	−.12	—
Relative definition of variables (only)	.40	.49	.54	.651
Problem type (simplex = 0; complex = 1)	.30	.45	.45	.205
Strategic				
Transformation required to isolate unknown	.70	.45	.35	−.109

Constant ($\alpha = -2.167$).

by the eight variables. Three replicates of each word problem, equated on the schematic and strategic knowledge variables, were developed. These replicates were assigned to three separate test forms.

An intervention was developed on the schematic representation of the problems. The intervention was based on Reed's (1987) method of outlining problem relationships in a tabular form. These tables were required to complete the intervention items. Thus, external structures were imposed on actual test problems during the intervention stage.

Test forms were assigned to pretest, intervention, and posttest by a Latin square design, such as to counterbalance forms and occasions. Thus, three conditions were created that varied only in which forms were administered on each occasion. All tests and the intervention were administered by computer.

The subjects were 578 Air Force recruits, who were assigned to a condition by their Air Force flight numbers. All subjects received a pretest, cued intervention, and a posttest during a single session of about 60 minutes.

Results.   A preliminary analysis showed that five knowledge variables had moderate correlations (.34 < r < .61) with item difficulty (Rasch scale) for the word problems. These variables were then used as knowledge factors in MRMLC+. The MRMLC+ model was implemented as follows with two occasions and five knowledge factors:

$$P(X_{i(k)j} = 1) = \frac{\exp(\Sigma_{m=1}\theta_{jm} - \Sigma_m\beta_n u_{in} + \alpha)}{1 + \exp(\Sigma_{m=1}\theta_{jm} - \Sigma_n\beta_n u_{in} + \alpha)}$$

Where

θ_{j1} = initial ability for person j
θ_{j2} = modifiability for person j
u_{in} = score for item i on knowledge factor n
β_n = weight for knowledge factor n in item difficulty
α = intercept for item difficulty.

The results indicated that the model of item difficulty accounted for item difficulty quite well. MRMLC+ was compared to MRMLC (which estimates a difficulty value for each item). Fit decreased significantly by estimating item difficulty from only the knowledge factors. However, the knowledge variables yielded at least moderately good prediction of item difficulty, because a fit index value comparable to a correlation of .79 was obtained. The estimates of MRMLC+ weights for the knowledge variables, β_n, are shown in Table 7.1. The most important contribution to prediction was from the knowledge variables that were associated with the problem schema. Also shown in Table 7.1 are descriptive statistics and correlations with the Rasch model item difficulties for the eight knowledge variables.

The results on modifiability indicated a small, but statistically reliable impact of intervention on problem solving. Most central to the current goals, however, is the interpretability and scalability of modifiability in terms of problem solving skills. Figure 7.2 shows the relationship of simple gain scores to modifiability. It can be seen that simple gain is not uniquely associated with a modifiability. At each level of gain, varying levels of modifiability are observed, which depend on the initial status. The modifiability estimates, but not the gain scores, are controlled for initial level. Thus, the MRMLC modifiability scale clearly differs from raw gain.

Most important, modifiability may be linked to the substantive features of the items. That is, initial ability, modifiability, and the impact of the knowledge factors on item difficulty may be represented on a single scale. Figure 7.3 is a representation of the meaning of performance at various scale levels, in terms of knowledge requirements. As items and abilities are placed on a common scale in a latent trait model, representative items can be placed at the various scale points. As item difficulty is understood in terms of substantive features (i.e., the knowledge factors), the scale points are interpretable. It can be seen that difficult items all involve complex schematic types and

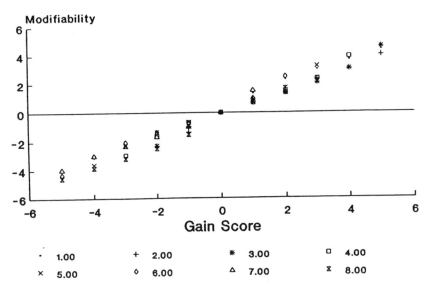

FIG. 7.2. Relationship of gain scores to MRMLC modifiability.

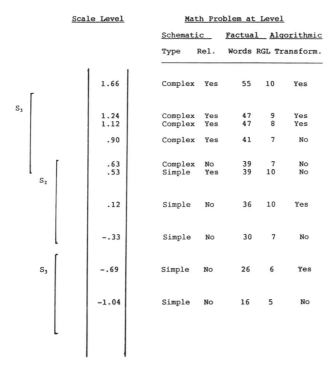

Scale Level		Math Problem at Level				
		Schematic		Factual		Algorithmic
		Type	Rel.	Words	RGL	Transform.
1.66		Complex	Yes	55	10	Yes
1.24		Complex	Yes	47	9	Yes
1.12		Complex	Yes	47	8	Yes
.90		Complex	Yes	41	7	No
.63		Complex	No	39	7	No
.53		Simple	Yes	39	10	No
.12		Simple	No	36	10	Yes
−.33		Simple	No	30	7	No
−.69		Simple	No	26	6	Yes
−1.04		Simple	No	16	5	No

FIG. 7.3. Relationship of item substantive features to item difficulty and to ability and modifiability.

relative definitions of variables. Moderate items involve simple schema but somewhat difficult algorithmic transformations or difficult factual knowledge.

Also shown in Fig. 7.3 are the initial competency and modifiability of three subjects from the sample. For S_1, with a low initial competency, the modifiability involves solving schematically simple items with more complex factual and linguistic knowledge. For S_2, with a moderate initial competency, modifiability involves increased competency on problems with complex schema but not on problems with relative definitions of the variables. Last, for S_3, with a moderate high initial competency, modifiability involves increased competency for all schematic variables.

Thus, for the mathematical word problems in this study, the Mayer et al. theory provides a meaningful framework from which to interpret individual learning. However, it should be noted that this interpretation depends on both an adequate psychometric model for linking modifiability to substantive features and the quality of the theory. For theoretical quality, not only must the theory be empirically plausible, but the representation of the variables in the items must yield interpretable scale points. These conditions were met in this example.

SUMMARY

Latent trait models have many desirable measurement properties in comparison to classical test theory. Increasingly, the models are being applied to measure abilities. A particularly intriguing possibility of latent trait models, however, is the possibility to interface measurement with substantive theory. Model-based measurement, as represented by latent trait models, interfaces well with the mathematical modeling approach of contemporary intelligence research.

Current theories of cognition and intelligence emphasize the multifaceted aspects of performance on complex tasks, particularly those that appear as test items. Further, the modifiability of performance over conditions, either concurrently or prior to measurement, is characteristic for most complex tasks. These substantive considerations require complex, multidimensional latent trait models.

In this chapter, two multidimensonal latent trait models were presented to link intelligence measures to cognitive-based measurement designs. The multicomponent latent trait model (MLTM and GLTM; Embretson, 1980, 1984) permits the estimation of abilities and item difficulties on processing components that underlie item performance. GLTM was illustrated by an application to a fluid intelligence test with progressive matrix items. The impact of two latent variables, general control processing and working memory capacity, on the construct validity of the test was studied. The multidimensional Rasch model for learning and change (MRMLC & MRMLC+; Embretson, 1991, 1995a) permits the estimation of initial ability and one or more modifiabilities that result from changing conditions of measurement. MRMLC+ was illustrated by an application to mathematical problem solving, in which a short intervention was administered. The results showed that individual learning could be linked to the substantive features of items.

REFERENCES

Andrich, D. (1988). *Rasch models for measurement*. Newbury Park, CA: Sage.
Belmont, J. M., & Butterfield, E.C. (1971). Learning strategies as determinates of memory deficiencies. *Cognitive Psychology, 2*, 411–420.

Bereiter, C. (1963). Some persisting dilemmas in the measurement of change. In C. Harris (Ed.), *Problems in measuring change* (pp. 3–20). Madison: Univerisity of Wisconsin Press.

Brown, A. L. (1978) Knowing when, where and how to remember: A problem of metacognition. In R. Glaser (Ed.), *Advances in instructional psychology* (Vol. 1, pp. 77–165). Hillsdale, NJ: Lawrence Erlbaum Associates.

Carpenter, P. A., Just, M. A., & Shell, P. (1990). What one intelligence test measures: A theoretical account of processing in the Raven's Progressive Matrices Test. *Psychological Review, 97.* 404–431.

Cliff, N. (1977). Further study of cognitive processing models for inventory responses. *Applied Psychological Measurement, 1,* 41–49.

Cronbach, L. J., & Furby, L. (1970). How should we measure change—or should we? *Psychological Bulletin, 74,* 68–80.

DeBoeck, P. (1981). Individual differences in the validity of a cognitive processing model for responses to personality inventories. *Applied Psychological Measurement, 5,* 481–492.

Dempster, A. P., Laird, N. M., & Rubin, D. B. (1977). Maximum likelihood estimation with incomplete data via the EM algorithm (with discussion). *Journal of the Royal Statistical Society, Series B, 38,* 1–38.

Embretson, S. E. (1980). Multicomponent latent trait models for ability tests. *Psychometrika, 45,* 479–494.

Embretson, S. E. (1983). Construct validity: Construct representation versus nomothetic span. *Psychological Bulletin, 93,* 179–197.

Embretson, S. E. (1984). A general multicomponent latent trait model for response processes. *Psychometrika, 49,* 175–186.

Embretson, S. E. (1991). A multidimensional latent trait model for measuring learning and change. *Psychometrika, 56,* 495–516.

Embretson, S. E. (1995a). A measurement model for linking individual learning to processes and knowledge: Application to mathematical reasoning. *Journal of Educational Measurement, 32,* 277–294.

Embretson, S. E. (1995b). *Processes in abstract reasoning: A test of the Carpenter, Just & Shell theory.* Unpublished manuscript, University of Kansas at Lawrence.

Embretson, S. E. (1995c). Working memory capacity versus general control processes in abstract reasoning. *Intelligence, 20,* 169–189.

Embretson, S. E., & DeBoeck, P. (1994). Latent trait theory. In R. J. Sternberg (Ed.), *Encyclopedia of intelligence* (pp. 4012–4017). New York: Macmillan.

Feuerstein, R. (1979). *The dynamic assessment of retarded performers: The learning potential assessment device, theory, instruments and techniques.* Baltimore: University Park Press.

Glaser, R. & Bassock, M. (1989) Learning theory and the study of instruction. *Annual Review of Psychology, 40,* 631–666.

Guthke, J. (1992). Developments in learning potential assessment: Theoretical, methodological, and practical issues. In J. H. M. Hamers, K. Sijtsma, & A. J. J. M. (Eds.), Ruijssenaars *Learning potential assessement: Theoretical, methodological and practice issues* (pp. 43–67). Amsterdam: Swets & Zeitlinger.

Hambleton, R. K., Swaminathan, H., & Rogers, H. J. (1991) *Fundamentals of item response theory.* Newbury Park, CA: Sage.

Jöreskog, K. G. (1970). Estimation and testing of simplex models. *British Journal of Mathematical Statistical Psychology, 23,* 121–145.

Kyllonen, P., & Christal, R. (1990). Reasoning ability is (little more than) working memory capacity?! *Intelligence, 14,* 389–434.

Maris, E. M. (1992, June). *Psychometric models for psychological processes and structures*. Dissertation award address, European meeting of the Psychometric Society, Barcelona, Spain.

Mayer, R., Larkin, J., & Kadane, P. (1984). A cognitive analysis of mathematical problem solving. In R. Sternberg (Ed.), *Advances in the psychology of human intelligence* (Vol. 2, pp. 231–273). Hillsdale, NJ: Lawrence Erlbaum Associates.

Pellegrino, J. W., & Glaser, R. (1980). Components of inductive reasoning. In R. E. Snow, P. A. Federico, & W. E. Montague (Eds.) *Aptitude, learning and instruction: Cognitive process analysis of aptitude* (pp. 177–218). Hillsdale, NJ: Lawrence Erlbaum Associates.

Reed, S. K. (1987). A structure mapping model for word problems. *Journal of Experimental Psychology: Learning, Memory & Cognition, 13,* 124–139.

Sternberg, R. J. (1985). *Beyond IQ: A triarchic theory of human intelligence.* Cambridge, England: Cambridge University Press.

CHAPTER 8

Models for an "Objective" Assessment of Treatment Effects Based on Item Response Data

Gerhard H. Fischer
University of Vienna

CHARLES SPEARMAN AND AFTER

Charles Spearman's contributions both to the quantitative methodology and to the theory of intelligence are part of the store of knowledge of any undergraduate in psychology. Most basic formulae of "classical test theory" are found already in his early publications (Spearman, 1904a, 1904b, 1907, 1910, 1913). In his seminal paper "General Intelligence," objectively determined and measured (Spearman, 1904b), Spearman started out from reviewing the work of early test psychologists, many of whom had reported considerable correlations between various kinds of intellectual abilities, and concluded that there must exist some common element in all of them, some sort of a general intellectual ability, the "g-factor."

Spearman's approach to the study of intelligence was a completely rational one, methodologically far ahead of the opaque manner in which many of his contemporaries approached psychological problems. The empirical analysis in Spearman (1904b) was based on a formal investigation of the attenuation of correlations by measurement error. Despite the undisputed importance of these results for the development of test theory and factor analysis, however, the empirical application of one of these attenuation formulas to the estimation of the true correlation between certain school grades and out-of-school cleverness on the one hand, and various sensory discrimination tests on the other, suffered from a serious misinterpretation. Spearman thought that the average correlations within each of the two groups of variables could be taken as estimates of reliabilities, which entailed a sizable underestimation of these reliabilities and, consequently, a considerable overestimation of the stepped-up correlation between both groups of variables. The latter seemed to support the hypothesis that both groups of variables were governed by one general intellectual ability, the g-factor. Spearman stated his conclusion as follows: "Thus we arrive at the remarkable result that the *common and essential element in the Intelligences wholly coincides with the common and essential element in the Sensory Functions*" (Spearman, 1904b, p. 269).

After some further data analysis he formulated the following "theorem": "*Whenever branches of intellectual activity are at all dissimilar, then their correlations with one another appear wholly due to their being variously saturated with some common fundamental Function (or group of Functions)*" (Spearman, 1904b, p. 273).

I see no contradiction between acknowledging Spearman's great importance as one of the fathers of psychometrics, of a rational approach to psychology as a science, and the statement of fact that his g-factor theory was not well-grounded empirically. It is history that the psychological model of intelligence that was most central to Spearman's work was refuted by later investigations and eventually had to give way to Thurstone's (1935) multiple factor model.

The latter, as a psychological theory, however, should not become too successful either: With the advent of computers in the late 1950s and early 1960s and the abundance of factor-analytic studies in the literature, the factor models of intelligence went to seed as it turned out that factor structures did not generalize over subject populations or over different samples of test variables. (In passing I remark that the presence of measurement error alone cannot account for this lack of generalizability, as was already seen in early computer simulations of factor models, e.g., Fischer & Roppert, 1965.) So, looking back now at 90 years of history of factor-analytic investigations of intelligence (and, similarly, of personality), we have to admit that we do not know which nor how many intelligence (or personality) factors there are, and we still have no proven technique for constructing unidimensional tests as measures of any single factor alone (except for very special cases).

This is an uncomfortable situation that seems to prevent us from doing well-grounded research in many applied areas, such as on the effects of environments or education with respect to the intellectual development in children, because we do not know within what coordinate system of primary abilities we should describe such development. This chapter is concerned with measuring change of trait variables as occurring, for example, in cognitive development, or in the process of formation or change of attitudes, or under the impact of clinical treatments. In the absence of any generally accepted reference system of factors within which to monitor change, I try to lay out a psychometric approach to this type of research problem, actually dispensing with any presumptions about the underlying factor structure of human traits.

THE LINEAR LOGISTIC MODEL
WITH RELAXED ASSUMPTIONS

I review certain psychometric tools with a broad range of use for typical applied research questions about the effects of educational or clinical treatments of training, of information, of environment, or of experimental conditions on abilities, personality traits, attitudes, or behaviors. In order to make my approach transparent, let me begin by stating my methodological creed: Given that there are almost as many factor models of intelligence (or personality) as there are researchers in the area, I abhor the idea of basing my methods on any particular model of "primary abilities" (or personality factors) that would invariably be at odds with almost everybody else's conception of intelligence (or personality). It appears to be a logical necessity that, if we want to construct a successful psychometric model for the measurement of treatment effects on intelligence or personality, we must avoid getting between the front lines of different schools of thought about the underlying trait dimensions; rather, we should formulate a model of maximum flexibility regarding the number and nature of the underlying latent dimensions and their possible interrelations.

Therefore, I assume only that such dimensions exist. The maximum meaningful number of latent abilities that can be assumed, for instance, in a study on intellectual growth of preschool children, obviously equals the number of test items in the test battery employed. I assume that the developmental psychologist who designs the test battery knows, from his general experience and from the literature, what set of test items is appropriate for describing the development of intelligence at the respective age level. So I start out with simply assigning one latent trait dimension to each and every item, yet refraining from making any assumptions about how these latent dimensions are related to each other. This approach covers everything between complete independence of the dimensions, at one extreme, and the case that all dimensions are linear functions of one common g-factor, at the other extreme. As a consequence, the historic debate about the nature and number of primary ability factors remains without influence on the present psychometric approach.

To make matters more concrete, let the test battery consist of
k dichotomous items, I_1 , . . . , I_k, and assume the existence of k latent
traits Θ_i, i = 1 , . . . , k, assigned one-one to the items. (The more
complicated case of polytomous items is taken up later.)

Now the latent trait dimensions have to be related to the observed
reactions. Let a logistic link function be chosen, for which a justifica-
tion will be given later. Then, the probability of a right response of
subject S_v to item I_i at time point T_1 (prior to the treatment) is:

$$P(+|S_v,I_i,T_1) = \frac{\exp(\theta_{vi})}{1 + \exp(\theta_{vi})} ,\qquad(1)$$

for v = 1 , . . . , N subjects and i = 1 , . . . , k items, where θ_{vi} is
subject S_v's level of that ability Θ_i, which is measured by item I_i.

This alone clearly would not yet constitute a meaningful model: If
we attempted to estimate the individual ability parameters θ_{vi} for any
given individual S_v by maximizing the likelihood of S_v's response, $\hat{\theta}_{vi}$
would tend to ∞ whenever the respective response was correct
(denoted by $x_{vi} = 1$), and to $-\infty$ whenever the response was incorrect
($x_{vi} = 0$).

Because it is our present aim to construct a model for *change*, for
instance, of cognitive functions under the influence of preschool
programs, we may assume that the children's responses to the same or
equivalent items are observed again at a later time point after the
treatment period, T_2. So we similarly write, for T_2,

$$P(+|S_v,I_i,T_2) = \frac{\exp(\theta'_{vi})}{1 + \exp(\theta'_{vi})} ,\qquad(2)$$

where the θ'_{vi} are S_v's abilities after the treatment. Still the model is not
estimable (for the same reasons as before), but if we introduce the
postulate that the treatment effects *generalize* over all latent traits Θ_i,
we may set

$$\theta'_{vi} - \theta_{vi} = \delta_v, \quad \text{for } i = 1, \ldots, k,\qquad(3)$$

where δ_v is the amount of change induced in S_v by the treatment(s).
Equation 3 means that *only one change parameter* δ_v *is assigned to each
subject* S_v, based on all items I_i, which makes δ_v—in principle—an
estimable parameter. If we undertook to estimate δ_v for each individual
separately, however, the estimates δ_v would be subject to large error,
and they would not be very interesting anyway, because our primary
object was to relate change to the treatments given rather than making
statements about individual amounts of growth. Therefore, we proceed
by writing δ_v as a function of the treatment effect parameters as follows:

$$\delta_v = \sum_j q_{vj}\eta_j + \sum_j \sum_1 q_{vj}q_{vl}\rho_{jl} + \tau \tag{4}$$

In Equation (4), the amount of change is modeled as a sum of treatment (main) effect parameters η_j, $j = 1$,..., m, weighted by the treatment dosages q_{vj}, and of treatment interaction effects ρ_{jl}, weighted by the products $q_{vj}q_{vl}$, and of a trend effect τ. (The dosages q_{vj} are considered given as they are part of the design of the study.)

This model has been called the Linear Logistic Model with Relaxed Assumptions (LLRA; Fischer, 1972, 1977). The name expresses the important fact that, in contrast to most other IRT models, the LLRA does not make any undimensionality assumption; rather, the items are allowed to be multidimensional and thus to represent all relevant factors. For instance, in a clinical study on the effects of intervention in depressive patients, the items should comprise all symptoms by which clinicians describe the state of a patient, or by which the patient describes himself. (It can be shown that the LLRA formally is a special case of a more general IRT model known as the Linear Logistic Test Model [LLTM]; Fischer, 1973, 1976, 1995a).

What can we gain from applying the LLRA, for example, in a pre-school education study? Upon testing children of one suitable treatment group and children of a control group prior to the training period, and repeating the testing again after the training period, it would be possible to obtain an estimate of one treatment main effect η and a trend effect τ, the latter measuring the combined effects of all causes of change that are unrelated to the treatments (e.g., natural cognitive development of the children). If several treatments or treatment combinations are given to respective treatment groups, one independent effect parameter per group could be estimated, and these parameters could be decomposed into main effects, interactions, and trend, given that the treatment design suffices certain minimum requirements.

An immediate question is, by what method should we estimate the effect parameters, and when does a unique solution to the estimation problem exist? Fortunately, these questions can be answered quite satisfactorily (Fischer, 1977, 1983). Without going into technical details, the main findings can be summarized as follows:

Noting that δ_v in Equation 4 is a linear function (a weighted sum) of effect parameters $(\eta_j, \rho_{jl}$, and $\tau)$ we may, for formal convenience, rewrite Equation 4 as

$$\delta_v = \sum_{j=1}^{M} q_{vj}\eta_j, \tag{5}$$

where the η_j, $j = 1, \ldots, M$, now may be main effects, or interactions, or a trend, and where the q_{vj} are redefined accordingly. (For instance, the trend parameter τ now might be parameter η_M with weights $q_{vM} = 1$ for $v = 1, \ldots, N$; in other words, the trend formally is understood as the effect of a treatment that is given to all S_v's with the same dosage 1.) The conditional likelihood of the item-score matrices $\mathbf{X}_1 = [(x_{vi1})]$ and $\mathbf{X}_2 = [(X_{vi2})]$, given their sum $\mathbf{X}_+ = \mathbf{X}_1 + \mathbf{X}_2$, assuming local stochastic independence of the items, can be seen to be

$$L = \prod_v \prod_i \left[\frac{\exp(x_{vi2}\delta_v)}{1 + \exp(\delta_v)} \right]^{(x_{vi1} - x_{vi2})^2}, \tag{6}$$

where the exponent $(x_{vi1} - x_{vi2})^2$ serves for filtering out all those pairs of responses (x_{vi1}, x_{vi2}) where no change was observed (i.e., where $x_{vi1} = x_{vi2}$), which are uninformative with respect to the effects of the treatments.

An important property of this conditional likelihood function is its independence of the latent trait parameters θ_{vi}. The model underlying Equation 6, which obviously refers to a subset of the data (all pairs of responses $x_{vi1} = x_{vi2}$ have been disregarded) and comprises only the effect parameters η_j, is called the *conditional model* of the LLRA. Taking logarithms of Equation 6 and differentiating with respect to the η_j, immediately yields the conditional maximum likelihood (CML) equations:

$$\sum_v q_{vj} \sum_i (x_{vi1} - x_{vi2})^2 \left[x_{vi2} - \frac{\exp(\delta_v)}{1 + \exp(\delta_v)} \right] = 0, \tag{7}$$

for $j = 1, \ldots, M$ effect parameters η_j, keeping in mind that the δ_v are functions (weighted sums) of the η_j (see Equation 5).

It is readily seen that the conditional estimation equations (7) of the LLRA are unconditional estimation equations of a logit model (cf. Cox, 1970) with parameters η_j. That the individual person parameters θ_{vi} have now been eliminated implies a central property of the LLRA for measuring change: The effect parameters η_j can be consistently estimated independently of the actual values of the unknown person parameters θ_{vi} if the sequence of the θ_{vi} satisfies certain mild restrictions.

This means that we should get roughly the same results from any subsample (or, more precisely, by sampling randomly from any subpopulation) of subjects. In the preschool education example, we should expect approximately the same treatment effect estimates for children from underprivileged homes and for children from more privileged environments—if the treatments actually are equally effective in both subpopulations. If, on the other hand, the treatments happen to be more effective in children who received a lesser degree of intellectual stimulation from their parents, we should find larger effect parameters in the latter subgroup. Hence, the model serves for testing the null hypothesis of generalizability of treatment effects over subgroups of subjects.

Another important consequence is that we really need not know whether and in what way the θ_{vi}, $i = 1, \ldots, k$, are mutually related or dependent. So, as I have stressed from the outset, the present approach remains valid whatever factor structure should happen to hold, and even whether or not the sample is a mix from subpopulations with different factor structures.

It is important to note that in this model items and subjects are completely symmetric. Hence, we may similarly test the hypothesis of generalizability of treatment effects over items (or, to be more precise, over the latent traits that are measured by items).

The symmetry of items and subjects in the LLRA has important consequences for the statistical properties of the estimators of the effect parameters: It implies that, as long as the model does hold, increasing the sample of subjects is equivalent to increasing the sample of items. This assures that the asymptotic results about the estimates $\hat{\eta}_j$ can be applied even in small samples of subjects if the test comprises sufficiently many items.

One might ask what sample size is the minimum requirement for an application of the LLRA. The minimum requirement obviously is that the estimation equations possess a unique solution $\hat{\eta}$. Necessary and sufficient conditions for the existence of a unique solution of the CML equations (7), which, however, are complicated and therefore not easy to apply, were given by Fischer (1983). But for most practical LLRA applications, the following sufficient result will be satisfactory: A unique CML solution $\hat{\eta}_1, \ldots, \hat{\eta}_M$ exists if (a) the design comprises at least M treatment groups G_g, $g = 1, \ldots, M$, with linearly independent dosage vectors $\mathbf{q}_g = (q_{g1}, \ldots, q_{gM})$, and if (b) for each treatment group G_g there exists at least one item I_s and one subject $S_v \in G_g$, such that $x_{vs1} = 1$ and $x_{vs2} = 0$, and at least one item I_t and one subject $S_w \in G_g$, such that $x_{wt1} = 0$ and $x_{wt2} = 1$.

This sufficient condition is quite weak: Condition (a), the linear independence of the M dosage vectors, is an obvious restriction on any design for measuring M treatment effects, and (b) only requires that, within each treatment group, there has been observed at least one change from a correct response $(+)$ to an incorrect response $(-)$, as well as one change from an incorrect response $(-)$ to a correct response $(+)$. Hence, we may be assured that we find a unique solution of the CML equations even in most small-sample applications.

Large-sample properties of the effect parameter estimates $\hat{\eta}_j$ are also known: If the design comprises at least M treatment groups G_g, $g = 1, \ldots, M$, with linearly independent dosage vectors $\mathbf{q_g}$, and if all the numbers of subjects per groups, n_g, tend to ∞, then $\hat{\eta}$ is asymptotically multivariate normal around the true parameter vector η with asymptotic covariance matrix $\mathbf{I}^{-1}$, where $\mathbf{I}$ is the information matrix.

This result is important when it comes to testing hypotheses on the treatment effects η_j: Asymptotic likelihood ratio tests of a large class of hypotheses, formulated as linear contrasts of the treatment effect parameters, are easily carried out as follows: Let a H_0 about some or all treatment effect parameters be formulated by way of a linear contrast, $\Sigma_j g_j \eta_j = 0$, and let the maximum of the conditional likelihood function $\mathbf{L}(\mathbf{X_1},\mathbf{X_2}|\mathbf{X_1} + \mathbf{X_2} = \mathbf{X'_+})$, obtained under H_0, be denoted by L_0, and similarly, the maximum under H_1, by L_1. Given that the aforementioned conditions for the asymptotic normality of $\hat{\eta}$ hold, H_0 can be tested by means of the asymptotic likelihood-ratio statistic

$$\chi^2 = -2\ln\left[\frac{L_0}{L_1}\right] \text{ with } df = M_1 = M_0,$$

where M_1 is the number of effect parameters under H_1, and M_0 the respective number under H_0.

Examples of typical hypotheses testable in this manner can be found in Fischer (1991a). Many applications of the LLRA have been made in the past 15 years in studies on the effect of preschool education (El-Ganady, 1979; Rop, 1977; Zeman, 1976), of therapy in speech-handicapped children (Heckl, 1976), of sports training (Vodopiutz, 1977), of teaching at school (Formann & Spiel, 1989; Pendl, 1976), of the training of learner drivers (Grabner, 1980; Rella, 1976), of group dynamics (Witek, 1980), of psychotherapy (Mutschlechner, 1987; Widowitz, 1987; Zimprich, 1980), of personality and behavior training for employees of various companies (Schmied, 1987; Iby, 1987), of information on attitude (Barisch, 1989), of jogging in alcoholics (Doff, 1992), and of test wiseness in intelligence tests (Pölderl, 1992). These studies have shown that the LLRA provides a very flexible and powerful framework for the assessment of treatment effects and for monitoring change in latent traits.

This is not to say that there are no problems involved. One problem arises when change is very large, as, for example, in developmental studies: Then many changes from "incorrect" to "correct" responses, $x_{vi1} = 0$ and $x_{vi2} = 1$, are observed, but hardly any changes in the other direction, $x_{vi1} = 1$ and $x_{vi2} = 0$. In such cases the treatment effect estimates $\hat{\eta}_j$ become very large and, at the same time, are estimated very poorly. (In extreme cases, there might be only pairs of responses $x_{vi1} = 0$, $x_{vi2} = 1$, but no pairs $x_{vi1} = 1$, $x_{vi2} = 0$, so that the η_j would no longer be estimable (see the uniqueness theorem shown earlier). Fortunately, there is a remedy to that problem: If we can find, by means of a pretest calibration study, pairs of items (I_i, I_i^*), each pair separately sufficing a Rasch model with test length $k = 2$, where the respective item parameters β_i and β_i^* are sufficiently different, we can present the easier item of each pair, I_i, at time point T_1, and the more difficult one, I_i^*, at T_2; hence, at each time point only items of appropriate difficulty are presented. It is then an easy matter to incorporate the differences $\beta_i^* - \beta_i = \Delta_i$, known from the pretest calibration study, as constants in the model, requiring a trivial generalization of the estimation equations (7). This model is referred to as the Hybrid LLRA. (We cannot, however, go into its technical details here; see Fischer, 1977, 1989.)

Another problem is the way that "generalizability over time" (or over subjects) has been defined. Most empirical studies did not find full generalizability over items, that is, subgroups of items differed in their sensitivity as indicators of change (or, in other words, the underlying latent traits were differently susceptible to change). Nevertheless, results about the relative effectiveness of treatments, that is, the quotients η_j/η_ℓ, still might be generalizable over the items. For finding out whether this weaker form of generalizability holds, we might estimate the η_j separately for each and every item, obtaining estimates $\hat{\eta}_{ij}$, and then check whether these estimates satisfy, at least approximately, $\hat{\eta}_{ij} = \hat{\lambda}_i \hat{\eta}_j$. The $\hat{\lambda}_i$ could then be interpreted as measures of the "susceptibility" to change of the traits Θ_i, and the $\hat{\eta}_j$ (as before) as measures of generalizable treatment effects. Unfortunately, the parameters λ_i and η_j appearing in multiplicative form cannot be separated in the same way as the θ_{vi} and η_j parameters were separated via the CML approach. (Again, it is not possible to deal here with the technical questions involved.)

In concluding this overview of the LLRA, I would like to mention that a similar logistic model of change has been developed for unidimensional tests (item sets) also. Formally, this model is a Linear-Logistic Test Model (LLTM; Fischer, 1973). The technical problems involved are more demanding than in the LLRA, but they have been solved quite satisfactorily (see Fischer, 1983, 1989). This model, however, has a lesser range of applicability due to the underlying unidimensionality assumption, and hence is not discussed here further; yet there exist interesting applications (see Gittler, 1992).

SPECIFIC OBJECTIVITY AS A BASIS OF THE LLRA

The LLRA has a number of advantageous properties—separability of trait and effect parameters, availability of existence and uniqueness results, convenient asymptotic behavior of the CML estimators, asymptotic likelihood-ratio statistics for a large class of hypotheses—but still the choice of the logistic link function in Equations 1 and 2 and of the additivity of treatment effects in Equations 4 or 5 may seem arbitrary. As is shown next, this objection is not justified: Within a certain formal framework, the LLRA is the only possibility for obtaining specifically objective results about treatment effects. The term *specific objectivity* (SO) was coined by Rasch (1967, 1968, 1972, 1977) in connection with the one-parameter logistic or Rasch model; it has a precisely defined meaning that can best be translated as "generalizability of comparisons between items over samples of subjects, and of comparisons of subjects over item samples." In the same sense, I call comparisons between treatment effects specifically objective if they are generalizable over subjects and items. It can be shown that both the logistic link function and the parametric additivity are necessary consequences if SO has been adopted as an axiom (Fisher, 1987). Within the scope of the present chapter on the measurement of treatment effects, SO can be defined as follows:

Suppose that the impact of a treatment or training program on the patients or trainees, hereafter referred to as treatment effect, can be fully characterized by one scalar parameter α. Suppose further that the treatment transforms a given level ξ on one latent dimension, Ξ, into another level, ξ'. If we assume that this change is systematic then there should exist a function F yielding ξ' as the resultant of ξ and α,

$$F(\xi,\alpha) = \xi';$$

$F:\mathbf{R}^2 \rightarrow \mathbf{R}$ will be assumed to be continuous and strictly increasing in both parameters and is called an effect function.

Our basic methodological postulate will be the following: If we observe two subjects, S_1 and S_2, with different initial levels of the trait, ξ_1 and ξ_2, and if the effect of the treatment, α, is the same for both subjects, then any scientifically meaningful measure U of the difference between the two subjects before the treatment, and the same measure U applied to their difference after the treatment, should yield the same result,

$$U[F(\xi_1,\alpha),F(\xi_2,\alpha)] = U(\xi_1,\xi_2), \tag{8}$$

independent of the size of the treatment effect, α. In other words, U: $\mathbf{R}^2 \rightarrow \mathbf{R}$ is a function by means of which the comparison between the two subjects is carried out, and hence is referred to as a comparator function. Again, U will be assumed to be continuous, strictly increasing in ξ_2, and strictly decreasing in ξ_1. Our basic axiom that the result of the comparison be independent of the treatment effect α, will be called specific objectivity of the comparison of the two subjects. It can be shown that this is equivalent to the assumption that, for any two subsequent treatments with effects α_a and α_b, respectively, applied to a subject S_v with trait parameter ξ_v, there exists a function H, independent of ξ_v, such that

$$\alpha_{ab} = H(\alpha_a, \alpha_b), \tag{9}$$

where α_{ab} is the effect of a third treatment that produces the same result as the two separate treatments. This is an alternative equivalent formulation of SO (Fischer, 1987). It has an important consequence in regard to the measurement properties of the effect paramters: We may view Equation 9 as representing a sort of a concatenation operation for treatment effects, implying that effects are measurable on a ratio scale.

The theory of specific objectivity can be developed with mathematical rigor, and nontrivial consequences can be deduced. We are not going into mathematical technicalities here; the interested reader is referred to Fischer (1987, pp. 565–587). The central result is that, upon an appropriate rescaling of the latent trait, $\xi \to \theta$, and of the treatment effect, $\alpha \to \eta$, the model can always be brought into the following simple form,

$$\theta' = \tilde{F}(\theta, \eta) = \theta + \eta, \tag{10}$$

$$\tilde{U}(\theta', \theta) = \eta = \theta' - \theta,$$

where $\tilde{F}$ is the new reaction function defined in terms of θ and η, and $\tilde{U}$ the respective comparator. This means that the state of the subject after the treatment can be predicted by simple addition of the parameters θ and η, and that two subjects (or the same subject at two time points) are appropriately compared by means of their numerical parameter difference. Moreover, it can be shown that the scale of θ is an interval scale, and that of η, a ratio scale. For two treatments with effects α_a and α_b and a joint effect α_{ab}, one obtains the additive relation

$$\eta_{ab} = \eta_b + \eta_b. \tag{11}$$

On first sight, all this might look quite obvious and might seem to correspond to a long-standing practice of statistical analysis of psychological data; but note that the underlying measurement problem is not at all trivial. The simple additivity of trait and treatment effect parameters, and the similar additivity of two treatment effects, hold only after an appropriate rescaling of the parameter dimensions, but certainly not for the raw scores and their differences, which are typically used in classical approaches to measuring change.

Logically, the next question is how to find the transformed scales θ and η for measuring change on a ratio scale. As we shall see, again there exists a satisfactory answer to this question. Before we can present this answer, however, we have to return for a moment to the assumptions. When defining specific objectivity, we have not yet made assumptions about the nature of the data on which the comparison is be based. Let the following further specifications be introduced: (a) the items are dichotomous (reaction categories "right"-"wrong"), (b) the ICCs are strictly monotone increasing without guessing, (c) the responses are locally independent, and (d) the assessment of change is based on a likelihood function of the responses.

From these assumptions it can be deduced mathematically that the link function (or IC curve) must be logistic if additivity of the parameters is to hold. This means that the interval scale properties for θ and the ratio scale properties for η are obtained only if the logistic link function is employed. Additivity, however, may be assumed without loss of generality if the SO axiom is presumed (see Equation 8). Hence, logistic models like the LLRA are the only answer to the quest for specifically objective results on change within the formal framework specified by assumptions (a)-(d), and treatment effects may be assumed to be additive. (The reader interested in further formal details may wish to consult Fischer, 1987).

RECENT DEVELOPMENTS

The LLRA as described so far was already developed and available in the 1970s. I now briefly describe some more recent developments of this methodology for measuring change.

One limitation of the original LLRA was that it allowed for only two occasions or time points. In many longitudinal studies, however, subjects are observed on more than two occasions, such as prior to, immediately after, and 6 months after a treatment period. It was therefore necessary to extend the LLRA to any number of time points. This extended LLRA is

$$P(+|S_v, I_{\text{lit}}, T_t) = \frac{\exp(\theta_{vi} + \beta_{\text{lit}} + \delta_{vt})}{1 + \exp(\theta_{vi} + \beta_{\text{lit}} + \delta_{vt})}, \tag{12}$$

where

P denotes the probability that S_v responds right to item I_{lit}, that is, to the l-th item measuring subdimension (or domain) D_i, presented at time point T_t,

θ_{vi} has the same meaning as before (ability on dimension D_i),

β_{lit} denotes the difficulty parameter of item I_{lit} in a dichotomous Rasch model for items from domain D_i, and

δ_{vt} is the amount of change induced by the treatments in S_v up to time point T_t.

The amount of change can again be decomposed, for example, in the form

$$\delta_{vt} = \sum_j q_{vjt}\eta_j + (T_t - T_1)\tau, \tag{13}$$

where q_{vjt} is the dosage of treatment B_j as applied to S_v up to time point T_t.

All the essential properties of the LLRA are preserved in this generalization: The treatment effects and the trend effect again are measured on a ratio scale and are consistently estimated independently of the actual values of the abilities θ_{vi} in the sample of subjects (as long as the sequence of θ_{vi} parameters satisfies certain mild restrictions, see Pfanzagl, 1994, p. 254). Hence, generalizability of treatment effects over subgroups of subjects and/or subsamples of items can again be tested. Equation 12 is also general enough to accommodate cases of unidimensional item sets, that is, where all $\theta_{vi} = \theta_v$ for $v = 1, \ldots, N$. But, as said before, in applied studies this is an exception rather than the rule.

Another restriction of the original LLRA was that the items, or symptoms, have to be dichotomous. This restriction is acceptable in most domains of educational testing, but in other areas of research, models for polytomous item responses are indispensable, for instance, in clinical studies where patients rate their subjective feeling of illness on a five or seven point rating scale. We have therefore adapted the so-called Rating Scale Model (RSM; Andrich, 1978a, 1978b; Rasch, 1961) by embedding a linear structure in the item parameters, yielding the Linear Rating Scale Model (LRSM):

$$P(H_{vi} = h|\theta_v;\beta_i;\omega_0, \ldots, \omega_m) = \frac{\exp[h(\theta_v + \beta_i) + \omega_h]}{\sum_{l=0}^{m} \exp[l(\theta_v + \beta_i) + \omega_l]}, \tag{14}$$

where

H_{vi} is the response variable of subject S_v on item I_i that can take on values 0,1,2, . . . ,m, representing the respective category of item I_i chosen by subject S_v,

β_i is the item parameter of item I_i in the RSM, and

ω_h, $h = 0,1, \ldots ,m$, are general attractivity parameters of the response categories, C_h.

The item parameters β_i are then construed as weighted sums of certain "basic" parameters η_j, namely,

$$\beta_i = \sum_{j=1}^{M} q_{ij}\eta_j + c, \tag{15}$$

where q_{ij} is a weight of the basic parameter η_j for item I_i.

It can be shown that it is possible to estimate the basic parameters η_j consistently along with the category parameters of ω_h, again independent of the actual values of the person parameters θ_v. Essentially this model preserves the property of specific objectivity and all other properties discussed in connection with the LLRA. The technical problems of parameter estimation and hypothesis testing, however, are far more complicated than in the dichotomous models, but they have been solved: a detailed account of that work is found in Fischer and Parzer (1991).

The usefulness of Equation 15 for measuring change is obvious: We may simply reinterpret the weights q_{ij} as dosages of certain treatments, and the η_j as effect parameters. In order to turn this unidimensional LRSM again into a multidimensional model of change, where any subject S_v has many trait parameters $\theta_{v1}, \ldots ,\theta_{vk}$, we resort to a useful formal trick: We reinterpret the responses of subject S_v to one item I_i at all time points $T_0,T_1, \ldots ,T_t, \ldots$, on the one hand, and S_v's responses to another item I_t at $T_0,T_1, \ldots ,T_t$, on the other hand, as stemming from different subjects S_{vi}^* and S_{vl}^*, that is, we introduce the notion of "virtual subjects." It can be seen that the LRSM then becomes, without any formal change of the model, a multidimensional polytomous model for change, completely analogous to the LLRA. (For further details, see Fischer & Parzer, 1991.)

Applications of Equation 14 to measuring change are still scarce. But first tentative applications have shown that the model is hard to fit. Therefore, recently the model was once more extended by replacing the basic RSM with the so-called Partial Credit Model (PCM; Andersen, 1983; Masters, 1982). The PCM is defined by

$$P(H_{vi} = h|\theta_v; \beta_{ih}) = \frac{\exp(h\theta_v + \beta_{ih})}{\sum_{l=0}^{m} \exp(l\theta_v + \beta_{il})} ,$$
(16)

where all notation is as in Equation 14, except that β_{ih} is the attractiveness of response category C_h of item I_i. This model is more flexible and therefore easier to fit to data because it has one separate parameter β_{ih} for each category by item combination, that is, it allows different attractiveness of the response categories in each item. By decomposing the β_{ih} into a weighted sum of basic parameters,

$$\beta_{ih} = \sum_j q_{ihj}\eta_j + hc,$$
(17)

we obtain the Linear Partial Credit Model (LPCM) that again can be used for measuring effects, for instance, of clinical treatments on the rating of symptoms by psychiatrists or by patients. A detailed account of this recent development and a sample application can be found in Fischer and Ponocny (1994).

Cases where the number of response categories is unbounded have also been considered, as, for example, when the data are frequencies of critical events, such as paroxisms in a clinical study, or outbursts of anger in children in an educational study. For such frequency data, multiplicative Poisson models turn out to be very well suited. It can be shown that they possess the same favorable properties as the LLRA and its extensions described earlier. Again it is possible to formally define a framework for SO such that the Poisson models result as the only practical answer to the quest for measuring change in frequency data. This framework was treated in Fischer (1991b, 1995b).

CONCLUSION

Nine decades lie between the beginning of Spearman's psychometric work and the present models for measuring treatment effects. These two psychometric approaches, and the psychologically motivated aims at their bases, are quite dissimilar. Yet there is one common element in them, the attempt to formalize and, as a consequence, to treat rigorously the scientific questions in the domain of psychology. This is what still can be learned today from studying Spearman's work.

REFERENCES

Andersen, E. B. (1983). A general latent structure model for contingency table data. In H. Wainer & S. Messick (Eds.), *Principals of modern psychological measurement* (pp. 117–138). Hillsdale, NJ:Lawrence Erlbaum Associates.

Andrich, D. (1978a). A rating formulation for ordered response categories. *Psychometrika, 43*, 561–573.

Andrich, D. (1978b). Application of a psychometric rating model to ordered categories which are scored with successive integers. *Applied Psychological Measurement, 2*, 581–594.

Barisch, S. (1989). *Einstellung zur Epilepsie und Einstellungsänderung durch Information* [Attitudes and attitude change towards epilepsy]. Unpublished master's thesis, University of Vienna.

Cox, D. R. (1970). *The analysis of binary data*. London: Methuen.

Doff, B. (1992). *Laufen und psychische Gesundheit* [Jogging and psychic health]. Unpublished master's thesis, University of Vienna.

El-Ganady, M. (1979). *Die Wirkung der Förderung des logischen Denkens auf die Sprechentwicklung im Vorschulalter* [The effects of preschool training of logical thinking and of verbal abilities]. Unpublished doctoral dissertation, University of Vienna.

Fischer, G. H. (1972). A measurement model for the effect of mass-media. *Acta Psychologica, 36*, 207–220.

Fischer, G. H. (1973). The linear logistic test model as an instrument in educational research. *Acta Psychologica, 37*, 359–374.

Fischer, G. H. (1976). Some probabilistic models for measuring change. In D. N. M. de Gruijter & L. J. Th. van der Kamp (Eds.), *Advances in psychological and educational measurement* (pp. 97–110). New York: Wiley.

Fischer, G. H. (1977). Linear logistic latent trait models: Theory and application. In H. Spada & W. F. Kempf (Eds.), *Structural models of thinking and learning* (pp. 203–225). Bern, Switzerland: Huber.

Fischer, G. H. (1983). Logistic latent trait models with linear constraints. *Psychometrika, 48*, 3–26.

Fischer, G. H. (1987). Applying the principles of specific objectivity and of generalizability to the measurement of change. *Psychometrika, 52*, 565–587.

Fischer, G. H. (1989). An IRT-based model for dichotomous longitudinal data. *Psychometrika, 54*, 599–624.

Fischer, G. H. (1991a). A new methodology for the assessment of treatment effects. *Evaluación Psicológica-Psychological Assessment, 7*, 117–147.

Fischer, G. H. (1991b). On power series models and the specifically objective assessment of change in event frequencies. In J. P. Doignon & J. C. Falmagne (Eds.), *Mathematical psychology* (pp. 293–310). New York: Springer-Verlag.

Fischer, G. H. (1995a). Linear logistic models for change. In G. H. Fischer & I. W. Molenaar (Eds.), *Rasch models: Foundations, recent developments, and applications* (pp. 157–180). New York: Springer-Verlag.

Fischer, G. H. (1995b). The derivation of polytomous Rasch models. In G. H. Fischer & I. W. Molenaar (Eds.), *Rasch models. Foundations, recent developments, and applications* (pp. 293–305). New York: Springer-Verlag.

Fischer, G. H., & Parzer, P. (1991). An extension of the rating scale model with an application to the measurement of change. *Psychometrika, 56*, 637–651.

Fischer, G. H., & Ponocny, I. (1994). An extension of the partial credit model with an application to the measurement of change. *Psychometrika, 59*, 177–192.

Fischer, G. H., & Roppert, J. (1965). Lineare Strukturen in Mathematik und Statistik [Linear structures in mathematics and statistics]. Vienna: Physica-Verlag.

Formann, A. K., & Spiel, C. (1989). Measuring change by means of a hybrid variant of the linear logistic model with relaxed assumptions. *Applied Psychological Measurement, 13*, 91–103.

Gittler, G. (1992). *Testpsychologische Aspekte der Raumvorstellungsforschung—Kritik, Lösungsansätze und empirische Befunde* [Test-psychological aspects of research on spatial ability—critique, approaches, and empirical findings]. Habilitations thesis. Vienna: University of Vienna.

Grabner, I. (1980). *Erfassung der Komplexität von Verkehrssituationen* [The assessment of the complexity of traffic situations]. Unpublished doctoral dissertation, University of Vienna.

Heckl, U. (1976). Therapieerfolge bei der Behandlung sprachgestörter Kinder [Therapy effects in the treatment of speech-handicapped children]. Unpublished doctoral dissertation, University of Vienna.

Iby, M. (1987). *Die Effektivität von Kommunikationsseminaren in der innerbetrieblichen Ausbildung der Zentralsparkasse* [The efficacy of communication seminars for employees of the "Zentralsparkasse"]. Unpublished doctoral dissertation, University of Vienna.

Masters, G. N. (1982). A Rasch model for partial credit scoring. *Psychometrika, 47*, 149–174.

Mutschlechner, R. (1987). *Der Patient im Krankenhaus—Ein Versuch, die Wirksamkeit einer psychologischen Betreuung nachzuweisen* [The patient in hospital—an attempt to assess the effects of psychological treatments]. Unpublished doctoral dissertation, University of Vienna.

Pendl, P. (1976). *Effektivität des Sprachlabors an Höheren Schulen* [The efficacy of a language laboratory in high schools]. Unpublished doctoral dissertation, University of Vienna.

Pfanzagl, J. (1994). On the estimation of parameters in certain latent trait models. In G. H. Fischer & D. Laming (Eds.), *Mathematical psychology: New developments* (pp. 249–263). New York: Springer-Verlag.

Pölderl, R. (1992). Lern und Trainingseffekte bei Intelligenztestleistungen [Effects of experience and of practice in the taking of intelligence tests]. Unpublished master's thesis, University of Vienna.

Rasch, G. (1961). On general laws and the meaning of measurement in psychology. *Proceedings of the Berkeley symposium on mathematical statistics and probability, Vol. IV*, (pp. 321–333). Berkeley: University of California Press.

Rasch, G. (1967). An informal report on a theory of objectivity in comparisons. In L. J. Th. van der Kamp & C. A. J. Vlek (Eds.), *Measurement theory*. Proceedings of the NUFFIC international summer session in science in "Het Oude Hof," The Hague, July 14–28, 1966 (pp. 1–19). Leyden: University of Leyden.

Rasch, G. (1968, September). *A mathematical theory of objectivity and its consequences for model construction*. Paper presented at the European Meeting on Statistics, Econometrics, and Management Science, Amsterdam, The Netherlands.

Rasch, G. (1972). Objectivitet i samfundsvidenskaberne et metodeproblem [Objectivity in the social sciences as a methodological problem]. *Nationaloekonomisk Tidsskrift, 110*, 161–196.

Rasch, G. (1977). On specific objectivity. An attempt at formalizing the request for generality and validity of scientific statements. In M. Blegvad (Ed.), *The Danish yearbook of philosophy* (pp. 58–94). Copenhagen: Munksgaard.

Rella, E. (1976). *Trainierbarkeit des Antizipierens von Gefahrensituationen im Straßenverkehr* [Trainability of anticipating of dangerous situations in traffic]. Unpublished doctoral dissertation, University of Vienna.

Rop, I. (1977). The application of a linear logistic model describing the effects of preschool curricula on cognitive growth. In H. Spada & W. F. Kempf (Eds.), *Structural models of thinking and learning* (pp. 281–293). Bern, Switzerland: Huber.

Schmied, C. (1987). *Die Effektivität von Managementseminaren—durchgeführt bei den Österreichischen Bundesbahnen* [The efficacy of management seminars for employees of the Austrian Federal Railways]. Unpublished doctoral dissertation, University of Vienna.

Spearman, C. (1904a). The proof and measurement of association between two things. *American Journal of Psychology, 15,* 72–101.

Spearman, C. (1904b). "General Intelligence", objectively determined and measured. *American Journal of Psychology, 15,* 201–293.

Spearman, C. (1907). Demonstration of formulae for true measurement of correlation. *American Journal of Psychology, 18,* 161–169.

Spearman, C. (1910). Correlation calculated with faulty data. *British Journal of Psychology, 3,* 271–295.

Spearman, C. (1913). Correlations of sums and differences. *British Journal of Psychology, 5,* 417–426.

Thurstone, L. L. (1935). *The vectors of the mind.* Chicago: University of Chicago Press.

Vodopiutz, A. (1977). *Komplexbildung im motorischen Lernen* [The formation of complex movement in motor training]. Unpublished doctoral dissertation, University of Vienna.

Widowitz, E. (1987). *Der Effekt autogenen Trainings bei funktionellen Erkrankungen* [The effect of "autogenous training" on the functional syndrome]. Unpublished doctoral dissertation, University of Vienna.

Witek, J. (1980). Die Effektivität des gruppendynamischen Sensitivity Trainings [The efficacy of a group-dynamic sensitivity training]. *Zeitschrift für Experimentelle und Angewandte Psychologie, 27,* 335–345.

Zeman, M. (1976). *Die Wirksamkeit der mathematischen Früherziehung* [The efficacy of early mathematics training]. Unpublished doctoral dissertation, University of Vienna.

Zimprich, H. (1980). Behandlungskonzepte und-resultate bei psychosomatischen Erkrankungen im Kindesalter [Designs and effects of treatments of psychosomatic diseases in children]. In H. Zimprich (Ed.), *Kind und Umwelt* (pp. 131–198). Vienna: Springer.

CHAPTER 9

Predicting Occupational Criteria: Not Much More Than g

Malcolm James Ree
James A. Earles
Armstrong Laboratory

Charles Spearman is perhaps best remembered for his contribution to our understanding of intelligence by advancing the concept of general cognitive ability, g. He noted that this was the general or common portion of all cognitive ability tests. Although Spearman first derived g in the educational setting, the importance of g in the prediction of occupation criteria has been and continues to be the center of a controversy (Calfee, 1993; Green, 1994; Jensen, 1993; McClelland, 1993; Ree & Earles, 1992; Ree, Earles, & Teachout, 1994; Schmidt & Hunter, 1993; Sternberg & Wagner, 1993).

In hierarchical models of ability (Ree & Carretta, 1994; Vernon, 1969), g occupies the highest level with first-order factors at lower levels. These first-order factors are frequently highly g saturated. Others have chosen to study first-order factors such as spatial ability, verbal ability, working memory, or elemental cognitive components. We have chosen to study g because research demonstrates that it is ubiquitously predictive of important theoretical and practical criteria and it is readily estimable in large existing databases. Measurement of g requires no special equipment such as computers and is inexpensive to accomplish. It is no surprise that others find additional cognitive components of interest. However, the long list of correlates of g, presented by Brand (1987; see also Jensen, 1987), compels attention. Some correlates presented are expected, such as ability scores, reaction times, and memory. Others are not expected, such as dietary preferences, practical knowledge, altruism, and smoking. O'Toole (1990) and O'Toole and Stankov (1992) presented the eschatologically interesting positive correlation of g with life span.

METHODOLOGICAL ISSUES IN ABILITY RESEARCH

There are three issues that make the study of g more difficult. Confusion over these issues often leads to erroneous conclusions about the utility of a predictor. Cautions must be provided about each and recommendations for rectification offered. The issues are rotated factors, censored samples, and unreliability of measurement.

The first issue is rotation in factor analysis. When factors are rotated, the variance of the first unrotated factor, almost invariably g in ability tests and other cognitive measures, is distributed across the other factors. The first factor, g, therefore seems to disappear, but in fact it usually becomes the dominant source of variance in each of the rotated factors. The other factors become g and something else. It is usually the "something else" that the factor is named for, and the g in the factor is not acknowledged. For example, V, the verbal factor consistently found in multiple aptitude tests, is mostly g as a consequence of rotation. Ree and Carretta (1994) showed that the total proportion of reliable non-g variance in a representative multiple aptitude battery (the U.S. Armed Services Vocational Aptitude Battery [ASVAB]) was only 16%, whereas the proportion of g variance was 64%. In large part, g accounts for the correlation of the factors in multiple aptitude tests and for the correlation of topographically dissimilar linear composites in multiple aptitude batteries. To be accurate, we should call verbal not V but

$$\mathbf{g} + v.$$

with g written large to indicate its contribution to the variance of the factor (Ree & Carretta, 1994).

This is not unique to paper-and-pencil aptitude tests. A wide variety of computer-administered elementary cognitive tasks based on cognitive component theory has been shown by Kranzler and Jensen (1991) to be mostly g. Kyllonen (1993) provided a battery of computerized cognitive component tests for which g accounts for a greater proportion of variance than g accounts for in paper-and-pencil aptitude tests.

To avoid the problem of the disappearing g associated with rotation, one should either not rotate and use unrotated first principal components principal factors or use residualized hierarchical factors. Residualization (Schmid & Leiman, 1957) removes the effects of the higher order factor, g in cognitive measures,[1] from the lower order factors.

The second concern in research on ability is caused by the almost unavoidable use of censored samples. Censored samples can create artifacts that lead to erroneous conclusions about ability. A sample is censored when the variance of one or more of the variables has been reduced due to prior selection. For example, if the experimental subjects were all students in a university, they would have been subjected to prior selection on the basis of test scores and academic achievement. The variance associated with the causes of test scores and academic achievement has been reduced.

Correlations computed in censored samples are substantially downwardly biased estimators and can even change signs from their population value (Ree, Carretta, Earles, & Albert, 1994). Thorndike (1949) provided a good discussion of the phenomena with an example from a large World War II military sample. Interpretation of correlations computed in range restricted censored samples frequently leads to erroneous conclusions about the sign and magnitude of the relationships of variables.

Brand (1987) observed that many studies seeking to isolate ability components factorially or to evaluate the efficacy of g and other variables have been conducted in samples that have been censored with respect to g. The subjects, frequently university students, were selected, at least in part, on the basis of g. The variance of the censored variable, g, is reduced and this artificially reduces observed correlations. Goldberg (1991) observed with regard to one highly g loaded measure, the Scholastic Aptitude Test (SAT), "in other words, one can always filter out—or at least greatly reduce the importance of a causal variable, no matter how strong that variable, by selecting a group that selects its members on the basis of that variable" (p. 132). He further reminded us that the more the variance of a variable is restricted, the less its apparent validity.

Military, college and university students, and almost all other occupational samples used in studies have been selected to some frequently large degree on g and ineluctably, the variance associated with g has been dramatically reduced. In U.S. Air Force samples, it is usual to find ASVAB[2] test variances reduced from the normative 100 to 25 by prior selection. This range restriction often leads to a false conclusion that g is not strongly related to other variables. Actually

---

[1]Residualization is also appropriate for noncognitive measures that display a hierarchical structure.

[2]The ASVAB is the U.S. military enlistment qualification test battery.

the conclusion is the consequence of a statistical artifact. Echoing McNemar's (1964) famous American Psychological Association presidential address, meta-analysts (Hunter & Schmidt, 1990) have sounded the most recent warning on this problem. To avoid range restriction problems due to censored samples, statistical corrections should be applied. In some cases the "univariate" corrections (Thorndike, 1949) are appropriate if censoring has occurred on only one variable. If censoring has occurred on more than one variable, as is almost always the case in studies conducted in operational settings, the multivariate correction (Lawley, 1943; Ree, Carretta, Earles, & Albert, 1994) is appropriate. These corrections have been shown to be better estimates of the population parameters and in general to be conservative estimators (Linn, Harnish, & Dunbar, 1981). They tend to underestimate the population parameters and, therefore, are an undercorrection.

A third problem that leads to erroneous conclusions about correlates of g is the use of tests or cognitive tasks, or other measures that are sufficiently unreliable that they cannot correlate with g (or any other tests), falsely giving the appearance of uniqueness. Spearman (1904) demonstrated that such tests must be made more reliable. The remedy to this problem is to lengthen the test by including more items or to remove ambiguity from the extant items. Failing these remedies, discard the test. All experimental tests and cognitive tasks should be administered twice to the same subjects to estimate reliability for use in the correction-for-attenuation formula (Spearman, 1904). Although the appropriate time interval for retest is not agreed on, we believe that several days separation that allows for practice effects to diminish, is more desirable than same day retesting. The corrected-for-attenuation correlation should be used to answer theoretical questions.

ESTIMATING g FOR INDIVIDUALS

To conduct comparative or validity studies it is often necessary to estimate the general cognitive ability, g, of individuals. Using large samples of young adults (n = 9,173) we have shown (Earles & Ree, 1991; Ree & Earles, 1991a) that with ordinary multiple aptitude tests any positive weighting (see Wilks, 1938) of the tests will yield almost identical estimates, in a ranking sense, of g for the subjects. Common weighting schemes to estimate g are usually derived from the statistical procedures of component or factor analyses. The methods we used estimated g as the first unrotated principal component, the first unrotated principal factor, and the highest factor from 12 hierarchical factor analyses. Correlations among g estimates never dropped below

.93 and more often than not exceeded .99! We also computed coefficients of congruence and all were above .99. This was because all the tests, regardless of title, overt content, and form, measured g in large part. This commonality of measure accounts for the uniformly positive correlations among all tests first reported by Spearman (1904) and ever since. We have yet to see cognitive tests that do not measure g to some large extent, usually the major portion of the variance.

Recently, Kranzler and Jensen (1991) demonstrated the positive correlation of elementary cognitive tasks (ECT) and g. They administered the Multidimensional Aptitude Battery (MAB), Raven's Matrices, and a battery of 37 cognitive tests to a sample of 101 college students. They extracted the unrotated first principal component from the MAB and Ravens and a simple linear composite from the 37 cognitive tasks. The correlation between the unrotated first principal component, g, and the simple linear composite of the ECTs was .558. This showed the high g saturation of the ECTs.

After g is statistically removed from tests and other cognitive measures what remains is non-g, that portion of the score due to intelligence but strongly enough influenced by experience to be factorially distinct (Cattell, 1987). The non-g portions readily fall into two categories: specific abilities (spatial, perceptual, etc.) and job knowledge (electronics, shop, mechanics, instrument comprehension, etc.). These non-g portions can be represented by common factors or principal components. We have chosen to use principal components because they include all the variance, thereby giving the non-g portions maximal opportunity to show validity and incremental validity. In most instances the g portions of tests (or cognitive tasks measuring cognitive components) account for more variance than any other portion. In many instances the g portion exceeds the sum of the non-g portions. For example, the g portion of the American military enlistment battery is about 64% (Ree & Carretta, 1994), whereas the American commissioning battery has a g proportion of about 41% (Carretta & Ree, 1996). The rest of the variance is either error or specific that is distributed among the various subtests. Having demonstrated ways to measure g and non-g portions for tests and for individuals, we have investigated the utility of g and non-g for predicting job performance, and other occupational criteria.

Job performance has several components. One is possessing the knowledge, skills, and techniques required by the job. Training and retraining for promotions, lateral reassignment, as well as learning to stay even with changing responsibilities of the same position are significant aspects of most employment. The second component is the application of the knowledge, skills, and techniques to achieve personal and organizational goals. Determinants of job performance such as physical strength, individual motivation, personality, or other nonintellectual components will not be addressed as other researchers and a rich literature cover those topics.

PREDICTING TRAINING OUTCOMES

A test's ability to predict training success, the first aspect of job success, comes predominantly from the share of the test which measures g. The g loadings of the 10 tests comprising the U.S. military's enlistment selection and classification battery (ASVAB) were correlated with their average validity for predicting the training success of more than 24,000 enlisted subjects in 37 diverse jobs (Jones, 1988; Ree & Earles, 1992, 1994). Final grades in training were the criteria. Included were jobs classified as administrative, electrical, general technical, and mechanical. Test g loadings were derived on the normative sample (Ree & Wegner, 1990) by means of the unrotated first principal component. The sample was range restricted because the subjects were selected in large part on the basis of these tests. In many cases the test variances were reduced by as much as 75%. Therefore, the validities of the 10 tests for each job were corrected for multivariate range restriction using Lawley's theorem (1943). This provides far superior estimates of the correlation parameter. The rank order (Spearman) correlation between the loadings and the average validity was .75 (Jones, 1988). When the loadings were corrected for the unreliability of the tests, the coefficient became .98 (Ree & Earles, 1994). This same rank order correlation was estimated in another sample of more than 78,000 subjects across 150 jobs and computed to be .96. When computed within the job families of mechanical, administrative, general–technical, and electronic, the correlations were much the same (Jones, 1988). Tests with higher g loadings were more valid. Further, the variability of the correlation of g loading and average validity within the job families was the same as across the job families. Ree and Earles (1992) suggested that this uniformity of prediction is the foundation of most validity generalization (Hunter & Schmidt, 1990).

ASVAB data were used to study the incremental validity of non-g to g (Ree & Earles, 1989). Usually the first requirement in a job is to learn the technical and practical aspects of job performance. Training and learning job skills continues during almost all jobs even if only to keep even with developments in the field or to use new tools and techniques. Consequently, job training is an important primary criterion.

Technical job training performance in a sample of 78,049 airmen in 89 technical job training courses was predicted by both g and non-g portions of the ASVAB. The average sample size was 876. This study was done by computing 89 individual regressions with only g and comparing the results to 89 additional regressions containing g and specific abilities. Psychometric g was uniformly determined to be the most valid predictor for each technical training course and the contribution of the non-g portions was small or nonexistent. Because the ASVAB had been used for selection, it was necessary to correct the correlations for the effects of range restriction. The average corrected-for-range-restriction correlation of g with the criterion was .76. The predictive validity of g for job training performance was high and was incremented little by non-g. An average increase of .02 in correlation was found by adding the non-g portions to the 89 prediction equations. The second principal component was the most frequent incremental predictor and it is mostly a measure of job knowledge as opposed to a measure of specific ability. The job knowledge measured was electronics information, auto and shop information, and mechanical comprehension. One job was found for which the non-g portion added .10 to prediction; however, for one third of the jobs, g was the only significant predictor. An estimate of the expected variance of the additional predictive power of non-g was not made. The hypothesis that the small variance of the incremental validity of non-g was expected sampling variance cannot be rejected.

A study on a sample of 78,041 Air Force enlisted troops was conducted to determine if g predicted job training performance in about the same way regardless of the difficulty or the kind of job (Ree & Earles, 1991b). It might be argued that g was acceptable for some jobs, but that other specific aptitudes were compensatory or more important for other jobs. An analysis that sought to determine if g were equally predictive of all jobs and if some jobs required specific abilities would help evaluate the hypothesis. Linear models statistical analyses were used to test whether the relationships of g to training success criteria were the same for 82 jobs. This was done by imposing the constraint that each of the 82 regression coefficients for g be the same and then releasing the constraint and allowing the 82 regression coefficients to be individually estimated and potentially to vary. Although there was statistical evidence that the relationships of g to the criteria differed by job, these differences were small and appeared to be of no practical predictive consequence. The relationship of g to performance was nearly identical for all jobs. Aggregating the jobs using a single prediction equation for all the jobs reduced the correlation less than one half of 1%.

More recently, a meta-analysis was conducted[3] of the validity coefficients for various ASVAB composites and training success criteria. There were 150 Air Force enlisted jobs and 88,724 male and female subjects. Two simple-weighted composites and a best-weighted regression-based composite were meta-analyzed across the 150 jobs. The two simple-weighted composites were a unit-weighted verbal and quantitative measure from four tests, almost purely g, and an integer-weighted sum of all 10 ASVAB tests, a more diverse and hence more complete g measure. An individual regression-weighted composite of all 10 ASVAB tests was estimated for each of the 150 jobs. The Hunter and Schmidt (1990) meta-analytic model was used in which each correlation was individually corrected. For the two simple-weighted composites the mean validities were .760 and .767 and 100% of the variability in correlation coefficients was accounted for by study artifacts. The mean validity of the set of regression based multiple correlations was .768 and 73% of the variance in correlations was accounted for by study artifacts. Clearly there is some small amount of predictive efficiency to be gained from best-weighting. However, in about 85% of the regression equations negative regression weights penalized good performance on tests despite the instructions to the examinee to achieve the highest score possible.

Non-g portions of ASVAB have been found to add little validity beyond g in prediction of training success. However, special classification tests have been developed to augment the predictiveness of ASVAB for some Air Force jobs. Two additional test measures, one for the selection of computer programmers and one for the selection of intelligence operatives, were investigated to determine if they measured something other than g (Besetsny, Earles, & Ree, 1993; Besetsny, Ree, & Earles, 1993) and to determine their validity incremental to g. In these studies training performance was the criterion. In each job, multiple regression equations containing g alone and then g and specifics together were tested to determine if specific abilities incremented the validity of g. The samples were comprised of 3,547 computer programming trainees and 776 intelligence operatives trainees. For the two jobs, regression analyses showed incremental validity gains for specifics beyond g of .00 and .02, respectively. Although intended to add unique measurement, these two tests contributed little or nothing beyond g.

Because some jobs require college degrees, Brodnick and Ree (1995) studied the relationship among academic performance, g, and socio-economic status. The sample was 339 students in a small Catholic

---

[3]This study was conducted by Fenske and Ree and is being prepared for publication.

college in Texas. Nine observed variables including three aptitude measures from standardized college entry tests, three measures of socioeconomic status from federal financial assistance forms, and three measures of first-year academic performance in the form of grades on mandatory classes were collected for each subject. Confirmatory factor analyses disclosed that g was a good predictor of academic performance. Despite common knowledge such as contained in the Coleman report, a specific latent variable for socioeconomic status added nothing to the structural models. The model with the best fit to the data included only the latent variables of g and academic performance.

PREDICTING WORK SAMPLES

The second component of job success, the accomplishment of the job's primary tasks, has been much less studied, particularly for the role played by g. This is frequently because of the difficulty and expense of obtaining criterion measures.

A study of the incremental validity of non-g to g in prediction of work sample criteria was conducted (Morales, 1991; Olea & Ree, 1994). The Air Force Officer Qualifying Test (Carretta & Ree, 1996), a multiple aptitude battery measuring g and the five factors of verbal, mathematics, perceptual speed, spatial, and aircrew knowledge was used in this study. A sample of approximately 5,500 college graduate lieutenants, 4,000 in Air Force pilot training and 1,500 in Air Force navigator training, was studied to determine how well g and non-g predicted six flying and six navigation criteria. The subjects were tested from a few months to as much as 4 years prior to collection of the criteria.

For the pilots, the criteria were actual samples of flying and academic performance. For the navigators, the criteria were work samples of day and night celestial navigation and academic performance. In addition, the sum of the five individual criteria for each job comprised a composite criterion. Very few students fail training for academic reasons; most fail for inability to control the aircraft (pilots) or inability to correctly use the navigational instruments (navigators) on check rides.

Similar results were found for prediction of pilot and navigator academic and job sample performance as for technical training performance; g was the best predictor. For the composite criterion, the broadest and most meaningful measure of performance, the validity was .40 for pilots and .49 for navigators. The non-g portions provided an average increase in predictive accuracy of .08 for pilots and .02 for navigators. Examination of the non-g portions adding to validity for pilots revealed that they were measures of job knowledge (aviation information and instrument comprehension) and not specific abilities (verbal, mathematics, perceptual speed, spatial).

Ree, Earles, and Teachout (1994) also investigated the validity and incremental validity of g and non-g for several job performance criteria across a variety of jobs. A sample of 1,036 airmen with approximately 2 years' job experience was used to determine if g were the best predictor of on-the-job performance in seven jobs; from the mechanical, administrative, general–technical, and electrical job families as used by the Air Force. Subjects were administered the aptitude test (ASVAB) 2 to 4 years prior to criterion data collection. The criteria were hands-on work samples that measured job performance, technical interviews in which the incumbent explained how job tasks were done step-by-step, and a composite of the work sample and technical interviews. There were several reasons for using multiple criteria. Hands-on work sample measures have the highest fidelity with on-the-job performance and the greatest face validity. The technical interviews sampled a greater number of job tasks than the hands-on work samples, particularly those that would have removed machinery from service, were expensive to test, or presented a danger. As for pilots and navigators, the composite criterion was deemed the most complete and therefore, the best overall measure of job performance. As before, g and non-g or s were used to predict the criteria using multiple regression equations. Multiple regression equations using g and s were compared to multiple regression equations using only g. Again, g was the best predictor (the range-restriction-corrected average correlation was .44) of all the job performance measures. The mean increase in predictiveness after adding non-g was .03 for the work sample measures, nothing for the interviews, and .02 for the composite criterion. These incremental values were similar to the value found in the pilot–navigator study and in the technical training study.

AUGMENTING THE PREDICTIVENESS OF g

Many occupational psychologists have searched for predictors of job performance to augment or replace g (see, e.g., McHenry, Hough, Toquam, Hanson, & Ashworth, 1990). Two of the most familiar are psychomotor tests and interviews.

Because psychomotor tests and interviews look different than paper-and-pencil tests, they are frequently believed to measure something different. The belief that appearances necessarily indicate what is being measured is an example of the *topographical fallacy* (Walters, Miller, & Ree, 1993).

A recent study (Carretta & Ree, 1994) investigated the incremental validity of psychomotor scores from a computer administered pilot selection test, the Air Force Basic Attributes Test (BAT; Carretta, 1990),[4] above g for predicting passing–failing pilot training. The Air Force Officer Qualifying Test (AFOQT) was used to estimate g for this sample of 678 pilot trainees. An increment to the validity of g of .02 (uncorrected for range restriction) was found, which was similar to the increment found in previous studies and to the increment reported by the Army (McHenry et al., 1990) for psychomotor ability. In a sample of 4,039 male and female Army enlisted troops, psychomotor tests added (corrected for range restriction) no more than .02 to any of their five criteria with a mean increment of .014 across all nine jobs considered.

The hypothesis that psychomotor tests were measures of g as well as psychomotor skill was investigated (Ree & Carretta, 1994). If this hypothesis were sustained, it would explain the relatively small incremental validity psychomotor tests offer. A sample of 354 first-term male and female airmen was administered a battery of psycho-motor tracking tests yielding eight scores and two verbal and two mathematics tests as the measure of g. These psychomotor tests; two-hand coordination, complex coordination, and time-sharing have a long history (Thorndike & Hagen, 1959) and are well known and regarded (Fleishman & Quaintance, 1984). The observed correlations of the psychomotor tests and g averaged .21 uncorrected for range restriction and .34 after correction for range restriction.

A confirmatory factor analysis showed that all the psychomotor and paper-and-pencil tests loaded, as expected, on the first factor. A congruence analysis showed that the paper-and-pencil loadings were almost identical to the loadings found when paper-and-pencil tests were analyzed alone, with no difference greater than .04. This demonstrated that the first factor of the cognitive tests and the psychomotor tests analyzed together was g.

Finally, a confirmatory residualized (Schmid & Leiman, 1957) hierarchical factor analysis disclosed that g contributed to each test, psychomotor as well as paper-and-pencil. The g factor accounted for 39% of the variance. Additionally, there was a higher order psycho-motor factor that accounted for 29% of the variance.

A structured interview was investigated to augment current procedures for selecting pilot training candidates (Walters, Miller, &

---

[4]The BAT contains tests in addition to the psychomotor.

Ree,1993). The interview measured educational background, self-confidence and leadership, motivation to fly, and flying job knowledge. Additionally, three global ratings of probable success in pilot training, bomber–fighter flying, and tanker–transport flying were made. The sample was 223 U.S. Air Force pilot trainees who were administered the AFOQT, computer-based cognitive and personality tests, and the structured interview. The criterion was passing–failing pilot training. The seven interview scores had an average validity of .21, the 16 AFOQT tests had an average validity of .28, and the computer-administered tests had an average validity of .18. When the seven interview scores were added to the regression equation containing the AFOQT scores and the computer test scores, no incremental validity was found.

The lack of incremental validity resides in the lack of unique predictive variance beyond g in the interview scores. Linear regression analyses subsequent to Walters et al. (1993) comparing full and restricted regression equations for predicting pilot training success, showed that adding the interview scores to a measure of g extracted from the AFOQT did not improve prediction. Clearly the predictive power of the interview came from the measurement of g.

PERORATION

We have provided a body of evidence for the ubiquity and primacy of g in the prediction of several facets of job performance including technical training grades, flying performance ratings, navigation tasks ratings, technical knowledge, and hands-on work samples. Further, there is evidence that the predictiveness of some "noncognitive" measures such as psychomotor scores or interviews comes, in part or wholly, from g. As Brand (1987) observed "g is to psychology as carbon is to chemistry" (p. 257).

All research on the development of new predictors of job performance or other occupational criteria should include measures of g. The uniqueness of the predictors beyond g, and when appropriate, the incremental validity of the predictors beyond g should be investigated. All samples should be corrected for the pernicious effects of range restriction. The use of unrotated principal components or unrotated principal factors or residualized scores from hierarchical factor analysis is imperative to avoid erroneous conclusions.

Additionally, the utility of g and non-g predictors should be estimated in dollars where applicable or in terms of increases in expected job performance. Indeed, the increments to g reported could have large utility under specific large sample conditions. Nevertheless, the utility of g as a predictor of job performance is assured.

None of what has been reviewed should be construed to imply that g is the only construct worth investigating. Clearly, McHenry et al. (1990) demonstrated that personality and temperament measures can predict certain job related criteria such as "effort and leadership," "personal discipline," and "physical fitness and military bearing." However, for predicting training success, hands-on job performance and other measures of essential occupational criteria, not much more than g is needed.

ACKNOWLEDGMENTS

The opinions expressed are those of the authors and not necessarily those of the U.S. Air Force or the U.S. government.

We thank our colleagues and coworkers L. Besetsny, R. Brodnick, T. Carretta, A. Duke, S. Fenske, G. Jones, P. Kyllonen, M. Miller, M. Olea, D. Perry, W. Tirre, L. Valentine, L. Walters, J. Weeks, and J. Wheeler for their many conversations, ideas, efforts and help in the studies reported here. Special thanks are extended to A. Jensen, F. Schmidt, and H. Wainer.

REFERENCES

Besetsny, L., Earles, J. A., & Ree, M. J. (1993). Little incremental validity for a special test of abstract symbolic reasoning in an Air Force intelligence career field. *Educational and Psychological Measurement, 53,* 507–511.

Besetsny, L., Ree, M. J., & Earles, J. A. (1993). Special test for computer programmers? Not needed: The predictive efficiency of the electronic data processing test for a sample of Air Force Recruits. *Educational and Psychological Measurement, 53,* 993–997.

Brand, C. (1987). The importance of general intelligence. In S. Modgil & C. Modgil (Eds.), *Arthur Jensen: Consensus and controversy.* New York: Falmer.

Brodnick, R., & Ree, M. J. (1995). A structural model of academic performance, socioeconomic status, and Spearman's g. *Educational and Psychological Measurement, 55,* 583–594.

Calfee, R. (1993). Paper, pencil, potential, and performance. *Current Directions in Psychological Science, 2,* 6–7.

Carretta, T. R. (1990). Cross validation of experimental USAF pilot training performance models. *Military Psychology, 2,* 257–264.

Carretta, T. R., & Ree, M. J. (1994). Pilot-candidate selection method: Sources of validity. *The International Journal of Aviation Psychology, 4,* 103–117.

Carretta, T. R., & Ree, M. J. (1996). Factor structure of the Air Force Officer Qualifying Test: Analysis and Comparison. *Military Psychology, 8,* 29–42.

Cattell, R. (1987). *Intelligence: Its structure, growth, and action.* Amsterdam: Elsevier.

Earles, J. A., & Ree, M. J. (1991). *Air Force Officer Qualifying Test: Estimating the general ability component* (AL-TR-1991-0039). Brooks AFB, TX: Armstrong Laboratory.

Fleishman, E. A., & Quaintance, M. K. (1984). *Taxonomy of human performance: The description of human tasks.* Orlando, FL: Academic Press.

Green, B. F. (1994). g is not enough. *The Score, 17,* 12–15.

Goldberg, S. (1991). *When wish replaces thought.* Buffalo, NY: Prometheus.

Hunter, J. E., & Schmidt, F. L. (1990). *Methods of meta-analysis.* Newbury Park, CA: Sage.

Jensen, A. R. (1987). The g beyond factor analysis. In R. R. Ronning, J. A. Glover, J. C. Conoley, & J. C. Dewitt (Eds.), *The influence of cognitive psychology on testing and measurement* (pp. 87–142). Hillsdale, NJ: Lawrence Erlbaum Associates.

Jensen, A. R. (1993). Test validity: g versus "tacit knowledge." *Current Directions in Psychological Science, 2,* 9–10.

Jones, G. E. (1988). *Investigation of the efficacy of general ability versus specific abilities as predictors of occupational success.* Unpublished master's thesis, St. Mary's University of Texas, San Antonio, TX.

Kranzler, J. H., & Jensen, A. R. (1991). The nature of psychometric g: Unitary process or a number of independent processes? *Intelligence, 15,* 397–422.

Kyllonen, P. C. (1993). Aptitude testing inspired by information processing: A test of the four-sources model. *Journal of General Psychology, 120,* 375–405.

Lawley, D. N. (1943). A note on Karl Pearson's selection formulae. *Proceedings of the Royal Society of Edinburgh. Section A, 62,* Pt. I, 28–30.

Linn, R. L., Harnish, D. L., & Dunbar, S. (1981). Corrections for range restriction: An empirical investigation of conditions resulting in conservative corrections. *Journal of Applied Psychology, 66,* 655–663.

McClelland, D. C. (1993). Intelligence is not the best predictor of job performance. *Current Directions in Psychological Science, 2,* 5–6.

McHenry, J. J., Hough, L. M., Toquam, J. L., Hanson, M. A., & Ashworth, S. (1990). Project A validity results: The relationship between predictor and criterion domains. *Personnel Psychology, 43,* 335–354.

McNemar, Q. (1964). Lost: Our intelligence. Why? *American Psychologist, 19,* 871–882.

Morales, M. (1991). *The function of general and specific abilities in the validity of the Air Force Officer Qualifying Test.* Unpublished master's thesis, St. Mary's University of Texas, San Antonio, TX.

Olea, M. M., & Ree, M. J. (1994). Predicting pilot and navigator criteria: Not much more than g. *Journal of Applied Psychology, 79,* 845–851.

O'Toole, B. I. (1990). Intelligence and behavior and motor vehicle accident mortality. *Accident Analysis and Prevention, 22,* 211–221.

O'Toole, B. I., & Stankov, L. (1992). Ultimate validity of psychological tests. *Personality and Individual Differences, 13,* 699–716.

Ree, M. J., & Carretta, T. R. (1994). The correlation of general cognitive ability and psychomotor tracking tests. *International Journal of Selection and Assessment, 2,* 209–216.

Ree, M. J., & Carretta, T. R. (1994). Factor analysis of ASVAB: Confirming a Vernon-like structure. *Educational and Psychological Measurement, 54,* 457–461.

Ree, M. J., Carretta, T. R., Earles, J. A., & Albert, W. (1994). Sign changes when correcting for range restriction: A note on Pearson's and Lawley's selection formulae. *Journal of Applied Psychology, 79,* 298–301.

Ree, M. J., & Earles, J. A. (1989). *The differential validity of a differential aptitude test* (AFHRL-TR-89-59). Brooks AFB, TX: Armstrong Laboratory, Manpower and Personnel Research Division.

Ree, M. J., & Earles, J. A. (1991a). The stability of convergent estimates of g. *Intelligence,*

15, 271-278.

Ree, M. J., & Earles, J. A. (1991b). Predicting training success: Not much more than g. *Personnel Psychology, 44*, 321-332.

Ree, M. J., & Earles, J. A. (1992). Intelligence is the best predictor of job performance. *Current Directions in Psychological Science, 1*, 86-89.

Ree, M. J., & Earles, J. A. (1994). The ubiquitous predictiveness of g. In C. Walker, M. Rumsey, & J. Harris (Eds.), *Personnel selection and classification* (pp. 127-135). Hillsdale, NJ: Lawrence Erlbaum Associates.

Ree, M. J., Earles, J. A., & Teachout, M. (1994). Predicting job performance: Not much more than g. *Journal of Applied Psychology, 79*, 518-524.

Ree, M. J., & Wegner, T. G. (1990). Correcting differences in answer sheets for the 1980 Armed Services Vocational Aptitude Battery reference population. *Military Psychology, 2*, 157-169.

Schmid, J., & Leiman, J. M. (1957). The development of hierarchical factor solutions. *Psychometrika, 22*, 53-61.

Schmidt, F. L., & Hunter, J. E. (1993). Tacit knowledge, practical intelligence, general mental ability, and job knowledge. *Current Directions in Psychological Science, 2*, 8-9.

Spearman, C. (1904). "General intelligence," objectively determined and measured. *American Journal of Psychology, 15*, 201-293.

Sternberg, R. J., & Wagner, R. K. (1993). The g-ocentric view of intelligence and job performance is wrong. *Current Directions in Psychological Science, 2*, 1-5.

Thorndike, R. L. (1949). *Personnel selection.* New York: Wiley.

Thorndike, R. L., & Hagen, E. (1959). *Ten thousand careers.* New York: Wiley.

Vernon, P. E. (1969). Intelligence and cultural environment. London: Methuen.

Walters, L. C., Miller, M., & Ree, M. J. (1993). Structured interviews for pilot selection: No incremental validity. *International Journal of Aviation Psychology, 3*, 25-38.

Wilks, S. S. (1938). Weighting systems for linear functions of correlated variables when there is no dependent variable. *Psychometrika, 3*, 23-40.

CHAPTER 10

Matching Abilities, Instruction, and Assessment: Reawakening the Sleeping Giant of ATI

Robert J. Sternberg
Yale University

Everyone who has gone to school has, in one way or another, paid the price of the mismatch among abilities, instruction, and assessment. The only question is how much the person has paid, and in what form the payment has been extracted.

In my own case, my most memorable payment was the receipt of a grade of "C" in my college-level introductory psychology course. It was a memorize-the-book kind of course, and I have never been very good at memorizing textbooks. The grade was enough to convince me to study mathematics instead of psychology, although I later discovered that I was even worse in math, and switched back to psychology. Ironically, although many courses in psychology and other sciences are memorize-the-book types of courses, as a scientist, one never has to memorize a book, and if one does not remember something, one can simply grab the book off the shelf.

Teachers as well as students in all subject matter areas have seen the costs of mismatching among abilities, instruction, and assessment. In science, students who are marvelously creative and ingenious in the design of experiments may receive low marks in courses requiring memorization of books. In history, students who could ably recognize the implications of past historical events for present foreign policy conflicts find that they are unable to remember the dates or treaty names required for high grades on multiple-choice tests. In foreign language learning, students who can easily pick up a language from context are subjected to a mimic-and-memorize method of presentation that is more foreign to them than the foreign language. In mathematics, students who could easily visualize complex relationships are forced to learn mathematical techniques algebraically, despite the availability of geometric isomorphisms. In any area of subject matter learning, I would argue, mismatching extracts a toll.

The toll to both the individual and society is great. Potentially highly able scientists drop out of science, and people with natural foreign language learning facility conclude that they cannot learn another language. People who might have been great historians end up doing something else, and able mathematicians are streamed into humanities or other areas that do not require math. Mismatching can waste our most precious human resource: talent.

The question addressed in this chapter is whether we can realize compatibility among abilities, instruction, and assessment; if so, how; and, once we know how, what can we gain from doing so? The hypothesis proposed is that, yes, we can realize such compatibility, that it is not terribly hard to do, and that both students and teachers will gain by our doing so.

This hypothesis is far from universally accepted. Cronbach and Snow (1977) did a massive review of studies of aptitude–treatment interaction studies, and concluded that, for the most part, investigators had failed to show convincingly that such interactions exist. Where they had been shown to exist, for the most part, they did not go beyond the demonstration of an interaction with general ability. Thus, the claim being made here flies in the face of much past empirical evidence. Why should we be able to achieve any success where many have failed? We believe that, first, the large majority of studies did not actually match each of aptitude, instruction (treatment), and method of assessment, and that, second, having a strong and useful theory as a basis for a matching study may have given us a lever that some past studies did not have.

The remainder of the chapter is divided into three main parts. First, I describe a theoretical basis for achieving compatibility. In doing so, I consider both psychological and psychoeducational models that might serve as bases for achieving compatibility. Second, I describe an ongoing study we are doing, from which we have preliminary results, that attempts to instantiate the psychological and psychoeducational models I have described. And finally, I briefly talk about future directions and spell out some conclusions.

THEORETICAL BASES

Psychological Theories of Abilities

Perhaps the first question one needs to address in attempting to deal seriously with the question of aptitude–treatment interaction is what theory of aptitude will motivate one's work. There are a number of different kinds of theories from which one can choose (see Sternberg, 1990, for a review).

The most well-known theories are certainly psychometric ones (called geographic models in Sternberg, 1990). According to these theories, planning adequate instruction and assessment depends on an understanding of the mental map that comprises abilities. For example, Spearman's (1927) theory of general ability, g, has probably been the most popular theory of intelligence ever proposed. It states simply that among the various factors of intelligence, one stands out from all others in importance, namely, general intelligence, g. In planning an intervention, one would simply want to take into account different levels of this general ability. A more comprehensive attempt might be based on one of the multifactorial theories, such as those of Thurstone (1938) or of Vernon (1971). According to these theories, abilities are best understood as multiple in nature, with the exact abilities depending on the theory under consideration. As the number of abilities specified by the theory increases, however, the question of how to match abilities, instruction, and assessment becomes more complex, and a theory as complex as Guilford's (1967) structure-of-intellect theory will almost certainly be out of the bounds of practicality. At the same time, a theory as simple as Spearman's does not give us much hope of matching in any but a rather superficial way. But a problem with most of these theories is that they do not specify mental processes, at least in any detail, and to account adequately for the type of instruction one should give, it would seem to help to know what processes to teach. A second type of theory attempts to remedy this difficulty.

The second type of theory is epistemological. Piaget actually worked in the laboratory of Binet, one of the leaders of the mental testing movement, but was convinced that Binet paid too much attention to right rather than to wrong answers. Piaget (1972) developed a theory of how children and adults think, specifying two critical processes, assimilation and accommodation, which are used to incorporate new information into existing mental structures, and to form new mental structures to incorporate new information, respectively. Piaget proposed his well-known theory of stages to specify the levels of development that result from the equilibration (balancing) of assimilation and accommodation.

Although Piaget's theory specified mental processes, Piaget seemed to do so much more at the level of competence than of performance. For example, few people actually seem to think as logically as the stage of formal operations would imply for people of roughly 12 years of age and older. A third type of theory is more oriented toward performance than toward competence.

The third type of theory is the computational theory. According to this type of theory, instruction and assessment should be based on an understanding of the information processing done in actual learning and thinking. Computational theories deal with performance rather than competence. These theories range in the complexity of the information processing that they claim is central to the functioning of human intelligence. For example, Hunt (1978) proposed that verbal intelligence could be understood largely in terms of speed of lexical retrieval of information from long-term memory. He used a relatively low-level task, recognizing physical and name identities between letters (e.g., recognizing that "A" and "A" are both physically identical and identical in name, whereas "A" and "a" are identical only in name).

Some investigators have preferred to identify the basic processes at a higher level. Simon and Kotovsky (1963), for example, proposed that identification of the basic information processes of human intelligence would be better served by the consideration of higher level tasks, such as number series. Newell and Simon (1972) as well considered high-level tasks, such as theorem proving and playing chess. In my own earlier work (e.g., Sternberg, 1977; Sternberg & Gardner, 1982), I also looked at higher level information-processing tasks, such as analogies, series completions, and classifications.

Although the computational theories specify processes, they have tended to be at a molar rather than a molecular level. But several theorists have suggested that a complete theory of intelligence would have to specify the biological substrate underlying human information processing. Theorists such as Jensen (1982) have attempted to provide a link between information processing and the biological substrate through a fourth approach to human abilities, namely, a biological one. Jensen, for example, has suggested that individual differences in human intelligence may be understandable in terms of individual differences in speed of neural transmission. Eysenck (1986), in contrast, has emphasized the importance of accuracy of neural transmission.

Research using the biological approach has exploded in recent years, and some of the most exciting recent findings have been through the use of this approach. I do not consider it further, however, because it is not clear that it yet has straightforward implications for instruction or assessment of learning outcomes. We certainly do not know how to use these results either to teach or to assess what has been learned, except perhaps, at the loose metaphorical level suggested by those who talk about "left-brain" and "right-brain" learning. It is not clear that these loose metaphorical uses of biology in fact correspond to the biology of the human nervous system.

A fifth approach is an anthropological one, according to which intelligence is largely a cultural invention. For example, Berry (1974) suggested that we need to look at intelligence within each culture as an emic construct—as something arising out of that culture. This viewpoint of intelligence as inhering within a given culture is appealing, although it does not well account for biological findings suggesting at least some generality in mental mechanisms that cross-cut cultures. Although there may be some aspects of intelligence that are culturally specific (e.g., what is considered "smart" behavior in a given culture), there seem to be other aspects that are culturally universal (e.g., the need to define correctly the nature of a problem confronting one, taking into account that the correct definition may be culturally specific).

The sixth approach to abilities, and that which is taken here, is a systems approach. This approach attempts to combine some of the best elements of the approaches described previously. One theory under this approach, the theory of multiple intelligences of Gardner (1983), claimed that there are at least seven relatively independent intelligences, such as linguistic, logical–mathematical, musical, and interpersonal. My own theory, the triarchic theory (Sternberg, 1985), specified that three aspects of abilities are particularly important: analytical, creative, and practical. I do not claim that this theory is the only one that might be useful as a basis for matching abilities, instruction, and assessment. But I believe that it is one theory among others that may be particularly useful.

For one thing, positing three aspects of abilities is a feasible number of aspects for diversifying instruction and assessment. For another, I will argue that the implications of analytical, creative, and practical abilities for instruction and assessment across disciplines are quite clear, in contrast with the implications of other divisions of abilities. Finally, we have actually designed the instructional and assessment instruments that show the usefulness of this approach in practice as well as in theory, and therefore, we pursue the use of the triarchic theory here.

Psychoeducational Models Linking Abilities, Instruction, and Assessment

Several different psychoeducational models can be used to link abilities, instruction, and assessment. I consider seven such models here, and give an example of each.

No Model. Before considering alternative models, I should note that most frequently in the schools we find the use of no model at all. The teacher teaches and tests, making no particular effort either to link instruction or assessment to abilities. Often, the link between assessment and instruction is trivial at best, other than that the teacher attempts to assess what has been taught. But we can certainly go beyond having no model at all.

Model 1: Abilities.   This model underlies much of the ability–testing movement. Abilities are measured, but test scores go into a file and little attempt is made to use the test scores to individualize either instruction or assessment. No significant connection is made between abilities, on the one hand, and instruction and assessment, on the other.

Model 2: Instruction.   This model underlies most instructional attempts, as well as most attempts to improve instruction. A teacher decides what to teach and how to teach it, and no significant connection is made with abilities or even assessment. Many noteworthy attempts to improve instruction, such as the movement for emphasizing thinking skills or the movement emphasizing cultural literacy, draw on this model.

Model 3: Assessment.   This model has underlain most thinking about assessment. For example, the multiple-choice format used in group ability tests was not chosen in order to take into account abilities or instruction, but in order to facilitate ease of scoring and reliability of the assessments. Even the modern emphasis on performance testing and portfolios does not go beyond this model. As is so often true in education, we go from one trend (some might say "fad") to another without asking whether we are merely swinging the pendulum from one extreme to another.

Model 4: Abilities and Instruction.   This model underlies traditional aptitude–treatment interaction (ATI) research. The goal here is to fit instruction to level and often pattern of abilities of groups of students. Some teachers use this model intuitively. The problem with the model is that unless the teacher matches the assessment to the instruction, the value of the matching may never truly be known. So often in schools, for example, teachers try to teach for thinking, and then students are placed in the position of taking multiple-choice standardized achievement tests that measure little beyond rote recall.

Model 5: Abilities and Assessment.   This model is at the heart of truly multifaceted ability and achievement testing, where a variety of test contents (e.g., verbal, spatial), formats (e.g., multiple-choice, short-answer, essay), and often types (e.g., group, individual) are used to assess people. The idea is to make sure that people with different ability patterns will be equally benefited by the way testing is done. Teachers or psychologists using this approach recognize that different children benefit from different kinds of tests, and the testing reflects this fact.

Model 6: Instruction and Assessment. This model is the basis for programs that match assessment to instruction. For example, the Advanced Placement program of the College Board specifies what an introductory college course in a given discipline should contain and then provides examinations measuring this content. In the United States, many state mastery test programs specify the content to be taught in various courses and also provide tests measuring this content. Such programs almost never take into account either individual or group differences in ability and how they might impact instruction and assessment.

Model 7: Abilities, Instruction, and Assessment. This model is the one advocated here. It matches all of abilities, instruction, and assessment. It is the model that will be instantiated in the study to be described. In my view, this full model is rarely used in educational settings. In closing the discussion of models, I should note that, ideally, Model 7 would be implemented in such a way that children of varying patterns of abilities all receive a variety of kinds of instruction and assessments. In the ideal, you do not teach or test only to a person's strengths. Rather, you jointly help them to capitalize on strengths and to remediate and compensate for weaknesses. People need some instruction and assessment with which they are comfortable, but they also need to stretch themselves. As educators, we need to provide both. In our own experimental implementation, described later, children of all ability patterns received all kinds of assessments, but they were randomly assigned to a single kind of instruction. This design was, we believed, ideal for experimental purposes, but is not ideal in the classroom. Teachers should use a variety of instructional methods to meet varying ability needs, not just a single method of instruction.

APPLYING THE TRIARCHIC THEORY TO THE MODEL LINKING ABILITIES, INSTRUCTION, AND ASSESSMENT

In this section, I describe a study I have conducted in collaboration with Pamela Clinkenbeard that seeks to apply the triarchic theory of human abilities to Model 7—the model linking abilities, instruction, and assessment. The implementation was via a summer college-level course in introductory psychology, given to bright high school students selected and assessed in ways that measured analytic, creative, and practical aspects of performance. The course was taught during the summers of 1992 and 1993. At the time this chapter is being written, data have been analyzed for Summer 1992, but are still being collected for 1993. Hence, I summarize only the former data. The implementations were somewhat different, and so distinct as well as common aspects of the two implementations are discussed.

Method Design

The basic design was a three-way one. In the summer of 1992, students were selected for excelling in terms of either analytic, creative, or practical abilities. Students from the three identified ability groups were assigned at random to sections of an introductory psychology course that emphasized teaching for either analytical, creative, or practical thinking. And students of all three ability patterns in all instructional sections were assessed via assessments measuring analytic, creative, and practical accomplishments. Thus, the design was a 3 × 3 × 3 completely crossed one, with abilities and instructional assignment between subjects and assessments within subjects. In 1993, there were two additional ability groups: a balanced group, in which students were roughly equal in analytic, creative, and practical abilities; and an above-average control group, where students were not especially high in any of the abilities.

The prediction was that students who were matched in abilities, instruction, and assessment would perform better than those not so matched.

Selection Materials

All students were selected for participation in the summer program by virtue of their scores on a research form of the Sternberg Triarchic Abilities Test (Sternberg, 1993), High School–College level. The test itself is divided into a "process" facet and a "content" facet. There were three levels of the process facet and four of the content facet, which, when crossed, yielded 12 subtests. The three process facets were analytic, creative, and practical; the four content facets were verbal, quantitative, and figural (all multiple-choice), and essay.

Each of the multiple-choice subtests contained two practice items and four or more test items, whereas each essay subtest consisted of a single essay. A brief description of each test is:

1. *Analytic–Verbal.* LEARNING FROM CONTEXT. Subjects receive a brief paragraph with an embedded neologism (unknown word created especially for the test). Subjects had to infer the meaning of the unknown word.

2. *Analytic–Quantitative.* NUMBER SERIES. Subjects receive a series of numbers, which they must complete.

3. *Analytic–Figural.* FIGURAL MATRICES. Subjects receive a figural matrix with one entry missing. They must choose which of several figures belongs in the empty cell of the matrix.

4. *Analytic–Essay.* ANALYTICAL THINKING. Subjects are presented with a problem confronted by a school, and must analyze the problem systematically.

5. *Creative–Verbal.* NONENTRENCHED ANALOGIES. Subjects are presented with an analogy preceded by a counterfactual premise (e.g., "Suppose that villains were lovable," or "Suppose that sparrows played hopscotch"). Subjects need to solve the analogy as though the premise were true.

6. *Creative–Quantitative.* NOVEL NUMBER SYSTEMS. In the 1992 version, subjects were presented with number matrices into which were intermeshed novel symbols representing a new system of enumeration. Subjects had to fill in the missing entry in the matrix with either a normal number or one in the new system of enumeration. In the 1993 version, subjects had to do mathematics problems using novel number operations (e.g., two numbers x and y are added if x is less than y, multiplied if x is greater than y, and divided if x equals y).

7. *Creative–Figural.* SERIES WITH MAPPING. Subjects had to complete a figural series. However, the rule was illustrated in a series other than the one they had to complete, and subjects therefore had to transfer the rule from the old series to the new one.

8. *Creative–Essay.* CREATIVE THINKING. Subjects had to write a creative essay envisioning their ideal school.

9. *Practical–Verbal.* INFORMAL REASONING. Subjects read a paragraph describing a high school student with a life problem. They had to select which of several answer options provided the best solution to the student's problem.

10. *Practical–Quantitative.* EVERYDAY MATH. Subjects had to solve problems using everyday math, as in following recipes,

using train or bus schedules, computing costs of tickets to sporting events, and so on.

11. ***Practical–Figural.*** ROUTE PLANNING. Subjects were shown maps of amusement parks, portions of cities, and the like, and had to plan efficient routes for getting from one place to another, given constraints.

12. ***Practical–Essay.*** PRACTICAL THINKING. Students were given a practical problem faced in school, and asked how they would solve it.

The test had very liberal time limits for each subtest so that almost everyone was able to finish each subtest. Tests were sent to schools around the country (and to schools in other countries as well), and were administered by school personnel but scored by us. A person was labeled as "high" in an ability if his or her score in that ability exceeded his or her score in any other of the abilities by one standard deviation unit across subjects.

Instructional Materials

All students received two kinds of instructional materials: the text and the lectures. The instructional materials constituted the core of an advanced placement (college level) course in psychology.

The text was a higher level introductory psychology course for college students. The text, which I have written, was in preprint form. It consisted of 20 chapters covering the standard topics of an introductory psychology course. Students in the 1992 summer session got through only 12 of the chapters in their 3-week course, whereas students in the 1993 summer session completed the text. Emphases of the text were on (a) teaching students to think like psychologists, (b) helping students understand the dialectical evolution of ideas in psychology (and their origins in philosophy), and (c) understanding and applying scientific thinking in psychology.

All students also attended common morning lectures. The lectures were given by a Yale professor, Mahzarin Banaji, who has won an award for outstanding undergraduate teaching. The lectures were the same as she normally teaches in her introductory college lectures.

The differentiated treatment was in the afternoon, when students went to a section that emphasized either analytic, creative, or practical thinking in psychology. In the 1993 summer session an additional type of section emphasized memory for course content, more along the lines of a standard course. These sections were taught by advanced graduate students with experience teaching introductory psychology, and in 1993, as well by advanced placement high school teachers.

The sections emphasized a discussion format. In the analytic sections, the emphasis was on analyzing theories, critiquing experiments, evaluating concepts in psychology, and the like. In the creative sections, the emphasis was on generating new theories, thinking up new experiments, imagining how theories would need to be changed if certain assumptions were changed, and so on. In the practical sections, the emphasis was on using psychological concepts, theories, and data to inform and improve everyday life. In the standard sections (1993 only), the emphasis was on remembering and understanding course material.

Assessment Materials

Assessment materials were variegated according to the triarchic theory. There were four main assessments:

1. *Homework assignments.* There were two homework assignments, one involving reading and doing activities stemming from a study on cognitive dissonance, the other involving reading and doing activities stemming from a reading on alternative theories of depression. For each assignment, there was an analytical activity, a creative activity, and a practical activity. The analytical activity involved analyzing the experiment (Assignment 1) or theories (Assignment 2), or coming up with a new experiment (Assignment 1) or theory (Assignment 2), or discussing the relevance of the assigned experiment (Assignment 1) or theories (Assignment 2) for everyday life.
2. *Midterm.* The midterm consisted of multiple-choice test items basically emphasizing recall, plus two analytical, two creative, and two practical essays. The essays all were based on material studied in the course. Hence, the essays measured analytic, creative, or practical use of information.
3. *Final examination.* The final examination was parallel to the midterm, except longer. It contained more multiple-choice items, and three essays of each of the three kinds (analytic, creative, practical).
4. *Independent project.* Students were all required to do an independent project. Although they were free to choose the topic, they were required to explore analytic, creative, and practical facets of that topic.

All students in 1993 received a pretest on psychology knowledge because some of them had previously had high school psychology courses, whereas others had not. In 1992, none had prior psychology courses. Students also received a short battery of conventional ability tests.

In the 1992 summer program, students were ungraded, but received fairly extensive comments from their section leader describing their performance in the course. In the 1993 summer program, students also received these comments, and a letter grade (A–F) as well.

Subjects

Subjects in the 1992 summer program were roughly 65 students, mostly from the United States, but a few from abroad. One student was expelled from the program for behavioral reasons, leaving a final sample of 64. Subjects in the 1993 summer program were roughly 225 students, again both from around the United States and abroad. One student left voluntarily for homesickness. Three students acquired chicken pox and lost a few days for hospitalization. Students in both years were entering the junior or senior years of high school, meaning that they were roughly 16 to 17 years of age. All enrollments were voluntary, and parents generally paid for the children to attend. Generous scholarship aid was available. Students were diverse with respect to racial and ethnic groups.

In 1993, in order to make the program self-supporting and still provide scholarship aid, a few full-tuition paying students were admitted who did not fit into any treatment group. They were segregated into their own section.

Students were not aware of the experimental design, or even that there was any such design. They were informed that our goal was to try to use innovative methods for teaching psychology.

Main Results

We have now analyzed the data for the 1992 implementation. Because we used a small sample, we did not expect strong results. Indeed, the 1992 summer program was conceived of as a pilot for the full-scale 1993 summer study. Yet the results showed interesting trends that were either statistically significant or at least marginally significant.

The results for the creative-ability group conformed to our predictions. Students identified as creative who were placed in a section emphasizing teaching for creativity and who were assessed for creative performance excelled beyond all other groups on these creativity-based assessments.

The results were similarly promising for the practical–ability group. Subjects identified as high practical who were placed in a practically oriented section excelled above other groups in the practically based assessments.

The results for the analytic–ability group were at first puzzling. Quite simply, the high analytic students did worse on all the assessments than did members of any other group. Thus, the result was a main effect rather than an interaction, and in the wrong direction! However, interviews with the students' section leaders elucidated further why we got this result.

Students in the analytic–ability group were basically those who had always done well on standardized tests and, for the most part, in school, because both tests and schooling stress analytic abilities considerably more than creative or practical ones. Most of the high-analytic students had been labeled as gifted at some point in their school careers. Moreover, many of these students were ones who, in high school, were able to receive grades of "A" in their courses with very little effort. The lesson they had learned was that they could "ace" a course with very little work.

When students come to Yale as regular college freshmen, many of them encounter a rude awakening. They discover, usually after a first semester of mediocre grades, that they will not be able to get by as they did in high school, with just a minimum of effort. Our high-analytic summer students went through the same rude awakening. Believing that they could do well in the course without working hard, they did not work hard and discovered only too late that their cavalier attitude was not adequate to the demands of the course.

On the basis of these pilot results, we introduced regular letter grades in the summer of 1993 to emphasize to students the need to study hard, and we also warned them that the workload and difficulty they would face were very different from those to which they were accustomed in high school.

FUTURE DIRECTIONS AND CONCLUSIONS

We plan to continue the summer psychology program beyond the summer of 1993, although our funding for the project will extend for just 1 more year. We hope to refine our procedures, as the need arises. But we believe that the general benefits of matching extend beyond psychology and beyond a single age group. Hence, we would like to expand our work to other subject matter areas in order to show that matching is useful not just in psychology, but in other disciplines as well. Eventually, we would like also to extend the general plan to age levels other than the 16 to 17 year age level at which we have been working.

The results of the summer 1992 program are promising, although it remains to be seen whether the summer 1993 results replicate the 1992 results for the creative and practical groups, and provide the results we have predicted for the analytic group as well. Obviously, we have a long way to go in testing our ideas, but we believe that our data provide at least tentative evidence for the feasibility and desirability of matching abilities, instruction, and assessment.

ACKNOWLEDGMENTS

The work reported herein was supported under the Javits Act program (Grant #R206R00001) as administered by the Office of Educational Research and Improvement, U.S. Department of Education. The findings and opinions expressed in this report do not reflect the positions or policies of the Office of Educational Research and Improvement or the U.S. Department of Education. At the time this manuscript is going into production, the 1993 summer program has been run and the data analyzed: The results clearly and significantly show that students performed better if they were matched rather than mismatched in their course placement vis à vis their triarchic pattern of abilities.

REFERENCES

Berry, J. W. (1974). Radical cultural relativism and the concept of intelligence. In J. W. Berry & P. R. Dasen (Eds.), *Culture and cognition: Readings in cross-cultural psychology* (pp. 225–229). London: Methuen.

Cronbach, L. J., & Snow, R. E. (1977). *Aptitudes and instructional methods.* New York: Irvington.

Eysenck, H. J. (1986). The theory of intelligence and the psychophysiology of cognition. In R. J. Sternberg (Ed.), *Advances in the psychology of human intelligence* (Vol. 3, pp. 1–34). Hillsdale, NJ: Lawrence Erlbaum Associates.

Gardner, H. (1983). *Frames of mind: The theory of multiple intelligences.* New York: Basic Books.

Guilford, J. P. (1967). *The nature of human intelligence.* New York: McGraw-Hill.

Hunt, E. B. (1978). Mechanics of verbal ability. *Psychological Review, 85,* 109–130.

Jensen, A. R. (1982). The chronometry of intelligence. In R. J. Sternberg (Ed.), *Advances in the psychology of human intelligence* (Vol. 1, pp. 255–310). Hillsdale, NJ: Lawrence Erlbaum Associates.

Newell, A., & Simon, H. A. (1972). *Human problem solving.* Englewood Cliffs, NJ: Prentice-Hall.

Piaget, J. (1972). *The psychology of human intelligence*. Totowa, NJ: Littlefield Adams.

Simon, H. A., & Kotovsky, K. (1963). Human acquisition of concepts for sequential patterns. *Psychological Review, 70*, 534–546.

Spearman, C. (1927). *The abilities of man*. New York: Macmillan.

Sternberg, R. J. (1977). *Intelligence, information processing, and analogical reasoning: The componential analysis of human abilities*. Hillsdale, NJ: Lawrence Erlbaum Associates.

Sternberg, R. J. (1985). *Beyond IQ: A triarchic theory of human intelligence*. New York: Cambridge University Press.

Sternberg, R. J. (1990). *Metaphors of mind: Conceptions of the nature of intelligence*. New York: Cambridge University Press.

Sternberg, R. J. (1993). *Triarchic abilities test*. Unpublished test.

Sternberg, R. J., & Gardner, M. K. (1982). A componential interpretation of the general factor in human intelligence. In H. J. Eysenck (Ed.), *A model for intelligence* (pp. 231–254). Berlin: Springer.

Thurstone, L. L. (1938). *Primary mental abilities*. Chicago: University of Chicago Press.

Vernon, P. E. (1971). *The structure of human abilities*. London: Methuen.

Author Index

Subject Index